Social Life of Virginia

IN THE

Seventeenth Century

BY

PHILIP ALEXANDER BRUCE

CORNER HOUSE PUBLISHERS

WILLIAMSTOWN, MASSACHUSETTS

First Printed in 1907

Reprinted in 1968

by

CORNER HOUSE PUBLISHERS

PRINTED IN THE UNITED STATES OF AMERICA

Social Life of Virginia

IN THE

Seventeenth Century.

AN INQUIRY INTO THE ORIGIN OF THE HIGHER PLANTING
CLASS, TOGETHER WITH AN ACCOUNT OF THE
HABITS, CUSTOMS, AND DIVERSIONS
OF THE PEOPLE.

BY

PHILIP ALEXANDER BRUCE,

Late Corresponding Secretary of the Virginia Historical Society; and author of the
"Economic History of Virginia in the Seventeeth Century;" " Plantation
Negro as a Freeman;" " Rise of the New South;" " Short
History of the United States," etc., etc.

PREFACE.

No one who studies the purely social aspects of Virginian life in the seventeenth century can fail to be impressed with the paucity and poverty of the materials that touch directly upon the subject. Excepting a few brief summaries of personal observations in the Colony resembling those left by Colonel Henry Norwood, the Rev. John Clayton, and the author of *Leah and Rachel,* nothing that can be correctly described as Travels in the Virginia of that day, after it had become a populous community, with a definite character of its own, is in existence. Nor are there any extended biographies of the principal citizens belonging to the periods following the first colonization to supply indirectly information of value. The nearest approach to personal memoirs is to be found in the letter-books of William Fitzhugh and William Byrd, which, however, are, in substance, simply correspondence about dry business matters. Beverley's History, while full of vivid details, really relates to the last years of the seventeenth century and to the first of the eighteenth. To acquire an accurate conception of the Virginian social life from 1607 to 1700, the student must examine a very large mass of miscellaneous printed and manuscript materials which are primarily concerned with other subjects, such, for instance, as the pamphlets preserved in Force's Historical Tracts, the Virginian parish registers, the original colonial documents now in the custody of the British State Paper Office in

London, and above all, the several hundred volumes of the Virginian county records of the seventeenth century, which still survive. These are the chief, although not the only, sources of information; and to these, as well as to all other sources known to me, I have had access in person, with a view to the preparation of the present volume.

In one particular alone have I been compelled to rely on the special researches of others. The knowledge of American genealogy in general, as so far accumulated, is chiefly the result of the labors of students who respectively have devoted many years,—in some instances, indeed, a lifetime,—to the investigation of the history of a single family in all its ramifications. This is as true of those who have pursued their inquiries in the field of Virginia Genealogy as of those who have pursued their inquiries in the field of New England or New York. It is only quite recently that the study of Virginian family history has been carried on in a thoroughly scientific spirit, but we have already secured, by the zeal and industry of scholars so well known in this department of research as Alexander Brown, Rev. Philip Slaughter, Rev. Horace E. Hayden, Charles P. Keith, Edward Wilson James, William G. Stanard, Lyon G. Tyler, and others who might be named, a great volume of trustworthy genealogical information, which, when considered as a whole, throws a decisive light on the origin of the higher planting class of Virginia in the seventeenth century.

The conclusions touching this subject set forth in the present work are based on the results of the special investigations so far made by all those who have been active in this particular department; and I am confident that further investigations of the same character will only go to confirm more unmistakably the correctness of these conclusions.

In the present volume I have taken another step forward in the study of the conditions prevailing in Virginia in the seventeenth century begun in my *Economic History;* and I propose following it up with even more extended monographs on *Religion and Morals, Education, Legal Administration, Military System,* and *Political Condition,* which, under the general head of *Institutional History of Virginia in the Sevententh century,* would complete the study of the century as relating to that colony.

PHILIP ALEXANDER BRUCE.

NORFOLK, VA., APRIL 25, 1907.

CONTENTS.

  I. Size and Population, ... 13

 II. Influences Promoting English Emi-
        gration, ... 23

III. Origin of the Higher Planting Class, 39

 IV. Origin of the Higher Planting Class—
        Continued, ... 51

  V. Origin of the Higher Planting Class—
        Continued, ... 68

 VI. Origin of the Higher Planting Class—
        Continued, ... 83

VII. Social Distinctions, ... 101

VIII. Social Distinctions—*Continued*, ... 125

 IX. Social Spirit—Ties with the Mother
        Country, ... 140

  X. Social Spirit—Manner of Life, ... 157

 XI. Social Spirit—Hospitality of People, 170

XII. Popular Diversions—Drinking and
        Dancing, ... 177

XIII. Popular Diversions—Acting and Games, 186

XIV. Popular Diversions—Horse-Racing, ... 194

XV. POPULAR DIVERSIONS—HUNTING AND
FISHING, ... 211

XVI. PUBLIC AND PRIVATE OCCASIONS—THE
FUNERAL, ... 218

XVII. PUBLIC AND PRIVATE OCCASIONS—THE
WEDDING, ... 223

XVIII. PUBLIC AND PRIVATE OCCASIONS—
CHURCH, COURT-DAY AND MUSTER, ... 239

XIX. DUELLING, ... 245

XX. CONCLUSION, ... 250

APPENDIX. 258

BIBLIOGRAPHY.

The following is the list of works quoted in the Notes and References of the present volume as the authorities for specific statements made in the body of the text. The long list of works contained in the bibliography appended to the author's " Economic History of Virginia in the Seventeenth Century" was also carefully consulted:

Accomac County (Va.) Records for Seventeenth Century, original volumes, county court-house.

Allerton, Walter J., Allerton Family, Chicago, Ill., 1900.

Ancestor, The, A Quarterly Review, London and Philadelphia.

Baird, Rev. Charles W., Huguenot Emigration to America, New York, 1884.

Beverley, Robert, History of Virginia, Richmond, Va., 1855.

British Colonial Papers, originals, British State Paper Office, London.

Brown, Alexander—Genesis of United States, 2 vols., Boston, Mass.; First Republic in America, Boston, Mass., 1898.

Bruce, Philip Alexander, Economic History of Virginia in Seventeenth Century, New York, 1896.

Byrd, William, Letters of, Va. Hist. Soc., MSS. Coll.

Byrd Deed Book, Va. Hist. Soc. MSS. Coll.

Campbell, Charles, Spotswood Family, Albany, N. Y., 1868.

Chappell, E., Chappell Family, Kansas City, Mo.

Christ Church, Midalesex county (Va.) Parish Register.

Cogbill, James C., Family of Cogbill, Cambridge, Mass., 1879.

Crawford Family of Virginia.

Critic Newspaper, Richmond, Va.

Dinwiddie Papers, Va. Hist. Soc. Pubs.

Elizabeth City County (Va.) Records for Seventeenth Century, certified copies, Va. St. Libr.

Essex County (Va.) Records for Seventeenth Century, certified copies, Va. State Libr.

Farnham (Va.) Parish Register.

Fitzhugh, William; Letters of, Va. Hist. Soc., MSS. Coll.

Fulham Palace, London, MSS. relating to Colonial Virginia.

General Court (Va.) Records, Vol. 1670-76, Va. Hist. Soc., MSS. Coll.

Goode, Brown, Goode Family, Richmond, Va., 1887.

Goodwyn Family of America, compiled by L. G. Tyler, Richmond, Va., 1895.

Green, Raleigh T., Notes on Culpeper County, Va., 1900.

Green, Thomas M., Historic Families of Kentucky, Cincinnati, O. 1889.

Green, B. W., Word Book of Virginia Folk Speech, Richmond, Va.

Hayden, Rev. E., Virginia Genealogies, Wilkesbarre, Pa.

Henning, W. W., Va. Statutes at Large, Richmond, Va., 1812.

Henrico County (Va.) Records for Seventeenth Century, certified copies, Va. State Libr.

Horner, J., Blair, Banister and Braxton Families.

Hotten, J. C., Original Lists of Emigrants to America, 1600-1700, N. Y., 1874.

Hume, John Robert, Hume Family, St. Louis, Mo., 1903.

Isle of Wight County (Va.) Records for Seventeenth Century, originals, county court-house.

Keith, Charles P., Ancestry of Benjamin Harrison, Philadelphia, Pa., 1893.

Lancaster County (Va.) Records for Seventeenth Century, originals, county court-house.

Lambeth Palace, London, MSS., Relating to Virginia.

Lee, Edward J., Lee of Virginia, Phila., Pa., 1895.

Lower Norfolk County .Va.) Antiquary, edited by Edward Wilson James.

Lower Norfolk County (Va.) Records for Seventeenth Century, originals, Portsmouth, Va.

Maryland Archives, Proceedings of Council, Md. Hist. Soc., Coll.

Maury, Colonel R. L. Huguenots in Virginia, reprint.

Meade, Rt. Rev. William, Old Churches, Ministers and Families of Virginia, Philadelphia, Pa., 1857.

Middlesex County (Va.) Records for Seventeenth Century, originals, county court-house.

Montague, Peter, History of Genealogy of, Amherst, Mass., 1894.

Neill, Rev. E. D.—Va. Company of London, 1606-24, Albany, 1869; Va. Caralorum, Albany, 1869.

Northampton County (Va.) Records for Seventeenth Century, originals county court-house.

Northumberland County (Va.) Records for Seventeenth Century, originals, county court-house.

Page, Channing M., Genealogy of Page Family.

Parish Registers, Theological Seminary, Alexandria, Va.

Princess Anne County (Va.) Records for Seventeenth Century, originals, county court-house.

Randolph MSS., 3 volumes, Va. Hist. Soc. MSS. Coll.

Rappahannock County (Va.) Records for Seventeenth Century, certified copies Va. State Library.

Richmond County (Va.) Records for Seventeenth Century, originals, county court-house.

Sainsbury, E. Noel, Abstracts of Va. Colonial Documents in British State Paper Office, Va. State Libr.

Slaughter, Rev. Philip, History of Bristol Parish and History of S. F. George's Parish, Richmond, Va., 1890.

Smith, Captain John, Works of, Richmond, Va.

Spotswood, Letters of Governor, Va. Hist. Soc. Pubs.

Stanard, W. G., chart of descendants of Rev. Robert Rose, Richmond, Va., 1898.

Surry County (Va.) Records for Seventeenth Century, certified copies, Va. State Libr.

Thomas, Major R. S., Four Square and Fox Hunting, Smithfield, Va., 1905.

Tyler, Lyon G., Cradle of the Republic, Richmond, Va., 1900.

Upshur, T. T., Sir George, and Temperance Yeardley and Some of Their Descendants. Reprint, 1896.

Virginia Company of London, Abstracts of Proceedings, Va. Hist. Soc., Pubs.

Virginia Colonial Records, State Senate Document. Extra. 1874.

Virginia Land Patent Books, Va. State Capitol, Richmond.

Virginia Magazine of History and Biography, Va., Hist. Soc., Pubs.

Virginia, Present State of, 1697-8, by Hartwell, Chilton and Blair.

Waters, Henry F., Genealogical Gleanings in England, Boston, 1901.

Westmoreland County (Va.) Records for Seventeenth Century, originals, county court-house.

William and Mary College Quarterly.

York County (Va.) Records for Seventeenth Century, certified copies, Va. State Libr.

The SOCIAL LIFE *of* VIRGINIA

SEVENTEENTH CENTURY.

I.

SIZE OF POPULATION.

DURING the first decades following the earliest settlement of Virginia, when the number of its inhabitants had not expanded beyond a few thousands, it was not a difficult task to make out a complete and accurate roll even of their names. A census was taken in 1625, and also in 1634-'5, nearly ten years later, and there is no reason to think that the results of the counts made at these dates were not strictly correct, since the area stolen from the primeval foresι and occupied was still so narrow as to allow even a few enumerators to pass over it in a comparatively short time. But as the population grew, and the plantations spread out more and more widely and irregularly, thus pushing many families into remote and almost unknown corners of the frontier, it became less and less easy to find out from year to year, or decade to decade, the precise number of people having their homes in the Colony. The census of 1643-'5 was, perhaps, the last one of the seventeenth century taken after the manner of a modern census, which ascertains every fact with extreme exactness. As the century drew on there were several enumerations of population as well as of the different kinds of property owned by the Virginians, but they were the result rather of private calculation than of actual count.[1]

A statement was sent up to Jamestown each year from every county as to the number of its tithables that year. This information was required by the House of Burgesses, because the number of tithables in all the counties united constituted the basis of the public levy annually ordered by that body as the fountain head of the taxing power of the Colony. With this complete list of tithables at hand to go by, it was easy to fix with a fair degree of accuracy the size of the population at the time the list was taken. Throughout the seventeenth century the rule was to estimate the unknown number of inhabitants at thrice the known number of tithables, and this was for all practical purposes a trustworthy method of ascertaining. As long as the number of tithables was correctly re-

---

[1] A striking illustration of this will be found in the well-known enumeration given in the *New Description of Virginia*. The author of that pamphlet estimated the population in 1649 at 15,000 whites and 300 blacks; the number of cows, bulls, calves and oxen at 20,000; and the number of horses at 200, etc. By an act passed in 1645, and not repealed until 1648, not only tithables, but also land and live-stock of all kinds were made returnable for taxation. The calculation of the writer of the *New Description* was, doubtless, based on the figures entered in the tax lists of 1648, which were perhaps the most complete for all forms of property recorded in the history of the Colony previous to 1700, because it was during this short interval alone, that live-stock and land were subject to the levy. It was only in a narrow sense that the county commander could be looked upon as a census-taker, for his duty in this respect seems to have been confined to returning a full list of the persons eligible for military service.

turned, the colonial authorities felt no burning interest in the size of the population. That size was only
important ordinarily as forming the basis of taxation,
and extraordinarily, as forming the basis of a militia
muster to resist an attack by an Indian foe or invasion by a foreign enemy. In those distant times, when
political economy was yet to be reduced to a science,
the administrative authorities even in England concerned themselves but little with any aspect of population except such as related to the income required
for the support of government, or to the soldiers
needed for the defense of the soil. This was peculiarly so in a remote colony like Virginia, where the inhabitants were dispersed very thinly over the face of
a wide and uneven area of partially cleared plantations ; where there were neither cities, nor towns, nor
even villages or hamlets, and where the whole economic system showed a remarkable degree of simplic-
ity and monotony.

In 1619 it was estimated that the population of Virginia of English descent did not exceed twenty-four
hundred persons. About this time the annual addition
to it from the Mother Country was thought to be close
upon twelve hundred; and this was probably correct,
for in one year, 1621, for instance, everyone of the
twelve ships that came out to the Colony brought over
a detachment, more or less large, of new settlers.[2]
These yearly accessions, with the natural increase,
would have swelled the number of inhabitants at a
very rapid rate had not the mortality precipitated by
a change of diet and climate been extraordinarily great
even for that age, when so little care was exercised

---

[2] Broadside, Doct. 46, Colonial Papers, Vol. I.

in observing the general laws of health. It was computed by one contemporary authority that, during the first thirty years following the earliest settlement of Virginia, not less than five of every six persons landed on its shores soon succumbed to one disease or another, but principally to the debilitating influence of the period of seasoning, at which time the newcomer, accustomed from his birth to the more veiled rays of the English sun and the greater equableness of the English air, was first exposed to a semi-tropical blaze in the corn and tobacco fields in July, August, and September, or to those rapid alternations of the atmosphere marking the other parts of the year. The same writer asserts that, in the course of these thirty years, one hundred thousand persons died in the Colony.[3] If this statement was intended to apply to new settlers alone, it probably greatly exaggerated the mortality, but there is no room for doubt that the death rate, down to the middle of the century at least, was far beyond anything occurring in modern times within the temperate zone, and was only comparable to the rate prevailing among raw Europeans settled in the Delta of the Amazon or of the Niger. As the woods vanished before the axes of the colonists, and as the area of drained and cultivated soil spread back from the river banks to the foot of the higher lands, the hoarded malaria of the country steadily grew less; the people too gradually acquired from experience and observation a juster idea as to how to combat the poisonous influences of the newly upturned mould, the fetid marshes, and the burning sun; and the general healthfulness of all the plantations advanced. The rate of

---

[3] New Albion, p. 5, Force's Hist. Tracts Vol. II.

mortality for the whole population also steadily diminished as the number of persons born in the Colony,
and, therefore, accustomed to the climate from birth,
increased.

The death rate among those passing through the
period of seasoning must, however, have always remained high. As if the climate was not fatal enough
in its influence on the health of the new-comers during the first years after the earliest settlement, the
Indian tomahawk had to come into play to swell further the lists of the dead. A few months after the
Massacre of 1622 the number of inhabitants was supposed to be about twelve hundred and seventy-seven.[4]
The census of 1625 shows a population of only twelve
hundred and two, an actual decline as compared with
the population surviving the terrible catastrophe of
a few years before. During this brief interval famine
and disease had further cut down the number of inhabitants, and the massacre, together with the great
discouragements following it, had checked immigration from England. By 1628 the population, in spite
of the renewed flow of new settlers, had grown to only
three thousand.[5] In the following year an observer
upon the ground, who had long been a prominent
resident of Virginia, William Pierce, estimated the
number of people in the Colony at a figure ranging
from four to five thousand[6]; but only one year later
Governor Harvey stated that the population did not
exceed twenty-five hundred.[7] At the end of four years

---

[4] Colonial Records of Va. State Senate Doct. Extra, 1874, p. 89.

[5] British Colonial Papers, Vol. III., 1624-5, No. 32.

[6] British Colonial Papers, Vol. V., 1629-30, No. 24.

[7] Harvey to Privy Council, British Colonial Papers, Vol. V.,
1629-30, No. 95.

more the population was supposed to be fifty-one hundred and nineteen, which, if Harvey's calculation was correct, represented an annual increase since 1628 of about three hundred and fifteen only.[8] A formal count at this time (1634) revealed the fact that the population did not exceed four thousand, nine hundred and fourteen, but after the census was taken a Dutch ship brought in one hundred and forty-five persons from the Bermudas, and an English ship sixty from England.[9] The tide of new settlers then began to pour in in larger volume in consequence of the more orderly state of affairs and the rising prosperity of the Colony. In 1634 alone twelve hundred arrived.[10] Since 1619 the population of Virginia had doubled in size, but this had come about only after fifteen years had passed. In the course of the following fifteen the size of the population trebled; about five thousand in 1634, it rose to fifteen thousand in 1649, without including the three hundred slaves whom the planters then owned.[11]

The faster growth during this last interval was due, not to any great increase in the number of new settlers seeking homes in Virginia, but rather to the advance in the birth-rate among its inhabitants. There was by the middle of the century a large native population thoroughly seasoned to all the trying variations of the climate and inured to every side of plantation life,

[8] Sainsbury's Abstracts, Colonial Papers for 1628, p. 176, Va. St. Libr.

[9] British Colonial Papers, Vol. VIII., 1634-5, No. 55.

[10] British Colonial Papers, Vol. VIII., 1634-5, No. 3.

[11] New Description of Virginia, pp. 1-16, Force's Hist. Tracts, Vol. II.

however harsh and severe it might be in the struggle to press the frontier further and further outward. From an early date it had been observed that the fecundity of women residing in the Colony was remarkable, and this had not become less conspicuous as the conditions of existence grew more easy. Twelve years after the great Massacre of 1622, a catastrophe which had brought the Colony to the brink of ruin, the last trace of that appalling disaster had disappeared from the face of the country, and only the memory of the practical lessons in prudence and forethought which it taught remained. Every succeeding year now saw hundreds of new dwelling houses built, and new family circles, each beneath its own separate roof, formed under the protection of a firm and orderly local government, and supported in comfort and contentment by profitable labor in the field. The generous soil afforded an ample subsistence, however large the number of children gathered around the table at meal times; the more mouths there were to feed, the more hands there were to work; whilst the comparative loneliness of the life was an additional spur to marriage and the production of offspring.

In the course of the twenty years preceding 1649 but one event took place to check with great sharpness the growth of population. This was the Massacre of 1644; but that calamity fell on the planters dispersed along the line of the frontier, whilst the great body of the colonists escaped all loss of life and property. The peace and prosperity prevailing about the middle of the century, not only encouraged the rapid expansion of the native population, but also held out stronger inducements than ever before offered to persons in the

Mother Country to settle in Virginia.[12] The rate of growth observed in the Colony at this time continued to be maintained during the next fifty years. In 1675, after an interval of twenty-five, the population was estimated at fifty thousand by the three distinguished citizens, Morryson, Ludwell, and Smith, who had been commissioned to go to England to obtain a new charter[13]; and the general accuracy of this statement seems to be confirmed by one made by Culpeper a few years later. That Governor, in his report on the condition of the Colony about 1681, declared that the tithables then numbered about fourteen thousand, which would indicate a total population at the lowest of forty-two thousand, and at the highest of fifty-six thousand.[14] About 1697, according to the authors of the *Present State of Virginia, 1697-8*, the whole body of tithables had grown to twenty thousand, a proof that the population now ranged between seventy and eighty thousand.[15] It was perhaps really nearer the latter than the former figures, as some time had gone by since the number of inhabitants had been estimated at seventy thousand by Governor Andros in a report made to the Board of Trade.[16]

The preceding statements show that, during the interval of sixty-six years ending in 1700, the population of Virginia had increased to fourteen times its size at

---

[12] New Description of Virginia, pp. 1-16, Force's Hist. Tracts, Vol. II.

[13] Petition of Morryson, Ludwell and Smith, Colonial Entry Book, 1675-81, p. 33.

[14] British Colonial Papers, Vol. XLVII., No. 105.

[15] Present State of Virginia, 1697-8, Sect. 9.

[16] B. T. Va., 1697, Vol. VI., p. 161.

the beginning of that long period; in other words, that sixty-five thousand persons had been added to it at the average annual rate of one thousand, which seems a rather moderate degree of growth when it is recalled that the additions by births had been further swelled by immigration. Either the mortality among the natives themselves was very great, or the flow of new settlers into the Colony was comparatively insignificant, if we consider not the number who arrived in the English ships, but the number who survived the period of seasoning on the plantations. It is doubtful whether this number exceeded on the average five hundred a year, and it would perhaps be nearer the truth to estimate it at three hundred.[17]

It is no cause for surprise, that the average number of new settlers from year to year should have been greater in the time of the company than after the revocation of its charter. During the existence of the company there was a powerful body in England to employ all its energies and resources in encouraging emigration to the Colony; every means at the command of this body were used to set forth the advantages which Virginia had to offer to all who would remove thither

---

[17] If the land patents of the seventeenth century preserved in the Register's office at Richmond, made up the entire number issued during that period, it would be easy to estimate from year to year the additions to the population from abroad, since a full list of head-rights is either appended to each of these patents, or shown by the number of acres contained in the grant. This, however, would not throw any trustworthy light on the number of persons added permanently to the population, inasmuch as it is impossible to calculate with accuracy how many of the immigrants included in these lists of headrights survived the change of climate, diet and labor.

and make their permanent homes there; and every facility of transportation which that age afforded was extended to every person who wished to go out to become a citizen of the new country beyond the Atlantic. The greater the number of such persons sent oversea, the more rapidly the opening up of the forests would go on, and the more quickly the profits of the company itself, which were dependent on the growth of population, would be increased. When the letters-patent of that corporation were recalled, no similar organization arose in England to take its place in stimulating emigration to Virginia; no powerful influence, directed strenuously to that end by a single body of men on the ground, was left to do the same work. From 1624, when the company was abolished down to the end of the century, the only inducement, apart from political and social conditions, held out in England to promote emigration to Virginia was the general reputation of the Colony as a place where the fortune of the individual might be improved either by planting tobacco on one's own account, or by entering into indentures as an agricultural servant. As might have been expected, mere reputation, however favorable to the Colony, could not be as effective as the resources of a great company brought persistently to bear to fill the out-going ships with men, women, and children bent upon seeking new homes in Virginia.

II.

INFLUENCES PROMOTING ENGLISH EMIGRATION.

IN a former work[1] I dwelt at some length on the influence which led that great class of the colonial population known as the indentured servants, including
the mechanics as well as the agricultural laborers, to
leave their native England and bind themselves for a
term of years to planters in Virginia. What were the
influences that, from time to time, caused the emigration to the Colony of that large body of men who, immediately on their arrival, took a position of equality
with the foremost of the gentry there, a position to
which they were entitled by their social connections
in England, if not by the amount of wealth they had
brought with them? In short, what was the previous
social history of the founders of the families that controlled the highest social life of Virginia in the seventeenth century? By the end of that century, when
property had been accumulating during nearly one
hundred years, and a sufficient interval had passed to
allow at least two generations to be born and to grow
up in the Colony, a very considerable proportion of the
leading members of the landed gentry were natives of
the country who had inherited their estates from
fathers who, in their lifetime, were among its most
prominent citizens. But from 1619, when the community became for the first time free, down to 1700, per-

---

[1] See Bruce's " Economic History of Virginia in the Seventeenth
Century," Vol. I., Chapter 9.

haps not a period of twelve months went by that this class did not receive accessions by the arrival from England of men of equal social standing, who were in a position to acquire by patent or purchase an estate, large or small, according to the means at their command. And these men became at once as much a part of this class from a social point of view as if they had been born in the Colony in the same walk of life, or had risen to that walk after residing there during a long course of years. With few exceptions, the most distinguished families in the colonial history of Virginia were founded in the Seventeenth century. It was in this century that there emigrated from England the Armisteads, Banisters, Bassetts, Blands, Bollings, Beverleys, Burwells, Byrds, Carys, Corbins, Carters, Claibornes, Custises, Fauntleroys, Fitzhughs, Harrisons, Lees, Lightfoots, Ludwells, Masons, Pages, Peytons, Randolphs, Robinsons, Scarboroughs, Spencers, Thoroughgoods, Washingtons, and Wormleys—families that represented the nearest approach to an organized aristocracy which North America has seen, and which constituted in their association with the eighteenth, if not with the seventeenth, century, the stateliest social body known so far in American history.

The fundamental influence leading the founders of these families and families of equal social standing in the Colony to emigrate from England to Virginia was the active and enterprising spirit which has pre-eminently distinguished the English race immemorially. It was no longer possible in the seventeenth century to repeat the daring achievements of Drake and Hawkins, Frobisher and Cavendish, who had gathered around them the boldest and most gallant men in the

kingdom. Had James possessed the lion-heart of
Elizabeth, the bravest and stoutest in England would
have continued to find in the hot pursuit of Spanish
galleons on the ocean, or in the destruction of Spanish
cities along the seaboard, an outlet for their irrepres-
sible restlessness, untiring energy, and insatiable love
of adventure. Under this timid and calculating monarch, the only outlet remaining was the establishment
of colonies. Even this occupation, tame as it seemed
in comparison, was not, in the view of the more eager
spirits, entirely devoid of opportunities for romantic
action. How much a mere taste for strange experience
in a remote and unknown country entered into the
hearts of many who went out to Virginia in 1607 is
shown by the fact that the enterprise drew into that
company of voyagers John Smith, a man whose whole
previous life had been a series of episodes full of peril
and excitement. But Smith also illustrates how thoroughly practical the most adventurous Englishman
could be when the true work of settling the new land
began. Of all the European peoples in those times
the English possessed in the most marked degree the
bold and intrepid spirit which would move them to
leave their native soil behind and cross many thousand miles of sea, and also the patient and calculating
spirit which would enable them, when once fixed in
their new place of settlement, to make the most of its
advantages without any thought of returning to their
former homes. No people were more devoted to their
own country than they, and yet no people were quicker
to abandon it when the prospect of adventure, novelty,
or gain was held out before them. It was as if the
Englishman was more responsive to the primordial

impulses of Nature; as if civilization had not been able to repress in him that purely animal instinct which leads the bees to swarm forth from the original hive, and beasts to migrate blindly without any apparent motive in a search for food.

The wandering spirit of the Angles, who swept boldly southward unmindful of the dangers of the sea, and scornful of enemies, had been transmitted to their English descendants of the sixteenth and seventeenth centuries. The first great emigration of the race was from the sombre forests of the North; the second was from the beautiful hills and valleys of England itself; at bottom, the same impulse, hardly modified by the vast gap in time between the two movements, was at work,—an impulse which led the adventurer to rely blindly on his own fearless spirit to carve out a new fortune for himself in a new land, which allowed neither love of kindred nor devotion to familiar scenes, however thickly crowded with memories and associations, to shake his resolution to depart, and which directed his gaze cheerfully and firmly towards the star of hope in the West the very moment his native land sank below the horizon in the East.

It was no short and easy voyage in those times to pass from an English port to the Capes of Virginia; weeks must go by after the Scilly Isles had vanished behind the rim of blue waters before the pines along the Virginian coast would begin to loom above the waves; the hardships of a long sojourn in a contracted and uncomfortable ship must be endured; the dangers of violent storms at sea and the peril of wreck when land was approached must be risked; the debilitating influences of a hot climate on reaching the shore must be withstood,—not one of these discouragements served to lessen the tide of emigration which poured out of England, not only towards Virginia and Maryland, but also towards the English colonies in the North. The history of no other nation furnishes a movement of population comparable in magnitude and duration with that which led to the settlement of the whole Atlantic seaboard from Maine to Georgia. Vast as it was, it was only the beginning of English colonization. When the Revolution tore the American communities from the side of the Mother Country, the flood of English emigration westward slackened and practically died away, but before another hundred years had passed it had spread itself far into the Australasian seas; new English cities, crowned with all the triumphs of the modern arts, and teeming with a happy and prosperous population, had arisen under the Southern Cross; from Table Mountain to far beyond the Zambesi, English dominion had broadened out in South Africa; England's commissioned Viceroy was enthroned at Calcutta, her uncommissioned at Cairo; while in the West, in spite of Saratoga and Yorktown, she still owned half a continent and counted her loyal subjects by the millions. These were the achievements of her sons who had inherited that spirit of enterprise and adventure, not to be daunted by fear of a deadly climate or an Indian foe, which had sustained the souls of the men who, before the close of the seventeenth century had hewn down the forests in Eastern Virginia; had brought the land under cultivation; had established homes; had founded a carefully ordered social and political system, and thrown over all the aegis of English Law.

Give a people a bold, enterprising, and restless temper, and narrow the chances of fortune in their native land, then the disposition to emigrate, even when great obstacles are to be overcome and long distances to be traversed in doing so, will be irresistible. This was the general condition in England in the seventeenth cenutry. And no class in the community felt the influence of a contracted sphere in which to improve their pecuniary state more than that class which shared the most ancient blood in the kingdom. It was not merely the man who trimmed the hedges, dug the ditches, reaped the corn, followed the plough, and drove the teams afield who turned to Virginia as a spot where he might, after completing a term of indentured service, acquire an interest in the soil and build a home on his own estate, however small in area. The sons of long descended gentlemen residing on their own ancestral lands, the sons of men engaged in the professions of law, medicine, and the ministry, the sons of men who relied upon a small local trade, or an extended general business for the support of their families,—all these turned towards Virginia a gaze as hopefully and bravely expectant of better fortune there as the gaze of the common labourer dreaming of those remote plantations as he drove his loaded wagon to the barn, or scattered the seed far and wide from his open hand.

Then, as now, the families of the English were among the largest in the world; the manor house, the parsonage, the doctor's and the lawyer's residence overflowed with children. The women married young, and only too often died before middle age from the mere fatigue of child bearing; second marriage and

double sets of children in the same home were conditions observed everywhere. What careers were these
children to follow when they came to maturity? Where
were they to settle in order to earn a livelihood?
These were questions which pressed as anxiously
against the mind and heart of the parent whose income was transmissible as they did against the mind
and heart of the parent whose income was dependent
upon his life. In those times the foreign empire of
England had not spread entirely around the globe to
furnish an enormous number of civil offices to be filled
by the cadets of English families. The English regular army and navy were small, and in consequence
there was little room in these services for the host of
young men whose parents were seeking a pursuit for
them. What room was there for these young men in
the communities where they were born? The man
who owned a great landed estate was bound by the
chain of custom and pride, even if uncontrolled in his
own individual case by the law of primogeniture, to
leave that estate to his eldest son. As this son would
succeed him over the whole domain, however broad in
acreage or rich in soil, there would be no opening anywhere in that domain after his death for his other
children. The benefice of the clergyman, the practice
of the physician and lawyer died with them; at the
best, each could hope to establish only one son in the
calling which he himself followed.

It is no cause for surprise to find that under the pressure of this discouraging outlook for a large family,
so many sons of men of gentle birth were in that age
apprenticed in manual trades which, in modern England, are reserved for persons in the plainer walks of

life. No doubt many parents must have looked upon emigration as offering a far better chance of good fortune than the pursuit of a mechanical art in an English hamlet, or of business in a shop in some prosperous English town. Social prejudices must have played a strong part in those times in spite of the contracted field for employment. The younger brother of the heir to a landed estate was brought up in the same comfort and luxury as the heir himself. During their father's life time the home of the parents was the common home of all, where the footing and privileges of all were equal. The younger son was no more fitted than the elder to yield with equanimity to the claims of any occupation that would degrade his children to a level much lower than the one to which he himself was born.

As soon as Virginia began to acquire the reputation of a considerable community (and what was true of Virginia was also true of the other of the older English colonies in America), how natural that the English father of a large family, whether he was a land owner, clergyman, merchant, lawyer or physician, should have been disposed to weigh carefully the opportunities which it offered for an advantageous settlement of at least some of his sons. And there must have been periods when this disposition was far stronger than at others. During the supremacy of Cromwell what chance was there for the children even of those royalists who had enjoyed under happier conditions a high degree of power and influence? With all those kinsmen capable of advancing them, had Charles still been reigning at Whitehall, prescribed, and with their own immediate families under a ban because loyal to the monarchy, was it at all strange that so many young men, like the Washingtons, despairing of brighter days in their native country, and burning with ambition to improve their fortunes, and spurred on by a spirit of enterprise, should have looked upon emigration to Virginia as offering the only hope for the redress of the evils at home? One cavalier voiced the feelings of his whole class when he said that "Virginia was the only city of refuge left in his Majesty's dominions in those times for distressed cavaliers." [2] In 1649 alone, the year when the final blow was given to the cause of the royalists by the fall of the King's head on the scaffold, seven ships, heavily loaded with passengers, all, with few exceptions, there is reason to think, in sympathy with that cause, set sail for the Colony where Charles II. had been boldly proclaimed as soon as news of his father's death (which was at once denounced there as an impious murder) had arrived.[3] But long before this, and for many years afterwards, that stream had poured and continued to pour across the Atlantic to the "City of Refuge" among the plantations of Virginia.

There were special reasons why Virginia, after it began to grow in wealth and population, should appeal strongly to the interest of the English landed gentry as a body. First, it was firmly loyal to the monarchy in spite of the harsh and injurious operation of the Navigation Acts ; in spite of sweeping grants of its territory to independent proprietaries like Baltimore, or to pri-

---

[2] Ingram's Proceedings p. 34, Force's Hist. Tracts Vol. I.

[3] Interregnum Entry Book, Vol. XXXVI., p. 13, British State Papers.

vate beneficiaries like Arlington and Culpeper; in spite
of selfish denials of reasonable requests like that for
the cessation of tobacco culture for a time; and in
spite of royal Governors, like Howard and Culpeper,
bent upon their own enrichment in a few years by un-
just impositions upon the people.

Secondly, Virginia as a whole was devoted to the
Church of England. It is true that persecution of
none of the various dissenting sects was ever carried
to the same extreme in this Colony as in the colonies
of New England, but at no time previous to the Act of
Toleration was Virginia a comfortable spot for such
sects.[4] The controlling influences in her society hardly
needed the vehement and persistent co-operation of
Sir William Berkeley to give emphatic direction to the
disapproval felt by that society for all forms unsanc-
tioned by the Anglican Church. Much of the bitter
feeling aroused by the division of Virginia's territory
in favor of Baltimore was due to his profession of the
Roman Catholic faith; the foundation of Maryland signified not only a rupture of the original grant to Virginia, which might at any time be repeated as to the
unoccupied soil yet left to her, but also the establishment of a Roman Catholic community at her very
door. There is no reason to think that the violent
course of Berkeley towards Quakers and Puritans was
repugnant to the sentiment of a majority of the people,
or that the Toleration Acts of Charles and James were
regarded with entire satisfaction by any sections except those who thus obtained the right to worship in

---

[4] During the Protectorate, the Puritans enjoyed absolute exemption from interference, but neither the Quakers nor the Papists
were even then in so happy a condition.

the manner they preferred. The Virginians as a body were as conservative at heart as the English themselves, and conformity to the Church of England was but one phase of loyalty to the established order in the State.

Thirdly, the whole power of Virginian society even in the times when universal suffrage prevailed, was directed by the landowners. That society was composed entirely of the landed proprietors and their dependants. There were neither towns nor cities, and consequently the number ot persons following those special callings which thrive best in large and crowded communities was too small to be considered from a social point of view. The public sentiment was exclusively the sentiment of men who, like the landowners of England, looked to agriculture for the income which went to the support of their famlies, and whose only material interests were those associated directly with the soil. The member of the English landed gentry contemplating the advantages of sending his son out to Virginia deemed it a favorable circumstance that he would engage there in the pursuit which had occupied the time and thoughts of his forefathers in England for so many hundred years; nor was it a drawback that tobacco, and not wheat, would be the staple which that son would cultivate as soon as he had acquired an estate, for, in the course of a very few generations, the English people had seen a great community built up in Virginia entirely through the profits obtained from the sale of the plant. The young Englishman himself, accustomed from his birth to all the operations of the farm, perhaps discovered in the expectation of producing this plant a new fillip to

his interest in his own emigration. The mere fact that
it was unknown to him by practical experience in its
cultivation, no doubt, had a tendency to exaggerate his
idea of the pecuniary returns to be derived from it, to
which he would not for a moment have yielded had
the staple been one with which he was thoroughly familiar from childhood.

Letters resembling the one in which Fitzhugh gave
such a vivid description of the estate accumulated by
him in Virginia must have been constantly received in
England, and passed from hand to hand, with the in-
evitable result of stimulating in the breasts of many
persons the desire to share in a like good fortune by
emigrating to the Colony.[5]   Such testimony coming
from well-known citizens, without any motive to over-
state their happy condition, was not likely to have been
questioned.   A more critical attitude might have been
assumed towards an interested pamphleteer like William Bullock, but even his account of the advantages
to be derived from settlement in Virginia, supported
as it was by private information, must have made no
small impression.[6]   There were at least a dozen ports,
beginning with London in the east and Bristol in the
west, to which ships were annually returning from the
Colony loaded with cargoes of tobacco; though the
sailors might speak with disfavor of the heat of the
climate in summer, these cargoes were a tangible proof
of the fertility of the soil and of the ample reward of

---

[5] Bruce's Economic Hist. of Va. in the Seventeenth Century,
Vol. II., p. 243.

[6] Bruce's Economic Hist. of Va. in the Seventeenth Century,
Vol. I., p. 342, *et seq.*

labor. Any member of the English landed gentry who was debating in his own mind as to the advisability of sending his son out to settle there was not likely to be diverted from his purpose by the tale of a seaman touching the horrors of the "seasoning," for it was known that this period of bad health fell far more heavily on the ordinary agricultural servant, compelled by his contract to work in the fields under the rays of the sun soon after his arrival, than on the emigrant who had brought over means sufficient to enable him to employ others to till the ground for the production of his crops.

But there was still another reason why the Colony made a strong appeal to Englishmen who belonged to the landed gentry. In essentials the life which the Virginian led on his estate was the same as the life which the English gentleman led on his own. The comparative isolation of the plantation was considered by the latter to be no drawback, as it made possible that independence of individual action which was so highly valued by him in his native country; breadth of surface only assured the more certainly ampleness of room for the master to move in without touching elbows with his neighbours, to the diminution of his sense of personal supremacy. The life in Virginia, owing to the entire absence of towns, was even more rural in character than the life in England. The Englishman, accustomed to country pursuits, knew, in emigrating, that he was seeking a residence in a community where all the tastes and habits of the English rural gentry were in some respects only accentuated by the dispersion of the population. Love of home, as the centre of the most sacred affections, was perhaps not more fervent there than in England, but the bonds of kinship were much stronger because in that secluded existence ties of blood assumed a far higher degree of importance, while the pleasures of hospitality were more relished, for the presence of a guest was an event of greater rarity and distinction. And the Englishman was also aware that in no manor-house of Devon, Surrey, or Essex was the devotion to England and all things English deeper than in the plantation residences of Virginia; that the subtle tie of nationality was as binding there as in the Mother Country; that the recognition of class distinctions and social divisions was quite as clear; and that, as an English gentleman, he would at once take the same position in the society of the Colony as he had held in his native shire, and would hardly recognize in outward customs that he had made a change of habitation.[7] And this would also be true, not only of the amusements of indoor life, but also of the diversions of outdoor. All the immemorial games of England were pursued there with an equal zest, and all the manly sports with an equal energy. The various holidays that had been celebrated in England beyond the memory of man were without exception also observed in Virginia; and as in England so in Virginia, every occasion of a festive character, public or private, was used to the utmost to bring amusement and enjoyment into the lives of the people.

These different influences appealed with almost equal power to merchants debating in their own minds

---

[7] This seems to have been the impression of Colonel Henry Norwood and the other Cavaliers who were so liberally entertained after their arrival in Virginia.

as to settling either themselves or their younger sons
in Virginia. One of the earliest aspirations to rise in
the breast of an Englishman beginning to win success
in his trade was to own a country estate, a feeling that
sprang, not only from the immemorial love of rural
occupations and amusements characterizing the English people as a body, but also from a desire for the
increased social consideration which property of this
kind has always conferred in England. It was in the
power of the prosperous merchant to purchase land
for himself in one of the English shires, which,
naturally, he would prefer, but it was not always in
his power to purchase land for all his sons, even if he
had deemed this to be an advisable step to take. An
opening was presented in Virginia for establishing
some of these sons as landowners at a much smaller
expense than he could establish them in England, and
the wisdom of doing so seemed increased when he
recalled that the Colony was, from every point of view,
a mere corner of the Mother Country; that the habits
of the higher planting class were the habits of the
English rural gentry; and that the whole tone of the
social life there was practically the same as that prevailing in every English county. Like the father belonging to the circle of country gentlemen, he saw
that, in addition to the independence, heartiness, and
refinement of its social life, the Colony possessed in
tobacco culture a means by which a son starting there
with a fair estate might steadily improve his fortunes.
Many English merchants were by the course of their
business thoroughly informed as to the advantages to
be reaped by planters who engaged in trading in that
commodity. It was in this way chiefly, they knew,

that the largest properties held by citizens of the Colony had been accumulated; and the same opportunity, they felt sure, was open to a son who possessed the shrewdness and the capital to make the most of such chances as they arose from year to year.

III.

Origin of the Higher Planting Class.

EVEN in the earliest years of its settlement, Virginia was regarded with extraordinary interest by members of the most influential social classes in England. Of the three hundred and twenty-five incorporators whose signatures were attached to the charter of 1612, twenty-five were peers of the realm; one hundred and eleven, knights; sixty-six, esquires; and twenty, "gentlemen," a designation which, in those times, had a meaning distinctive of a special rank. Three-fourths of the persons who signed this document were embraced in the circle of the English gentry, while one hundred and twenty of the number had at one time been, or still were, members of Parliament, a position in that century, as in the present, generally filled by some one who was connected with the landed property of the kingdom.[1] In the charter of 1609 it was the trades of England which were chiefly represented; the commercial impulse given to colonization was then the most conspicuous; but three years later it was what was known in those times as the "gentle classes" which were principally interested. It followed very naturally that a very considerable proportion of those who took an active part in settling the country even in the beginning, when it stood in its primeval condition, were

---

[1] Charter of 1612, Brown's Genesis of the United States, Vol. II., p. 542.

men who had a right, whether from the point of view of birth, breeding, or education, to be called "gentlemen"; nor were they the less so because often impecunious, for as we have seen that was pre-eminently the age of hope, when it was thought that fortune would certainly come to anyone who would seek it in the unknown regions lying in the East or West,—the age when men gambled away their entire patrimony in a night, and sailed away by the first ship to recoup their losses.[2]

The calamities that had overwhelmed the colonists of Roanoke Island were still not forgotten, but not for one moment did this fact prevent a large number of Englishmen of good birth, who might have remained in ease and safety at home, from joining the expedition which set sail in 1606 from Blackwall for Virginia. Of the one hundred persons who went out on that adventurous voyage fifty-four were recorded as belonging to the station of a "gentleman," a term that was always used very guardedly in that age. Among these fifty-four were representatives of such distinguished English families as Archer, Sandys, Walthrop, Throckmorton, Brewster, Browne, Pennington, Wingfield, Waller, Wotton, Gower, and Frith.[3] At least one, George Percy, was the son of a nobleman of the highest rank in the kingdom.

In the First Supply, which arrived in the course of 1608, there were included thirty-three "gentlemen" in a total company of one hundred and twenty new set-

---

[2] Green's Short History of the English People, Sect. V., Chap. 7.

[3] Works of Captain John Smith, Vol. I., p. 153, Richmond edition.

tlers, a proportion of one-fourth of the whole as compared with the one-half who participated in the first
voyage.[4] Among these thirty-three were found men
bearing such well known English names as Featherstone, Abbot, Mollineux, Perkins, Bentley, Worley,
Killingbeck, Bayley, and Harper. As they were accompanied by a perfumer, they must have looked forward to the continued enjoyment on the banks of the
James of all their usual foppish refinements. Smith
has stated that most of the persons entered as "labour-
ers" in the First Supply were really footmen who were
in attendance on their masters; and that, of the entire
company, only a few dozen had been accustomed to
the rough manual work which the colonists were at
once called upon to do. Though Smith spoke at first
with impatient scorn of these gentlemen, with their
valets and perfumers, as men who were better fitted
"to spoyle a commonwealth than to begin or maintain
one," he was forced to acknowledge that the test of
practical experience showed that there was among
them more sensible minds and more industrious hands
than he had expected.[5]

In the Second Supply there arrived twenty-nine
"gentlemen" in a total company of seventy new settlers. Among the persons of gentle birth who came
out on this voyage was Francis West, a brother of
Lord De la Warr and a member of a family distinguished in the peerage. His companions in the same
station of life bore such well known names as Russell,

---

[4] Works of Captain John Smith, Vol. II., pp. 172-3, Richmond
edition.

[5] Works of Captain John Smith, Vol. I., p. 241, Richmond
edition.

Codrington, Philpot, Leigh, Harrison, Holt, Norton, Yarington, Phelps and Prat. Two alone, however, namely, Gabriel Beadle and John Russell, are designated by Smith as "gallants," the term applied in that age to young men of good family who had circumnavigated all the vices of the town, but in whom, in spite of waste or loss of fortune, a gay and adventurous spirit still survived.[6]

In the Third Supply a larger number of these reckless young fops found their way to the Colony. They had been hurried off by their friends, according to the same impatient chronicler, "to escape ill destinies," and were thus forerunners of a host of daring spendthrifts of fashion who, for several hundred years, have by their kinsfolk been packed away from the same island to remote corners of the globe, there, under new influences, to become, not infrequently, sober and honourable citizens. But the forests around Jamestown presented to these early gallants few inducements to lead a more useful life. Smith complained of them bitterly as creating factions among the settlers, and bringing confusion upon the objects for which the Colony had been founded.[7]

There was, however, in the conduct of the great body of the men of birth who came to Virginia in these first years nothing whatever to lead the authorities to discourage the introduction of the social element which they represented. "I would not have it conceived," declared De la Warr in a letter to the London

---

[6] Works of Captain John Smith, Vol. I., pp. 197, 203, Richmond edition.

[7] Works of Captain John Smith, Vol. I., p. 235, Richmond edition.

Company, "that we would exclude altogether gentlemen, and such whose breeding never knew what a day's labor meant, for even to such this country, I doubt not, but will give likewise excellent satisfaction, especially to the better and stayed spirits; for he amongst them that cannot dig, use the square, nor practise the axe and chisel, yet he shall find how to employ the force of knowledge, the exercise of counsel, and the operation and power, of his best breeding." [8]

The introduction into Virginia of persons belonging to the social rank of gentlemen went on as steadily after as before Smith's departure from the Colony. In the reply which the Grand Assembly made to the pamphlet entitled the *"Declaration of the State of the Colony in the Twelve Years of Sir Thomas Smythe's Government,"* it is expressly asserted that, among those who perished in Virginia during this period of its early settlement, were many persons sprung from "Ancyent Houses and born to Estates of £1,000 by the year, some more, some less." [9] Now an estate which in those times would assure an annual income of £1,000 would in these assure an annual income of £5,000, an income, as roughly estimated, equal to twenty-five thousand dollars.[10] That men so well placed in the point of fortune in their native land as this should have gone out to Virginia shows that they were either moved by a spirit of mere novelty and ad-

---

[8] Brown's Genesis of the United States, Vol. I., p. 411.

[9] Neill's Va. Co. of London, p. 408.

[10] One thousand pounds sterling in 1611 had the purchasing power of five thousand pounds at the present time.

venture, or expected extraordinary opportunities to arise there by which their means, already large, would be increased.

It is probable that every ship sailing for the Colony in the time of the company carried out a considerable number of persons who belonged in England to the social rank of gentlemen. It was not often that in the lists of passengers the social position of each was stated, but when it was, the proportion of gentlemen among them varied; sometimes it was small, and sometimes it was quite large. Of the band of thirty-five persons who came over in 1619 with the intention of settling at Berkeley on James River, the modern Harrison's Landing, only three were entered as of that station in life in the certificate which the Governor was required by law to draw up to show their arrival in the Colony. The names of these three were Toby Felgate, Ferdinando Yate, and John Blanchard. But in a second consignment of settlers which was made at a later date to the same plantation, thirteen, in a total company of fifty, were set down as men who had enjoyed high social position in England.[11] The ship *Margaret and John,* in crossing the ocean in 1620, with eighty-five emigrants on board bound for Virginia, was attacked by Spaniards, and in the fight that ensued eight persons among the English were killed. Of these eight it is incidentally mentioned that one was a "gentleman," whilst of the twenty who were simply wounded in the conflict five, or one-fourth of the number, were referred to as belonging to that

---

[11] Brown's First Republic, pp. 371, 413. Toby Felgate in a patent which he sued out in 1630 refers to himself as "mariner."

social rank.[12]   It is not improbable that this formed
the proportion of gentlemen in the full list of passengers.

Nor did that proportion fall off after the charter of
the company was recalled, if a trustworthy inference
can be drawn from the few instances in which any
light at all is thrown upon the social rank of the emigrants on board ship.   For instance, in 1636, when
Harvey set out for Virginia on his return after the mutiny which had expelled him, he was accompanied by
one hundred passengers, twenty of whom, or one-fifth of
the whole number, were declared by him to be "gentlemen of quality."   A large proportion of the remaining
passengers were perhaps the agricultural servants
whom these gentlemen were carrying out to the
Colony to work the lands which they intended to acquire by patent.[13]

Investigation of early Virginian genealogy has not
yet been searching enough to show fully and precisely
the social origin of every member of the memorable
Assembly which convened at Jamestown in 1619, the
first legislative body of a representative character to
meet on North American soil.   Enough, however, is
known to disclose the fact that, with few exceptions,
all had been of good, and some of high, social standing in England.   Yeardley, who as Governor was the
presiding officer of the Council sitting as the Upper
Chamber, seems to have been one of the few whose
beginnings were decidedly plain, but he had filled high
offices, and had been knighted for his valuable ser-

---

[12] Brown's First Republic, p. 416.

[13] British Colonial Papers, Vol. IX., No. 27, I.

vices.[14] On the other hand, Captain Francis West, a
member of the House of Burgesses, was a son of the
second Lord De la Warr. John Pory, the Speaker,
was not only a graduate of Cambridge University, and
an author of distinction, but also had been a prominent
member of the English Parliament, a position which
proved even more then than now that the incumbent
enjoyed high social consideration. Thomas Pawlett,
a Burgess, was the brother of John Pawlett, who was
afterwards raised to the rank of baron in the peerage.
Pawlett seems to have arrived in Virginia as recently
as 1618, and his election to the Assembly so soon
would indicate the power of social influence in the
Colony even in that early period, for he had hardly had
the time to make much impression by his personal
ability, independently of his conspicuous family connections.[15] Rossingham, another Burgess, was a

---

[14] The statement reported in the following deposition seems to
have been considered a slander:

" Deposition of Roger Marshall taken in open court: 'This de-
ponent saith that being at Mr. Littleton's house, Thomas Parkes
came into the kitchen and talked concerning Mr. Yeardley, saying,
" I have done the king better service than ever the sire of Yeardley
(i. e., Justice Yeardley) did," and, further, the said Parkes told
the people there present, saying, "Justice Yeardley's father (Sir
George) did work upon a taylor's stall in Burchin Lane in London." In a second deposition, Parkes is reported to have said:
"Alas! hee (i. e., father of Justice Yeardley, Sir George) was but
a taylor that lept off a shop board in Burchin Lane.' "

Northampton County Records, orders, Dec. 20, 1643.

A brother of Sir George Yeardley was an apothecary.

[15] Pawlett owned the famous Westover estate on James river,
which he devised by will to his brother, Lord Pawlett. He sat
in the Assembly of 1633 (N. S.) as the representative from Westover and Fleur de Hundred; see William and Mary College Quart.,
Vol. IV., pp. 151, 152.

nephew of Governor Yeardley, whilst Lieut. Gibbes, who was also a Burgess, is supposed to have been a son of Thomas Gibbes, formerly a member of the King's Council for the London Company. Captain Thomas Graves was of sufficient consideration to be included among the subscribers of the charter of 1609, and Captain William Tucker among those of the charter of 1612. John Jackson, or Juxon, was a kinsman of the Bishop who was to win such lasting fame as Charles the First's spiritual attendant when he ascended the scaffold under the windows of Whitehall. Walter Shelley, another Burgess, who had been among the earliest members of the London Company, is thought to have belonged to the family afterwards made so celebrated by the great poet of the same name, but one which had long enjoyed a conspicuous position among the landed gentry of England.[16]

Besides the Wests,[17] Pawletts, and Percies, who were either the sons or brothers of English noblemen, there were, in the interval between 1610 and 1623, numerous persons in the Colony connected by close ties of blood or marriage with members of the English baronetage. For instance, Henry Spelman was the son of Sir Henry Spelman, one of the most distin-

---

[16] See as authority for these various details the admirable article from the pen of the late William Wirt Henry, republished from the papers of the American Historical Association in the Va. Maga. of Hist. and Biog., Vol. II., p. 60.

[17] The family of West in Virginia traces descent from John West, one of the three brothers connected with the early history of the Colony; see Abstracts of Proceedings Va. Co. of London, Vol. I., p. 115, note.

guished antiquarians of that day.[18] Captain Jabez
Whitaker had married a daughter of Sir John
Bouchier.[19] George Thorpe, the manager of the College lands, an accomplished scholar and devoted philanthropist, who was destined to perish so miserably
by the tomahawk of the Indian, was a great-nephew of
Sir John Mason, of the English Council of State, and a
near kinsman of the titled families of Throgmorton
and Berkeley.[20] Thomas Willoughby, according to a
tradition which bears some evidence of authenticity,
was a nephew of Sir Perceval Walloton.[21] Henry
Fleet was, on the maternal side, the grandson of Sir
Thomas Wyatt, the celebrated rebel, and a great-great-
grandson of the almost equally famous Thomas
Brooke, Lord Cobham. William Strachey, who filled
the office of Secretary of State to the Colony, was a
direct descendant of Sir John Strachey, and belonged
to a family which has maintained by its talents and
wealth a conspicuous position among the landed
gentry of England down to the present day.[22] William Davison, who was also Secretary of State in Virginia, was a son of William Davison, who held the
same office in England, and was one of the most faithful and trusted advisers of Queen Elizabeth.[23] John
Rolfe, celebrated as the husband of the lovely Indian

[18] Va. Maga. of Hist. and Biog., Vol. I., p. 196.

[19] Va. Maga. of Hist. and Biog., Vol. II., p. 78.

[20] William and Mary College, Quart., Vol. IX., p. 209.

[21] Va. Maga. of Hist. and Biog., Vol. I., p. 448.

[22] William and Mary College Quart., Vol. X., p. 168.

[23] William and Mary College Quart., Vol. X., p. 199.

heroine Pocahontas, and as the first among the English
settlers to cultivate tobacco, was sprung from a family
of distinguished social connections, which had long
been seated at Heacham in Norfolk.[24] Captain Raleigh
Croshaw was probably a close kinsman of the famous
poet of the same name.[25]

In a petition to the Privy Council which the London
Company presented some time previous to the revocation of its charter in 1624 they declared that many of
the sub-patentees of the very extensive public land
grants, some of whom had gone out to Virginia, were
"men of noble and worthy families, and possessors of
such large fortunes that they were able to expend great
sums in settling and improving their plantations." [26]
The patents to private land grants recorded in the
Colony in the short interval between 1622 and 1624
were, in many instances, obtained by persons who
could justly lay claim to the same distinguished social
origin. Not only were a very considerable number of
these single patentees entered in their patents as "gen-

---

[24] William and Mary College Quart., Vol. X., p. 169. Among
those whose names are included in the list of dead at West and
Shirley Hundred, 1624-5, was "James Rolfe, slaine by the Indians."
This, there is little reason to doubt, was John Rolfe, a strange
fate for the son-in-law of Powhatan; British Colonial Papers, Vol.
III., No. 35.

[25] Va. Maga. of Hist. and Biog., Vol. I., p. 86. Croshaw is always
spelt with the o in the records, but the name was really Crashaw.

[26] Absracts of Proceedings of Va. Co. of London, Vol. I., p. 143,
Va. Hist. Soc. Pub. An instance is that of Sir Richard Worsley,
who, in 1622, was associated with other persons in patenting a
vast tract of land in Virginia, to which they had become entitled
by transporting to the Colony one hundred new settlers (Va.
Maga. of Hist. and Biog., Vol. II., p. 68). The Berkeley Grant
is another case in point.

tlemen," a term applied with legal precision in a public
document, but the searching inquiry into special genealogies now going on has shown that many of them possessed connections in England of a high social rank.
Among these patentees, for instance, were Maurice
Thompson, the father of the first Lord Habersham,
and Giles Allington, a member of the well known
family of Cambridgeshire formerly represented in the
peerage by the Barons Allington.[27]

---

[27] Va. Maga. of Hist. and Biog., Vol. I., pp. 189, 191: The title
now belongs to a different family. In estimating the proportion
of freemen among the persons whose names are mentioned in the
five hundred and one land patents issued between 1623 and July,
1637, Mr. William G. Stanard, in his abstracts of these patents
has declared that "of the names appearing in these 501 patents,
336 are positively known to have come to the Colony as freemen,
and were chiefly men and heads of families. There are 245 persons
whose names do not occur as headrights, and yet of whom it is not
positively shown that they were freemen, though probably the by
far greater number of them were. There were 2,094 whose transportation charges were paid by others. These included negroes,
wives, children, friends, etc. It would probably be fair to say that
of the names represented in the patents cited, there were 675
freemen, women, and children who came to Virginia, and about
2,000 servants and slaves." See Va. Maga. of Hist. and Biog.,
Vol. I., p. 441.

IV.

Origin of the Higher Planting Class.—*Continued.*

THE different records of the long period from 1624, when the company was abolished, until the close of the seventeenth century, show the continued emigration to Virginia of numerous persons who were connected by ties of blood or marriage with persons of high position in England. The Colony had reverted to the Crown only a few years when Sir John Zouch, a member of one of the most ancient families of Derbyshire, not only acquired a large tract of land on the James, but also took up his residence there, although it seems to have been only for a time.[1] Walter Aston, who lies buried at Westover, was a cousin of Lord Aston in the English peerage,[2] while Thomas Booth, the first of a name destined to become very well known in the social history of the Colony, was a cousin of the Earl of Warrington.[3] William Claiborne, who at different times filled the positions of Secretary of State, Commissioner of Parliament, and Deputy-Governor, and resisted so stoutly the partisans of Baltimore when they sought to dispossess him of Kent Island, was descended from the Cleburnes of Westmoreland, in England. His brother married a daughter of Sir Richard Lowther, of Lowther, situated in that county, a member of a family represented in the English peerage to-day by the Earls of Lonsdale, and long

---

[1] William and Mary College Quart., Vol. I., p. 222.

[2] Va. Maga. of Hist. and Biog., Vol. V., p. 313.

[3] William and Mary College Quart., Vol. II., p. 234.

one of the most powerful in the North.[4]   Adam
Thoroughgood, the owner of a large estate, and for
many years a very prominent figure in the affairs of
the Colony, was a brother of Sir John Thoroughgood,
of Kensington, who was attached to the Court.[5]
Samuel Mathews, who, like Thoroughgood, made a
large fortune by planting and trading, and, during the
Puritan Supremacy, became Governor of Virginia,
had married the daughter of Sir Thomas Hinton, the
son-in-law of Sir Sebastian Harvey, one of the most
distinguished Lord Mayors of London in those times.[6]

A leading member of the Council of Governor Harvey was Henry Finch, who was a brother of the Lord
Keeper of that name[7]; and Captain John West, referred to by Harvey as "the Uncle of the Late Lord
Lawar," was also a member of the same body.[8]   Sir
John Harvey himself had performed such valuable
services on the sea that he had been rewarded by his
elevation to knighthood.[9]   Henry Woodhouse, ancestor of the Woodhouse family of Virginia, who arrived
in the Colony about 1637, was descended from Sir
William Woodhouse, of Waxham, Norfolk.   Sir Wil-

---

[4] Va. Maga. of Hist. and Biog., Vol. I., p. 313.

[5] Thoroughgood's house was, until very recently, still standing
on Lynnhaven Bay, as solid and in as good repair apparently as
when it was first built.   It was from some points of view the most
interesting, as it was, perhaps, the oldest colonial residence in
Virginia at the time of its demolition.

[6] Neill's Va. Carolorum, p. 111; see, also, Va. Maga. of Hist.
and Biog., Vol. I., p. 91, Vol. XII., p. 88.

[7] British Colonial Papers, Vol. V., p. 95, II.

[8] British Colonial Papers, Vol. V., No. 95, II.

[9] Va. Maga. of Hist. and Biog., Vol. I., p. 87.

liam had married the widow of Sir Henry Parker, who was the daughter of Sir Philip Calthorpe; Woodhouse's son had married a daughter of Sir Nicholas Bacon (the famous Lord Keeper in the reign of Elizabeth), and the sister of the celebrated chancellor and philosopher, Francis Bacon. Captain Henry Woodhouse, the fruit of this marriage, and the father of the emigrant, was recommended for the chief command at Tilbury, became Governor of Bermuda in 1623, and aspired to the same office in Virginia.[10] Major Richard Morryson, who was for some years in charge of the fort situated at Point Comfort, was a son of Sir Richard Morryson by his wife, a daughter of Sir Henry Harrington. His brother, Colonel Francis Morryson, long one of the most prominent and useful citizens of the Colony, left England after the defeat of the royal cause, of which the Morrysons had been active and zealous supporters. A sister of these two brothers had married the accomplished Lord Falkland, who was so celebrated in the history of the Civil Wars.[11] A son of Major Richard Morryson settled permanently in Virginia, and when he died his estate passed to his nephew, Henry Morryson, who at the time occupied the rank of Lieutenant-Colonel in Lord Cutts's regiment of footguards.[12]

---

[10] British Colonial Papers, Vol. VIII., No. 75; Va. Maga. of Hist. and Biog., Vol. VIII., pp. 400-1; see, also, Lower Norfolk County Antiquary for numerous interesting facts about this ancient family, which is represented in Princess Anne county to-day.

[11] Va. Maga. of Hist. and Biog., Vol. II., p. 384.

[12] Elizabeth City County Records, Vol. 1684-99, p. 455, Va. St. Libr. Copy. The properties known as Fort Hill and Buck Roe were sold by Henry Morryson to Robert Beverley.

Among the principal families in Virginia previous to 1650 were the Calthorpes. Christopher Calthorpe, who was the first of that connection to settle in the Colony was the grandson of Sir James, and the uncle of Sir Christopher Calthorpe, of Stirston, in England. A cousin, Reynolds Calthorpe, had married the only daughter of Viscount Longueville.[13] Through his mother, who was a daughter of John Bacon, of Herset, in Norfolk, Christopher Calthorpe, of Virginia, was related to the Bacon family, one of the most powerful and distinguished in the Mother Country in that age, whether considered from a political or from a social point of view. George Reade, the earliest of that name to emigrate to the Colony, was a grandson of Sir Thomas Windebanke, of Harnes Hill, in Berkshire. This Sir Thomas had married a daughter of Sir Edward Dymoke, the hereditary champion of England, an honor which his descendants continued to enjoy until the last century.[14] Reade is invested with some personal interest as an ancestor of Washington. His brother was for some years the private secretary of his kinsman, Sir Francis Windebanke, who, as Secretary-of-State under Charles I., made himself, by his subserviency to that ill-advised monarch, so hateful to the popular party that, when the Long Parliament met, fiercely bent upon punishing him and his like, he was compelled, in order to escape arrest, to fly across the Channel to the Continent.

---

[13] William and Mary College Quart., Vol. II., p. 107, *et seq.*

[14] William and Mary College Quart., Vol. X., p. 171; Va. Maga. of Hist. and Biog., Vol. VIII., p. 300; see, also, Vol. VI., p. 408. There are interesting references to Reade in a letter of Secretary Kemp, which will be found in British Colonial Papers, Vol. IX., 1636-8, No. 97.

Richard Kemp, who filled the office of Secretary to the Colony about 1637, is believed on good evidence brought out by recent investigation to have been a brother of Sir Robert, of Gissing, who resided in Suffolk county, England.[15] Colonel William Barnard, one of the foremost citizens of Nansimond in 1640, was a brother of Sir Robert Bernard, of Brompton Hall, in Huntingdonshire.[16] Richard Bennett, a planter of large fortune, and at one time during the Puritan Supremacy Governor of the Colony, a man who occupied during a long life a conspicuously useful and honorable position in the community, was a member of the family upon which Lord Arlington had conferred so much social distinction and political power in England.[17] In 1635, in a letter describing the mutiny which ended in the expulsion of Governor Harvey, Secretary Kemp refers incidentally to Robert Lytcott as the "son of Sir John Lytcott, now bound out for England."[18] Among the wealthiest and most influential citizens of Accomac was Colonel Nathaniel Littleton, whom recent investigation shows to have been a brother of Sir Edward Littleton, Lord Chief Justice of England, and a son of Sir Edward, of Henley, in Shropshire. He was thus sprung directly from Sir Thomas Littleton, one of the earliest as well

---

[15] William and Mary College Quart., Vol. X., p. 171.

[16] Va. Maga. of Hist. and Biog., Vol. VI., p. 408.

[17] Bennett's kinship with Arlington (whose family name was Bennett) is referred to in a letter to Arlington from Thomas Ludwell, Va. Maga. of Hist. and Biog., Vol. III., p. 54.

[18] British Colonial Papers, Vol. VIII., No. 61.

as one of the most famous writers on law in the English language.[19]

Colonel Richard Lee emigrated to Virginia about 1641-'2, and there founded a family which has produced a larger number of celebrated men, whether in statesmanship or war, than any other family which England has furnished to America. Whether he was descended from the Lees of Coton or of Ditchley, he was sprung from a line of progenitors of whom it has been correctly said that they "were knights and gentlemen of high position before the ancestors of half the present peerage of England had emerged from obscurity." [20] There seems to have been no political motive in the emigration of Richard Lee, although about the year he went out to Virginia the Long Parliament was sternly calling to book all who had shown too much zeal in carrying out the intemperate and misguided policy of the King. It is possible that Lee foresaw the violent times that were approaching and desired to withdraw to a more peaceable spot beyond the sea. But it was not the habit of members of his family, whether they came before or have come after him, to

---

[19] William and Mary College Quart., Vol. VII., p. 230; Vol. IX., p. 62; New England Hist. and Gen. Register, Vol. XLI., pp. 364-9. See, also, Evelyn's Diary, March 24, 1688, for interesting references to the beautiful residences of one branch of this family in England.

[20] Lee of Virginia, p. 42. There is a letter still extant from Lancelot Lee to Tnomas Lee, which would seem to show that the emigrant was beyond doubt descended from John Lee, of Coton. See opinion of William G. Stanard, Va. Maga. of Hist. and Biog., Vol. VI., p. 256, an opinion confirmed by the more recent investigations of the same careful authority. The exact connection, however, has not yet been fully traced.

shrink from the shock of battle or the storms of public life, and it is more probable that, without any thought as to the rising commotion in England, which was finally to involve persons of his social rank in such a whirlwind, he was induced to go to Virginia by the assured prospect of great improvement in his pecuniary fortunes. That a man of his distinguished social antecedents and influential connections should have decided that the Colony offered greater advantages to persons of his class than England itself is one of the most remarkable proofs of the high consideration in which Virginia as a place of residence, and tobacco culture as a business, were held by Englishmen, who, in their native country, were surrounded by so much to make their lives agreeable and their occupations profitable. The portrait of Richard Lee, which is still in existence, presents as noble a type of the English cavalier as Vandyke or Lely ever immortalized on canvas. The dark hair, the swarthy complexion, the high forehead, the firm and regular features, the calm and proud expression,—all unite to form a countenance not surpassed in serene beauty by Rupert's, or in massive strength by Montrose's.

During the seventeenth century the Wormeleys were more prominent in the social and political life of the Colony even than the Lees. The first of this conspicuous family to settle in Virginia was Christopher Wormeley, who had filled the office of Governor of Tortuga in the interval between 1632 and 1635. He was accompanied by his brother Ralph. The two were sons of Christopher Wormeley, of Adwick-le-Street, in Yorkshire, and through him were directly descended from Sir John de Wormele, of Hadfield, situated in the same county.[21]   Ralph inherited the large estate of his brother, and at Rosegill, overlooking one of the noblest reaches of the broad Rappahannock, established what was perhaps the stateliest home in Virginia during the seventeenth century, a home adorned with all that the literature of the Mother Country and all that the mechanical arts of the Colony of that day could furnish, and celebrated far and wide for its hospitality and good cheer.[22]   Robert Throckmorton, the first of the Throckmorton family to arrive in Virginia, was the grandson of Gabriel Throckmorton, lord of the Manor of Ellington, in Huntingdonshire, who traced his pedigree to Sir Robert Throckmorton, of Coughton, Warwick.[23]   There was recorded in Accomac, in 1641, a deed from the widow of Sir Thomas Dale, in which she provided that one moiety of her property situated in Virginia should be divided among the children of Sir William Throckmorton.   This was the dividend which had been granted by the London Company to Dale as some return for his eminent services in the office of Governor.[24]   In 1650 Edward

---

[21] Lee of Virginia, p. 144; Va. Maga. of Hist. and Biog., Vol. IV., p. 173.

[22] See later reference to the library at Rosegill. A description of the house and its contents will be found in Bruce's *Economic History of Virginia in the Seventeenth Century*, Vol. II., p. 156. It was at Rosegill that Colonel Henry Norwood, who had crossed from the Eastern to the Western Shore, found a band of newly arrived Cavaliers in the full enjoyment of Colonel Wormeley's hospitality. Howard, while Governor, spent much of his time here.

[23] Va. Maga. of Hist. and Biog., Vol. VIII., pp. 84, 88.

[24] Accomac County Records, Vol. 1640-45, p. 62, Va. St. Libr. Copy.

Digges emigrated to the Colony, where he became distinguished, not only for the agricultural improvements he sought to introduce, but also for his prominence in political affairs. When he died he left a large estate to his widow, which included a variety of household articles showing a considerable degree of luxury and elegance in the appointments of his home. Digges was a son of Sir Dudley Digges, Master of the Rolls in England, one of the foremost offices in the administration of English justice. Sir Dudley was also at one time Ambassador to Russia, and had taken a conspicuous part in the management of the London Company. The mother of Edward Digges was a daughter of Sir Thomas Kemp, of Chilham, Kent.[25]

Nathaniel Bacon, the elder, emigrated to Virginia about the time the Puritan Supremacy in England was at its height; and he was not the only member of his family connection to leave his native land in consequence of that distasteful fact. We find him, after his arrival in the Colony, surrounded by numerous cavalier kinsmen. Through his mother, Martha Woodward, he was nearly related to Thomas Woodward, late assay-master of the Royal Mint, who had recently settled in Virginia. Through his first wife, Mrs. Ann Smith, he is supposed to have been a brother-in-law of Captain William Bassett, a former officer in the royal army, who also had decided to try his fortune in the Colony; while, through his second, he had become closely related to Sir Philip Honeywood, another cavalier officer who had found Virginia a more agreeable

---

[25] Lee of Virginia, p. 311; for Digges' Inventory see Bruce's *Economic History of Virginia in the Seventeenth Century*, Vol. II., p. 182.

place of residence than the Mother Country under the rule of Cromwell. An aunt, the widow of Sir Thomas Lyddall, had married Colonel George Lyddall, who, under the influence of the same feeling, had left England, and made his home in New Kent county, where we find him at a later day especially active in repelling Indian invasions. Lyddall was not the only member of his immediate family who had sought an asylum in Virginia, for, in 1666, Sir Robert Peake, a wealthy citizen of London, devised a considerable estate to John Lyddall, who at this time resided in the Colony.

Bacon himself was a grandson of Sir James Bacon, and was thus a great-great nephew of the celebrated Chancellor. As I have already pointed out, the Woodhouse family, which emigrated to the Colony at an earlier date, belonged to the same distinguished connection. Bacon, like Richard Lee, was an Englishman of the highest order both social and intellectual. He had received as thorough an education as that age afforded; was a man of commanding personality, as shown by the great prominence enjoyed by him throughout a long life, and of unusual talents for business, as proven by the large fortune which he accumulated. He possessed moral characteristics, associated with great mental vigor, which would have carried him very far in the public life of England had he remained there until the Restoration. He appears to have been singularly shrewd, wise, politic, and self-possessed. In the great commotion raised by his cousin, the younger Bacon, he never for a moment seems to have allowed family feeling to sway him, but throughout pursued a course which not only maintained the confidence Berkeley placed in him, but also relieved his name of the shadow of suspicion which might well have been attached to it among those in authority.[26]

Sir Henry Chichely, who arrived in Virginia only a few years before Bacon, had served in the royal army, and was such a conspicuous adherent of the royal cause that the Puritan Council of State, in granting him a license to emigrate, required him to furnish security that he would do nothing prejudicial to the existing government. Chichely was the son of Sir Henry, and brother of Sir Thomas Chichely, of Wimpole, Cambridgeshire. Sir Thomas was a member of the Privy Council, Master of the Ordnance, and a man who possessed great influence after the Restoration. Sir Henry Chichely himself had been an alderman of London.[27] Among the other titled Cavaliers who emigrated to the Colony about the same time as Chichely were Sir Thomas Lunsford, Sir Dudley Wyatt, and Sir Gray Skipwith. Thomas Welsford, who also removed thither, was the second son of Sir Thomas Welsford, who had lost both life and estate in supporting the side of the King.[28]

The first members of the Washington family to make

---

[26] For Lyddall and Bacon, see Waters's Gleanings, p. 11; William and Mary College Quart., Vol. VII., p. 223.

[27] Interregnum Entry Book, Vol. XCII., p. 177; Vol. CXXXII., p. 8; British Colonial Papers, Vol. XXX., No. 70; Vol. XLVI., No. 97; Va. Maga. of Hist. and Biog., Vol. III., p. 39; Vol. VIII, p. 181; William and Mary Quarterly, Vol. VI., p. 152. These different authorities contain many interesting facts about the Chichelys. Sir Henry Chichely married Agatha, the widow of Ralph Wormeley.

[28] William and Mary College Quart., Vol. VI., p. 89; Ingram's Proceedings, p. 34, Force's Historical Tracts, Vol. I.

their home in Virginia were the two sons of the Rev. Lawrence Washington, who was the brother of two knights, and connected by ties of close friendship with the Spencers of Althorp. The aunt of the two emigrants, the wife of Sir William Washington, was a half sister of one of the most famous and brilliant noblemen of that day, George Villiers, Duke of Buckingham. Rev. Lawrence Washington had been ejected from his pulpit in 1642 as a "malignant loyalist," and his fidelity had exposed him to many hardships and privations. His sons shared his sympathies, and following the example set by so many of even higher social rank, removed to Virginia in the hope of there restoring the fortunes of their family.[29]

One of the most promient citizens of the Colony for many years was George Ludlow, a cousin of General Edmund Ludlow, an officer of great distinction on the Puritan side in the Civil Wars.[30] A brother of General Ludlow was the ancestor of the earls of that name, a title which became extinct as recently as 1842.[31]

Henry Isham, whose daughter married the first of the Randolphs to emigrate to Virginia, belonged to a family which had been long seated in Northamptonshire, and which has retained its high social position down to the present day, when it is represented in the English baronetage. He was a nephew of Sir Edward

---

[29] Waters's Gleanings, p. 372; Mr. Waters suggests that the two emigrants mighc have been influenced in some measure to go to Virginia by their connection by blood with the Sandys and Vernon families, at one time so prominently represented there, or so deeply interested in its affairs.

[30] William and Mary College Quart., Vol. I., p. 190.

[31] Revived in recent years in favor of another family.

Brett, who had been knighted by Charles I. for brilliant services as an officer, and who by his will seems
to have devised a considerable estate to Isham's two
daughters. Isham resided in Virginia for a time, but
appears to have returned to England and died there.[32]
Thomas and Philip Ludwell, who became so distinguished in the social and official life of Virginia, were,
through their mother, great nephews of Lord Cottington, one of the most conspicuous figures in England
during the reign of the second Charles.[33] The first two
members of the Bland family to make their home in
the Colony were remote kinsmen of Sir Thomas Bland,
of Kippax Park, situated near the City of Leeds, who,
though knighted as late as 1642, was sprung from ancestry which had occupied the foremost place in that
part of England. A first cousin of the two emigrants
had married a titled member of the Herbert family.[34]

George Brent, one of the largest landowners residing in the Northern Neck, was a grandson of Sir John
Peyton, of Doddington, while his wife was a niece of
Sir William Layton, of Horsmandene, in Worcester-
shire.[35] John Clarke, who resided at Middle Plantation, was a son of Sir John Clarke, of Wrotham, in
Kent, and on the maternal side a grandson of Sir William Stead. Sir John was a brother of Sir William

---

[32] Waters's Gleanings, pp. 447-8.

[33] Lee of Virginia, p. 127; William and Mary College Quart.,
Vol. I., p. 110.

[34] Lee of Virginia, p. 138. See Waters's Gleanings for will of
the Herbert who intermarried with the Blands.

[35] Va. Maga. of Hist. and Biog., Vol. I., p. 124: Colonel St.
Leger Codd, of Northumberland county, was a grandson of Sir
Warham St. Leger, of Ulcombe, Kent; see same Vol. XI., p. 374.

Clarke, of the same place, and to the son of the latter, who inherited his father's title, the property of John Clarke in Virginia descended.[36]   The Scarborough family, long the most powerful on the Eastern Shore, furnished even after its arrival in Virginia at least one member to the titled class of England. Of the two sons of Edmund Scarborough, the emigrant, one, named Charles, settled in the Mother Country, where he became a scholar of great distinction, was elected a member of Parliament, and was appointed physician in turn to Charles II., James II. and William III. Knighted for his services, he rose to these high positions, not only by the force of extraordinary talents, but also through the influence of his family connection in England.[37]

Miles Cary, the first of that name to remove to Virginia, was related to the Cary family represented in the English peerage at that time by Robert Cary, Lord Hunsdon.[38]   Edmund Jennings, who arrived in the Colony when he was very young, and in later life became one of its Attorney-Generals, was a son of Sir

---

[36] William and Mary College Quart., Vol. XII., p. 37; York County Records, Vol. 1671-1694, p. 22, Va. St. Lbr: The incidental way in which these interesting items of family history come out in a single brief entry in tne York County Records show how slender are the materials which record the family connection with England of so many of the higher gentry of Virginia in the Seventeenth century. It also suggests how much valuable genealogical information has perished in the destruction of so many of the county records for this century.

[37] Va. Maga. of Hist. and Biog., Vol. IV., p. 316.

[38] This fact is shewn by the acknowledgment of Lord Hunsdon himself; see Keith's Ancestry of Benjamin Harrison, p. 39.

Edmund Jennings, of Ripon, Yorkshire, and through his mother, a grandson of Sir Edward Barkham, who had filled the office of Lord Mayor of London. Peter Jennings, a kinsman of Edmund, and like him at one time Attorney-General of Virginia, married a daughter of Sir Thomas Lunsford, the distinguished cavalier who had left England when the royal cause seemed hopeless.[39] George Luke, who, after his settlement in Virginia, became the husband of the widowed sister of William Fitzhugh, was a grandson of Sir Samuel Luke, of Woodend, in Bedfordshire, made famous in English literature by the pen of Butler as the hero of the great satire *Hudibras.*[40] Nicholas Spencer, who occupied the important post of Secretary of the Colony in the interval between 1679 and 1689, was, on the maternal side, the grandson of Sir Edward Gastwick, of Wellington, and was also related to the family in possession of the barony of Culpeper. His mother was Lady Mary Armiger.[41] A niece of Lord Culpeper had married Samuel Stephens, of Balthorpe, in Warwick county, in Virginia.[42] Joseph Woorey, of Isle of Wight county, was a nephew of Sir John Yeamans, of Bristol, a town which had sent many other emigrants of distinguished social connections to that part of Virginia. Woorey was also the great nephew of the brave and

---

[39] Lee of Virginia, p. 300; Va. Maga. of Hist. and Biog., Vol. IV., p. 366, Vol. VI., p. 399; William and Mary College Quart., Vol. III., p. 154.

[40] Va. Maga. of Hist. and Biog., Vol. III., p. 167.

[41] William and Mary College Quart., Vol. X., p. 173; see, also, will of William Spencer, brother of Nicholas, which will be found in Waters's Gleanings.

[42] Va. Maga. of Hist. and Biog., Vol. I., p. 83.

devoted loyalist who lost his life as the penalty for seeking to deliver up the city to Prince Rupert, an attempt which was thwarted by the Parliamentarians. Sir John Yeamans became celebrated in the colonial history of the Carolinas by founding the Clarendon settlement on Cape Fear River.[43] Among those who perished in the fight which took place in Lynnhaven Bay near the end of the century between the guardship *Shoreham* and a pirate vessel was Peter Heyman, a grandson of Sir Peter Heyman, of Kent, England, who had been appointed to the collectorship of Lower James River. Heyman had gone on board of the *Shoreham* to witness the battle.[44]

One of the most prominent families of Lower Norfolk county during the latter part of the seventeenth century was the Gutterick or Goodrich. In 1703 the affairs of Thomas Goodrich, probably of this family, then a minor and temporarily residing in England, were placed in the hands of his maternal uncle, Sir A. Danby, who had married a daughter of Abraham Moone, at one time a merchant of London, but afterwards, there is reason to think, identified for many years with Lancaster county, in Virginia.[45] Rowland Place, a member of the Council and a planter of large estate, had married the daughter of Sir John Brookes, of Norton, in Yorkshire. Place himself was the son of Francis Place, a painter of distinction residing in the city of York.[46] Lancelot Bathurst, who was set-

---

[43] William and Mary College Quart., Vol. VI., p. 131; Vol. VII., p. 212.

[44] Campbell's Hist. of Virginia, p. 361.

[45] Va. Maga. of Hist. and Biog., Vol. XI., p. 74.

[46] William and Mary College Quart., Vol. VII., p. 231.

tled in Essex county, was a son of Sir Edward
Bathurst, of Gloucestershire and member of a family
which continues to enjoy a position of social and political distinction in England.[47] The first of the Peyton family to emigrate was sprung from the Peytons
of Iselham, who traced back to the eleventh century.
He was also a descendant of Sir Thomas Osborne, the
founder of the family now in the enjoyment of the
dukedom of Leeds.[48]

[47] William and Mary College Quart., Vol. XII., p. 61.

[48] See Peyton Family, Hayden's Virginia Genealogies.

V

ORIGIN OF THE HIGHER PLANTING CLASS.—*Continued.*

A CONSIDERABLE proportion of the prominent families of Virginia in the sevententh century were sprung directly from the squirearchy of the Mother Country. It was the leading persons among this squireearchy who held the most conspicuous seats in the English parish churches, who filled the offices of vestryman and magistrate, who owned the bulk of the lands, who lived in manor houses which their forefathers had occupied, and who, like their forefathers, followed the hounds in season, and at times partook rather freely of the bottle. And it was their ancestors who lay in the chancels of the ancient rural churches, or under the defaced tombstones in the adjacent churchyards; whose memorial tablets gleamed on the interior walls of the churches themselves, and whose monuments rose in the shadow of the neighbouring yews planted far beyond the recollection of living men. From the massive gray church towers there could be seen in every direction in the surrounding country the homes, in most cases dating from the remote past, from which the younger sons of this local squirearchy had gone out to make their fortunes, some to the nearest town, some to the great mart of London to enter trade, and some over sea to plant tobacco in Virginia.[1]

---

[1] Sometimes the father would emigrate to Virginia and the son remain in England. A document recorded in Accomac county and signed by Earl of Derby, Duke of Richmond, etc., members of the

The emigration to that Colony had been especially large from the rural parishes of the southern and middle shires, so remarkable for their agricultural abundance and so productive of famous names in English history. From the great upland slopes that looked down upon the English Channel towards the south, and upon the Bristol Channel towards the west, the sons of the country gentlemen could see the white wings of the fleets of merchantmen bound out to Virginia, and gleaming for hours, even days, upon the blue waters before they melted finally from view. Doubtless, that annual spectacle was not without its effect upon the minds of many a susceptible youth, eager, in spite of the great natural beauty and wealth around him, and in spite of his ancient home haunted by a thousand memories and associations, to push out into some region never before visited by him, there to win fortune more easily than it could be done in his native land.

Among the prominent families of the Colony which traced their origin to the squirearchy of Devonshire, the most beautiful of these southern shires, was the

great Council of State, refers to "William Rydeing, late of Westerby in the county of Lancaster, gentleman, now of Accomac." His son, Hugh, lived at Westerby, and, in 1683, inherited his father's estate.—Accomac County Records, Vol. 1676-90, p. 371. Dr. Bennett W. Green, in his remarkable work, "Word Book of Virginia Folk Speech," declares that the slurring of the "r" shows that the ancestors of the Virginians "came chiefly from Southern England." Again he says (p. 9) : "There seems to be a distinctly southern, southwestern, and east midland character in the speech of the Virginians, little or none of the East-Anglian or Norfolk." See, also, William and Mary College Quart., Vol. IV., p. 28; Vol. VIII., p. 211.

Yeo. A Yeo had been a member of Parliament from Totness as early as 1557. One of the gentlemen who subscribed for the defense of the kingdom when the invasion by the Armada was threatened was Leonard Yeo, a leading citizen of the county at that date.[2] The first of the family to emigrate to Virginia, known also as Leonard, settled in Elizabeth City, but at a later period in the century the name was found in Accomac, for which county Hugh Yeo was at one time a member of the House of Burgesses. The family, long after its arrival in Virginia, continued to own property in England.[3] The Broadhurst family was sprung from Walter Broadhurst, who established his home in the Colony in 1650. He was the son of William Broadhurst, who resided at Lilleshall, in Shropshire, and whose social position was such that, in all formal legal papers, his name was always accompanied by the term "gentleman."[4] In 1678 he is found conveying property to the son who had settled in Virginia.[5] The first of the Peachy family to emigrate was the son of Robert Peachy, of Milden Hall, Suffolkshire.[6] The wife of Daniel Parke, the elder, belonged to the family made celebrated by the accomplished John Evelyn, of Wotton, a family, however, that had been long prominent among the country gentry of England. She was the

---

[2] Va. Maga. of Hist. and Biog., Vol. VII., p. 194; William and Mary College Quart., Vol. IX., p. 125.

[3] This fact appears in various depositions found in the Accomac Records. The Lear family, also very prominent, was from Devonshire.

[4] Va. Maga. of Hist. and Biog., Vol. IX., p. 333.

[5] Westmoreland County Records for 1678.

[6] William and Mary College Quart., Vol. III., p. 111.

daughter of George Evelyn, who was residing in Virginia as early as 1649, and where he still has descendants; thus, through him, she was the niece of John Evelyn, and the grand-daughter of Robert, of Long Ditton, in Surrey. Another member of this family connection, who also bore the name of Robert, was, in 1637, the Surveyor-General of the Colony. It is possible that these close personal ties made John Evelyn the more willing to accept an appointment to the Board of Trade and Plantations, of which he has left an interesting account in his famous diary.[7] The Corbins were sprung from Nicholas Corbin, who, in the reigns of Richard III. and Henry VII., owned Hall's End and other landed property in Warwickshire. The first of them to come out to Virginia was the grandson of Gawen Grosvenor, a distinguished name in that century as well as in this.[8]

John Page, the first of the Pages to make his home in the Colony, where he arrived in 1650, at the age of twenty-three, was the son of Francis Page, of Bedfont parish, in Middlesex. He is supposed on reliable evidence to have belonged to a branch of the Page family of Harrow-on-the-Hill, which had, during many generations, enjoyed a high position among the rural gentry of England. The Pages of Bedfont had been seated there from a date going back beyond the reign of Edward VI., during which period one member of the family, Rowland, had possessed manorial rights there.

---

[7] William and Mary College Quart., Vol. X., p. 172; Va. Maga. of Hist. and Biog., Vol. IX., p. 173. Robert Evelyn, the Surveyor-General, was entered at the Middle Temple in 1620; see Va. Maga. of Hist. and Biog., Vol. VII., p. 296.

[8] Lee of Virginia, p. 83.

The father of the emigrant was of sufficient consideration in the parish to have his tomb placed in the chancel of the parish church, an honour only paid to the remains of persons of high social standing.[9] The Beverley family, which was represented in Virginia in the seventeenth century by several members of great political prominence, had been associated with the town of Beverley, in Yorkshire, as far back in the past as the reign of King John. Robert Beverley, the elder, was perhaps the wealthiest citizen residing in the Colony, while his son of the same name was the earliest native of Virginia to write a book possessing extraordinary merits.[10]

The first of the Harrisons to emigrate settled on the James River not many years after the Colony was founded, and the family acquired importance before the close of the century. Investigation has been unable to throw much definite light on the origin of this family, which has contributed so many distinguished men to the history of our country, but as the emigrant was soon after his arrival appointed clerk of the Council, a position only held in those times by men of influence and social prominence, it has been inferred that his social connections in England were such as entitled him to more than usual consideration.[11]

---

[9] Herald's College Report, Page Genealogy, p. 34: " Sir Richard Brown, in his will, requested to be buried in the churchyard, he being much offended at the novel custom of burying every one within the body of the church and chancel, that being a favour heretofore granted only to martyrs and great persons."—Entry Febry., 1683, Evelyn's Diary, Chandos Classics.

[10] Lee of Virginia, p. 319.

[11] Keith's Ancestry of Benjamin Harrison, p. 46; British Colonial Papers, Vol. III., 1624-5, No. 26.

John Carter arrived about 1649. There is no trustworthy information as to his origin, though he is conjectured, apparently without any ground, to have been a member of the Carter family long seated in Hertfordshire.[12] The prominence of this family in Virginia, which has been almost exclusively social, really began early in the eighteenth century with Robert Carter, who combined with extraordinary wealth (partly inherited and partly accumulated by his own foresight) a remarkable personal impressiveness. The two together led to his receiving the name of "King Carter." Robert Carter and the second William Byrd, who were the most distinguished members of their families, were both born in the last quarter of the seventeenth century, and their characters were largely moulded by the influences which then prevailed. In their affluent style of life, great landed estates, troops of dependents, lordly deportment, and far reaching authority, they were the equals of the first proprietors among the English country gentry of their day.

The family of Colonel Peter Ashton, of Westmoreland county, were sprung from the Ashtons, of Spalding, in Lincolnshire, one of the most ancient families residing in that part of England, whilst the Burwells traced their descent immediately to a family equally ancient in Bedfordshire.[13] The Smiths, of Abingdon parish, in Gloucester county, were, through Elizabeth

---

[12] This claim is set forth in the Carter Family Tree, but does not appear to be substantiated; see William and Mary College Quart., Vol. I., p. 138.

[13] For Ashtons, see Letters of William Fitzhugh, Jan'y 30, 1686-7. For Burwells, see Neill's Virginia Carolorum, p. 260.

Cox, an offshoot of the Stracheys, of Sutton Court, in Somersetshire.[14]

A considerable number of the leading families of Virginia in the seventeenth century were directly descended from Englishmen who were distinguished in the professions, but who, in most cases, can be traced back to the landed gentry. William Fitzhugh, who accumulated a large estate, left a long series of interesting letters, and founded a representative family, was the son of a lawyer in practice at Bedford. As his brother, Henry Fitzhugh, enjoyed considerable interest at Court, it is probable that the family connection possessed social and political influence. There is some reason indeed to think that the Fitzhughs of Bedford were a remote branch of the Fitzhughs of Ravensworth, who had been raised to a barony.[15] The Douthats also appear to have borne a close relation to the legal profession in England.[16] Philip Lightfoot, the first of the Lightfoot family to come over, was the son of John Lightfoot, a barrister of Gray's Inn, in London.[17] Charles Harmar, who settled on the East-

---

[14] Va. Maga. of Hist. and Bicg., Vol. VII., p. 400.

[15] Lee of Virginia, p. 89; The Fitzhugh Family, Va. Maga. of Hist. and Biog., Vol. VII. One of the former homes of the Fitzhughs in Virginia is named Ravensworth. It is now the property of Mrs. William H. Fitzhugh Lee.

[16] York County Records, Vol. 1657-62, p. 187, Va. St. Libr: Margaret Pryor, daughter of William Pryor, of York county, returned to England and married Thomas Edwards, of "Inner Temple, Gentleman." She sold the lands which she had inherited in Virginia. See York County Records, Vol. 1657-62, p. 392, Va. St. Libr.

[17] William and Mary College Quart., Vol. II., p. 91; Va. Maga. of Hist. and Biog., Vol. VII., p. 397.

ern Shore, was the cousin of John Harmar, professor of the Greek Language in Oxford University.[18] Thomas and Henry Batte, the earliest of their name to arrive in Virginia, and the progenitors of a distinguished family connection, were the sons of Robert Batte, Vice-Master of University College at the same great seat of learning.[19] Christopher Robinson, who emigrated to the Colony in 1666 and established himself in Middlesex, where he at once became one of the leading members of the community, was a brother of John Robinson, Bishop of London. Robinson showed his attachment to his old home in England by naming after it his new home in Virginia—Hewick.[20] Isaac Bargrave, one of the earliest settlers in the Colony, was a brother of the Dean of Canterbury.[21] Peter Montague, the emigrant, was the second cousin of Richard Montague, who was the Bishop, first of Chichester, and afterwards of Norwich.[22] William Juxon, of York county, was a kinsman of Bishop Juxon, who received the last words of Charles I. As early as 1625 William Pinder, rector of Mottisfount, Southampton, left ten pounds sterling to his nephew, Thomas Singleton, then in Virginia.[23] Bequests of this kind constantly occur in the later history of the Colony. For instance, in 1672 Edward Newman received a like sum under the will of his uncle, a canon of Windsor Castle; and in 1691 William Bolton, a clergyman residing at Harrow-on-the-Hill, in Middlesex, England,

---

[18] Va. Maga. of Hist. and Biog., Vol. III., p. 274.

[19] William and Mary College Quart., Vol. I., p. 196.

[20] Va. Maga. of Hist. and Biog., Vol. III., p. 13.

[21] See Bargrave, Waters's Gleanings.

[22] History of Peter Montague, pp. 30, 49.

[23] Pinder Will, Waters's Gleanings.

made his brother in Virginia his residuary legatee.[24]
About 1669 a prominent citizen of York county provided in his will that, should his children die before
they came of age, one hundred pounds sterling should
be paid by his executors to his kinsman, Prebend Ter-
rill, of Windsor.[25]

There were in Virginia during the seventeenth century a considerable number of prominent families
sprung from English military officers. I have in a previous chapter referred to those of this origin who were
descended from Cavaliers with titles indicating social
rank; but there were numerous others descended from
Cavalier officers who were without such titles. Some
of the supporters of the royal cause who found their
way to the Colony were, like Robert Jones, merely
common soldiers, but, perhaps, like him, had been
wounded in battle in the King's service. After his
capture, Jones was shipped to the plantations, but
seems to have returned to England before the death of
Charles II.[26] An officer of distinction who found an
asylum in Virginia was General Mainwaring Hammond. He arrived about 1649, the very year Charles I.
perished on the scaffold, and was accompanied by Sir
Philip Honeywood, who also had been an officer in
the royal army. Other officers of high rank abandon-
ing England under the influence of their hatred of the
existing government were Majors Philip Stevens,
John Brodnax, and Richard Fox, and Colonels Guy
Molesworth, Joseph Bridger and Henry Norwood. In
the band of Cavaliers seeking a home in the Colony
there were a number who had been active supporters

---

[24] See Waters's Gleanings, years 1625, 1672, and 1691.
[25] York Records, Vol. 1669-72, p. 160, Va. St. Libr.
[26] British Colonial Papers, Vol. XLV., No. 3, 31.

of the King without, however, possessing a military title. Such were Anthony Langston, Henry Bishop, Alexander Culpeper, and Jeremiah Harrison; such also quite probably were the nine gentlemen, whose names, with the prefix of "mister," an indication at that day of social position, are included in the list of headrights offered by Sir Thomas Lunsford to secure a land patent in 1650, the year of his arrival. Some of these companions of Lunsford, himself a Cavalier officer of distinction, had, no doubt, held commissions in the royal army, while all had, in one capacity or another, either military or civil, striven to advance the royal cause. Jeremiah Harrison had married the daughter of the man by whose fidelity and coolness Charles II. had been saved just after the battle of Worcester, which had proved so disastrous to his fortunes. Henry Bishop became a citizen of Virginia previous to 1646, in which year he was commissioned by the House of Burgesses to return to England in order to deliver a letter addressed by that body to the English Parliament. He seems to have remained, for, in 1660, he filled the high office of Postmaster-General of the Kingdom.[27]

Among the most active supporters of the royal cause

[27] For the various details about the different Cavaliers mentioned in the previous sentences of this paragraph, see Va. Maga. of Hist. and Biog., Vol. III., p. 266, Vol. VIII., p. 390, and William and Mary College Quart., Vol. VI., p. 90. Major John Brodnax, the first of his distinguished name in Virginia, which is still associated with Brunswick county, died in York county. Mr. Lyon G. Tyler has called attention to the interesting fact that the will and inventory of Brodnax show his possession of all those articles of dress which are associated with the popular conception of the fashionable and dashing Cavalier. See William and Mary College Quart., Vol. VI., p. 61.

were the Randolphs, a family which enjoyed some distinction in England, not the smallest part of which was derived from the fame of a member who had become celebrated as one of the first poets of that day. They were, to use the words of one of their number, "entirely broken and dispersed" by the upshot of the Civil Wars;[28] but in emigrating to Virginia, William Randolph had taken the first important step, not only towards restoring the fortunes of the family, but also towards raising those fortunes to a point which had not been reached in England. Before the close of the colonial period a series of noble plantations in the most fertile part of the country along the Lower James River had become the property of the Randolphs in their various branches. Here they had lived in a state of affluence remarkable even in the most prosperous days of the Colony; had filled a succession of high public offices; had received the honor of knighthood; had intermarried with all the most powerful families; and had enjoyed a degree of social and political influence unsurpassed in those times. Nor did their distinction come to an end with that memorable era. Among the most prominent names in the period of the Revolution and the foundation of the national government were Peyton and Edmund Randolph; and in the great crisis of Secession there was an equally brilliant representative of the same family in George Wythe Randolph, the first Confederate Secretary of War.[29]

[28] Va. Maga. of Hist. and Biog., Vol. III., p. 266; see obituary notice of Sir John Randolph, of Virginia, in the *Virginia Gazette.*

[29] The present senior P. E. Bishop of Southern Virginia, the Right Rev. A. M. Randolph, D. D., so distinguished for great learning, moving eloquence, and saintly piety, is a member of this family.

The Mason family is descended from Colonel George Mason, who, according to an unconfirmed tradition, only after the crowning defeat of the royal cause at the battle of Worcester left England to settle in the Colony. He had been preceded by Gerard Fowke, a cousin who had been a member of the royal household as well as a colonel in the royal army.[30] Thomas Landon, the first of the Landon family to go out to the Colony, had been the eldest groom of the King's buttery, a position of a higher social character in that age of extravagant loyalty than it would be in these times when so much of the divinity that hedged a monarch has passed away.[31] The wife of the elder William Byrd was the grand-daughter of a clergyman, who, like Rev. Lawrence Washington, had, in 1643, been ejected from his benefice on the ground that he was a "malignant loyalist." A number of these clergymen appear to have settled in Virginia.[32]

These emigrants to Virginia, who had taken an active part in the Civil Wars, or had openly sympathized with the royal cause in the great conflict between King and Parliament, enjoyed an influence in the social life of the Colony which was out of proportion to their mere number. Some of these men, as we have seen, were persons of rank in England; others were untitled officers in the royal armies, and, with few exceptions, all were sprung from the English landed gentry. They

---

[30] Dinwiddie Papers, Va. Hist. Soc. Coll., p. 23.

[31] Va. Maga. of Hist. and Biog., Vol. II., p. 431.

[32] William and Mary College Quart., Vol. IX., p. 10: Berkeley wrote in 1671: "We had few (clergymen) we could boast of since the persecution in Cromwell's tyranny drove divers worthy men thither;" Hening's Statutes, Vol. II., p. 517.

brought with them to Virginia the tastes and habits of
the society in which they had moved, and to which
they had belonged by birth as well as by association,
the society of the English country gentlemen. The
most characteristic features of that society had, in
no small measure, been already introduced into the
Colony by those among the previous English settlers
who had mingled in it in their native land. The plantation life in which men like Lunsford, Honeyman,
Skipwith, Norwood, Stevens, Mason, Molesworth,
Brodnax, and Fowke found an asylum must have appeared to them as marked by much that was familiar in
spirit, custom, and habit as compared with that life
which they had so recently left behind. There was the
same disposition to enjoy with heartiness all the
sources of happiness and pleasure which life afforded;
the same love of overflowing good cheer; the same
taste for dancing, card-playing, and other indoor
amusements; the same interest in horse, dog, and gun,
in racing, coursing, and shooting; and the same loyalty to King and Church, which had prevailed among
the Cavaliers of England. These gentlemen of recognized position in England, these soldiers who bore
upon their persons the scars which proved the firmness of their courage and the strength of their devotion to their sovereign, must, in the homes of the principal planters, have possessed an extraordinary pres-
tige on account both of what they had suffered and
what they had represented in the Mother Country.
The participation of such men in the current of the
social life around them must have given it a stronger
impulse in the direction it was already running; and
also have done much to confirm and accentuate those

peculiarities which already existed. Emigrants, like Richard Lee and the elder Nathaniel Bacon, sprung from distinguished families, although without military reputation, no doubt, soon after their arrival, became the social leaders of the community, and by the dignity of their personal appearance and bearing, and thorough knowledge of all the refinements of the best society of that day made a lasting impression upon the social life of the Colony.

Nor, in describing the social influence of the Cavaliers, should Sir William Berkeley be forgotten. Appointed to the Governorship about 1642, he remained in office, with the exception of the interval of the Protectorate, until 1676. All the accounts unite in representing him as having enjoyed a great popularity down to the last ten years of his administration, when he allowed himself to fall so completely under those reactionary influences which arose both in Virginia and England after the Restoration. He was, from many points of view, a type of the extreme Cavalier. Sprung from one of the oldest and proudest families in England; the favorite of royalty and trained in the atmosphere of a Court; headstrong, irascible, impulsive, domineering, yet capable of assuming all the conciliatory graces of one long accustomed to the best society of his times; a man of imposing appearance and bearing on all occasions; an aristocrat in every feeling and opinion; brave to recklessness, and ready at any moment to maintain his honor with the sword at his side,—such are the outlines of a character, which, stamping itself deeply in many ways upon the contemporary social life of the Colony, must have served, like the presence of the emigrant Cavaliers, to strengthen the sympathies of the Virginian planters with all those ideas, standards, and habits which had immemorially distinguished the great body of the English people.

VI.

Origin of the Higher Planting Class,—*Continued*.

PERHAPS the most important section of the higher planting class during the seventeenth century were the families sprung directly from English merchants. Many of these descendants of English merchants, however, traced their pedigrees back, and that, too, not remotely, to landed proprietors in the different shires, for in that age a very large proportion of those engaged in trade in the cities had come in from the rural parishes. The law of primogeniture, which was, perhaps, more deeply rooted in England in those times than in these, had, as already stated, a powerful influence in causing many of the younger sons of the landed gentry to emigrate to Virginia in search of fortune; but it had an even more powerful influence in forcing many of these younger sons into mercantile, and even into mechanical, pursuits in order to earn a subsistence without leaving their native country.

From a very early period, the trade guilds had filled a conspicuous place in all the larger English towns, and nowhere was their supremacy within their own sphere of operation more absolute than in London; in that city, no one was permitted to cast a vote for municipal officers unless he had served an apprenticeship in one of the livery companies or crafts; and this regulation prevailed generally in all the other cities of the kingdom. This privileged exclusiveness made the mercantile and mechanical callings uniformly profitable. When there were three or four sons to be provided for by a father who was a country gentleman, it was usual, in the seventeenth century, to keep the eldest at home if he was to inherit the whole of the landed estates; the second was sent to one of the great universities, in order to prepare himself to enter a learned profession, such as law, physic, or divinity; the third was apprenticed to a local solicitor, apothecary, or surgeon; the fourth to a pewterer or watch-maker, or the like. It will be observed that the employments selected were graduated in social importance according to the relative ages of the sons; the youngest fared the worst in the dignity of the calling chosen for him, but in order that he might acquire the highest skill in his mechanical craft, it was customary for him to be dispatched to London (the greatest centre of business in the kingdom, and the finest school in which to learn an art), because it was known that there he would enjoy every opportunity of perfecting himself in his special pursuit. At the end of his time, he would return to the village or town nearest to his former home.[1] As the purely manual crafts were not admitted to the guilds, and the membership of the guilds themselves was confined to men who had enjoyed a long and careful training, there was no disposition to shut out from genteel society those persons belonging to these corporations who followed the lower branches of the arts; whilst so much wealth was accumulated by the persons who followed the higher, that they were able, not only to inter-- marry with the noblest families in the kingdom, but also to found new families of great distinction.

All of the London guilds (which included in their membership persons who had, in early life, come to that

---

[1] See Mrs. Gaskell's Life of Charlotte Brontë, chap. III.; also the Life of Sir Humphrey Davy.

great centre of trade from every part of England) were deeply interested in the early settlement of Virginia; this is shown by the fact that, among the subscribers to the charter of 1612, were ten mercers, twelve goldsmiths, seventy grocers, twenty drapers and tailors respectively, ten skinners, two salters, ten ironmongers, twelve haberdashers, sixteen clothworkers, and four vintners. These merchants and manufacturers were sagacious enough to perceive that the Colony would, in time, raise up a host of new purchasers for their goods and products. Throughout the seventeenth century, it was the tradesmen of London who took the leading part in supplying the various needs of the Virginian planters; their principal rivals in this traffic were the tradesmen of Bristol, who were among the most active and enterprising in that age; while following at a distance in sharing the profits of this commerce were the tradesmen of Weymouth, Dartmouth, Hull, Plymouth, Biddeford, and Barnstaple.

Many of the merchants engaged in trade with Virginia visited the Colony in the course of their business, and a very considerable proportion, already having relatives there, or forming new ties, or discovering in this new field a better chance of fortune than in the old in England, remained there permanently.[2]

---

[2] That these visits on the part of English merchants were very numerous was shown by the wills which they made before setting out on so long and so dangerous a voyage, and which were afterwards recorded. An example will be found in the will of Nathaniel Braddock, Va. Maga. of Hist. and Biog., Vol. XI., p. 149, and of William Wraxall, Idem, p. 361. See for the wills of other visiting merchants the "Virginia Gleanings in England," published in Va. Maga. of History and Biography. John Brewer, formerly a grocer of London, was, at his death, in 1635, a member of the Va. Council; Va. Maga. of Hist. and Biog., Vol. XI., p. 317.

During periods of extraordinary commotion in England, which brought about a disturbance of trade and encouraged severe exactions, many English merchants removed to the Colony in order to secure peace and quiet; this was especially the case at the beginning of the armed conflicts between Charles I. and his Parliament, which, following upon a period of remarkable prosperity, was to cause so much ruin and confusion by the interruption of foreign commerce, the sacking of cities and the passage of predatory troops in all directions.[3]

Among those engaged in business in Virginia at a very early date, after, perhaps, some experience of the like pursuits in England, were George Menifie, John Chew, and Abraham Piersey, men whose names are always coupled with the term "merchant" in the records. All three rose to wealth and prominence in the Colony, and at least one, Chew, founded a family of distinction and influence.[4]

Berkeley Hundred, which spread over eighty thousand acres, was, in the beginning, taken up under a patent granted to seven well-known merchants of London, and of the seven, all probably, but certainly three, William Tucker, Maurice Thompson, and Cornelius Lloyd, went out to Virginia in search of fortune.[5] The first patent to Martin's Brandon was acquired by three English mer-

---

[3] Tyler's Cradle of the Republic, p. 47. For prosperity in England about 1630, see Green's Short History of the English People, chap. viii, sect. 5. Clarendon also dwells upon it in his history.

[4] The Virginia Land Patent Books. The same is observed in the county records in the case of leading men like Cornelius Lloyd, of Lower Norfolk county; see Records of that county, orig., Vol. 1646-51, p. 81.

[5] Va. Maga. of Hist. and Biog., Vol. VI. p. 185.

chants, one of whom, Richard Quiney, was a kinsman of Shakspere's son-in-law of that name.[6]

The earliest of the Ferrers to settle in the Colony was nearly related by blood to Nicholas Ferrer, who, sprung from an old family of Hertford, had, when very young, been apprenticed to a skinner of London to become, in time, the master of the skinner's guild, a merchant of great eminence, and the trusted friend of many of the most celebrated seamen and statesmen of those times, among others, Drake and Hawkins, Sandys and Raleigh. He was one of the most distinguished members of the London Company, and among the most earnest and constant, as well as wisest supporters of that great enterprise. Even after the revocation of the charter, the Ferrers in England continued to show an active interest in every scheme that would advance the welfare of Virginia.[7]

The father of Captain Ralph Hamor, who, escaping with his life by a hair's breadth from the frightful massacre of 1622, wrote an account of the early history of the Colony, was the son of a merchant tailor.[8] William

---

[6] Va. Maga. of Hist. and Biog., Vol. VI., p. 187.

[7] Va. Maga. of Hist. and Biog., Vol. VII., p. 320; Bruce's " Economic Hist. of Va. in the Seventeenth Century," Vol. I., p. 365, *et seq.* For a remarkable account of the Ferrer religious establishment at Little Gitting, see Shorthouse's "John Inglesant." The history of Nicholas Ferrer's career shows what was done in England in those times with so many young men of good family, when they had to be settled in life, and also the fortunes which so many acquired in trade. Nicholas married Mary Woodenoth, who was of very ancient lineage.—Va. Maga. of Hist. and Biog., Vol. VII., p. 320.

[8] Abstracts of Proceedings of Va. Co. of London, Vol. I., p. 118, note, Va. Hist. Soc. Pubs.

Claiborne, at one time, as already mentioned, Secretary of Virginia, a Commissioner of Parliament and promi nent in many ways, had a brother who occupied a shop on Ludgate Hill, in London, where he was a dealer in clothing.[9] As the Claiborne or Cleburne family, from which these two brothers were directly sprung, was one of the most ancient in the English county of Westmoreland, the adoption of a trade by one of them as a pursuit in life, thus imitating the example of Nicholas Ferrer and so many other young men of gentle descent, serves to show both the greater social dignity of the ordinary crafts in the England of that day than in the England of this, and also the greater narrowness of the field of employment. In preferring to emigrate to Virginia rather than to follow in the footsteps of his brother in London, William Claiborne discloses how powerful was the influence leading so many young Englishmen in those times to seek their fortune in the Colony.

The Brooke family was already well known in Virginia in the seventeenth century. In a deed drawn up before 1650, John Brooke, of Essex-shire, referred to himself as "clothier," and named as his attorney in the Colony his relative, Henry Brooke, who resided there. We learn from this deed that Barnaby Brooke, a brother of John, died at sea, while on his way to Virginia in charge of a large quantity of merchandise. Nor were these the only kinsmen of Henry Brooke who were engaged in trade

---

[9] Governor Harvey, in a letter to Lord Dorchester, dated May 29, 1630, described him as a "stocking-seller." See British Colonial Papers for 1630, No. 5; see, also, Vol. V., No. 93. As Harvey was an enemy of Claiborne on account of a violent difference of opinion as to Baltimore's right to colonize Maryland, this term applied to Claiborne's brother was used contemptuously, without perhaps expressing the truth exactly.

in England; in a second deed, dated as early as 1638, we find him mentioning the name of Nicholas Brooke, who, it appears, was a merchant of London.[10]

Captain Robert Higginson, who was sent, in 1644, to build a palisade at the Middle Plantation, was the son of a painter-stainer, whose place of business was in London also.[11] In the same year, the earliest member of the Bushrod family to settle in Virginia entered his name in the records of the Eastern Shore as a merchant.[12] Richard Death, a well-known citizen of Isle of Wight County, about this time, in his will, devised property to a son belonging to the guild of Merchant Tailors in London.[13] Captain Robert Felgate, of York, who was even more prominent in the Colony, was a brother of William Felgate, of the guild of skinners in the same great city; in his will, bearing the date of 1644, he referred to himself as "gentleman," a term which had also been applied to Toby Felgate on his arrival in 1619.[14] Among the persons who acquired patents to lands situated within the boundaries of Shirley Hundred, was John Brewer, a member of the Grocer's guild of London, whose sons settled permanently in Virginia.[15] The Allertons, of the Northern Neck, a family of great distinction in the Colony, and possessing a wide and prominent connection

---

[10] York County Records, Vol. 1638-48, p. 63, Va. St. Libr. Copy.

[11] William and Mary College Quart., Vol. XII., p. 36.

[12] Northampton County Records, orders July 29, 1644.

[13] Isle of Wight County Records, Wills for 1647.

[14] York County Records, Vol. 1633-94, pp. 71-2, Va. St. Libr. Copy. Brown's First Republic, pp. 371, 413. Toby Felgate was alive in 1630, as we know from a land patent which he acquired in that year.

[15] Va. Maga. of Hist. and Biog., Vol. III., p. 183. Brewer himself died in Virginia.

through marriage, were sprung from Isaac Allerton, an English merchant-tailor.[16] Samuel Haywood, who intermarried with the Washingtons, and was himself the founder of an influential family, was the son of a wealthy merchant of London.[17]

Henry Corbin, of Westmoreland county, who, as we have seen, traced his pedigree to the Corbins of Hall End, in Warwickshire, a family of high standing among the English country gentry, had a brother in London who belonged to the guild of leather sellers.[18] A cousin of James Ashton, of the same county, a member very probably of the ancient family of Ashtons, of Spalding, in Lincolnshire, followed the trade of haberdasher in Covent Garden.[19] The Corbin and Ashton families, each in the full enjoyment of a distinguished social position in England, illustrated in the same striking way as the Claiborne family, the powerful influence that led some members to engage in trade in England, and others to seek their fortunes in Virginia. Cadwallader Jones, of Rappahannock county, was the son of Richard Jones, a London merchant.[20] A son of Richard Lee, the emigrant, left Virginia, and making his home in that city, remained in business there until his death.[21] The ancestor of the Booker family,

---

[16] William and Mary College Quart., Vol. IV., p. 39.

[17] Willliam and Mary College Quart., Vol. IV., p. 40.

[18] William and Mary College Quart., Vol. IV., p. 30.

[19] Letters of William Fitzhugh, Janry 30, 1686-7; Va. Maga. of Hist. and Biog., Vol. X., p. 292. The Ashton home in Virginia was known as "Chatterton," the name of the residence of the Lancashire branch in England, the original seat of the family.

[20] Va. Maga. of Hist. and Biog., Vol. II., p. 31.

[21] Lee of Virginia, p. 71.

which acquired prominence at a later date, was an English merchant, who carried on a large trade with Virginia about the middle of the seventeenth century.[22]

A brother of John and Henry Batte, sons of a Vice-Master of Oxford University, and the first of their name to remove to Virginia, was a member of the Grocers' guild in London.[23] Richard Bennett, who belonged to the family which Lord Arlington had made so conspicuous in England, was the nephew of an English merchant, who was interested in the trade with the Colony.[24] William Byrd, the founder of one of the most distinguished families in colonial history, was the son of a London banker or goldsmith[25], whilst the Blands, who traced back to English landed proprietors, were sprung directly from Adam Bland, a member of the skinners' guild in the same city. Of the two sons of Adam Bland, one followed the business of a merchant-tailor, the other, that of a grocer.[26] Both the father and uncle of Thomas and Philip Ludwell were participants in the trade of mercers; the father, as we have seen, had married a niece of Lord Cottington, one of the most famous public men of those times.[27] The first of the Fitzhughs was probably the grandson of a maltster of Bedford, through whom, however, he was, with equal probability, related

---

[22] Va. Maga. of Hist. and Biog., Vol. VII., p. 95.

[23] William and Mary College Quart., Vol. I., p. 79.

[24] Va. Maga. of Hist. and Biog., Vol. III., pp. 53, 54.

[25] William and Mary College Quart., Vol. IV., p. 153.

[26] Abstracts of Proceedings of Va. Co. of London, Vol. I., p. 83, note; Va. Hist. Soc. Pub. See, also, Hayden's "Virginia Genealogies."

[27] Waters's Gleanings, p. 719; Lee of Virginia, p. 127; William and Mary College Quart., Vol. I., p. 110.

to the Fitzhughs of Ravensworth, the possessors, as already stated, of a barony.[28]

Among the leading families which were associated with York county, were the Vaulx and Munford. The member of the Vaulx family, Thomas, by name, who was a justice of that county in 1670, seems to have been accompanied to Virginia by Humphrey and James Vaulx. The three were brothers of Robert Vaulx, a wealthy merchant of London, who, at one time, resided in the Colony, but perhaps only to obtain a practical knowledge upon the ground of the character of its business, for he returned to England.[29] William Munford came over to Virginia as the agent of his brother, John Munford, a London grocer; he describes himself in various deeds sometimes as "mercer," and sometimes as "tobacconist." It is possible that these two early merchants were brothers, or at least near relations, of Robert Munford, to whom the well-known family of Munfords of Virginia trace their origin.[30] Among the merchants trading in York county, who left descendants, were John Lockey and Thomas Griffith. Griffith had emigrated from London.[31] Hugh Stanford, who died in that county in 1657, was the brother of Anthony Stanford, a prominent merchant of the same great city.[32] The first members of the Washington family to emigrate, through the marriages of their cousins, the daughters of Sir William Washington, were also connected with the trades of London;

---

[28] Va. Maga. of Hist. and Biog., Vol. VII.; see Fitzhugh Family.

[29] York County Records, Vol. 1684-87, p. 170, Va. St. Libr. Copy. William and Mary College Quarterly, Vol. III., p. 14.

[30] William and Mary College Quart., Vol. III., p. 153, Vol. VI., p. 128; York County Records, Vol. 1657-62, pp. 28, 135, Va. St. Libr. Copy.

[31] William and Mary College Quart., Vol. VIII., p. 202.

[32] William and Mary College Quart., Vol. III., p. 14.

Susannah was the wife of Reginald Graham, a member of the draper guild, and her sister, of Colonel William Legge, a descendant of a Lord Mayor, who had accumulated a large estate by his talents for business.[33]

Among the leading citizens of York county was Peter Perry, a brother of Micajah Perry, who had also filled the same great office of Lord Mayor, and who was perhaps the most conspicuous English merchant engaged, during the seventeenth century, in supplying the plants during the seventeenth century, in supplying the planters of Virginia with goods of all kinds in exchange for tobacco, in which trade he succeeded in making a large fortune. It is probable that, like so many settlers in the Colony who were connected by ties of family with wealthy English merchants, Peter Perry combined the calling of a planter with the occupation of looking after his brother's interests in that part of Virginia. William Lee, a resident of the same county, was a brother of George Lee, a merchant of London, who enjoyed a profitable share in the Colonial trade.[34] Miles Cary, the first of the Cary family to leave England, and a relative of Lord Hunsdon, was the son of John Cary, a woolen draper of Bristol.[35] The Bollings, who, by the marriage of John

---

[33] Hayden's Virginia Genealogies, p. XVII. Colonel William Legge was the ancestor of the present Earl of Dartmouth. Sir William Washington had married a half-sister of the Duke of Buckingham. The marriage of his daughter Susannah shows the social standing of successful members of the London Guilds at that period.

[34] For Perry and Lee, see William and Mary College Quart., Vol. I., p. 80, *et seq.*

[35] The will of Alice Cary, of Stepney, Middlesex, bequeathed "to my grandfather, John Cary, of Bristol, woolen draper, one shilling, and to my uncle, Myles Cary, one shilling."—Waters's Gleanings, p. 1056.

Bolling with Jane Rolfe, descended from Pocahontas, and whose social prominence began in the seventeenth century, were probably derived from Robert Bolling, a silk throwster of London.[36]   The Peytons, who, like the Skipwiths, were represented in the Colony by a baronet, traced their ancestry back to Sir Edward Osborne, a member of the guild of cloth-workers, a Lord Mayor of London, and the founder of the ducal house of Leeds in the English peerage.   Henry Peyton, who settled in Stafford county, had before his emigration from the Mother Country, been a member of a trading guild.[37]   Henry Freeman, a landowner of York county, had formerly been a mercer at Chipping Norton in Oxfordshire, while Isaac Clopton, who was a justice of York county in 1676, had been a haberdasher before leaving England.[38]

The Harwar family was probably sprung from Samuel Harwar, a merchant tailor of London.[39]   Henry Sewell, a prominent citizen of Lower Norfolk county, where his name is perpetuated in Sewell's Point on Hampton Roads, was not only the son of a merchant, but also in early life, served a full apprenticeship to a trade in Yarmouth, England.[40]   The first of the Buckners to settle in Virginia was closely connected by blood with a wealthy family of the same name established in business in London, one of whom belonged to the guild of mer-

---

[36] Hayden's Virginia Genealogies, see Bolling Family.

[37] Hayden's Virginia Genealogies, see Peyton Family.

[38] William and Mary College Quart., Vol. II. p. 165; Vol. V., p. 80.

[39] York County Records, Vol. 1657-62, p. 458, Va. St. Libr.

[40] Lower Norfolk County Records, Vol. 1656-1666, p. 374[2].

chant-tailors.[41]   Thomas Wardley, of York county, was
the heir of Thomas Wardley, a leading member of the
same guild, and drew an income from property which
his father had bequeathed him in Cheapside.[42]   About
1665, James Bailey, a draper living in London, made a
grant of live-stock to his sister-in-law, who had gone out
to Virginia.[43]   Five years later, William Collin, a member of the weaver's guild in the same city, settled in the
Colony.[44]   John Sandford, a resident of Lower Norfolk
county, was a near kinsman of Richard Sandford, of
Exeter, who followed the trade of dyer, one of the most
important in England.[45]   The Booths were closely related
to Richard Booth, a leading merchant of London, and
member of a family which, as we have seen, numbered
among their kindred the Earls of Warrington.[46]

The sister of the elder Nathaniel Bacon married Anthony Smith, a member of the guild of tanners; her
grandfather, Sir James Bacon, of Freston Hall, the
nephew of the Chancellor, and grandson of the Lord
Keeper of the same surname, was the son of a member of
the guild of salters.   Richard Foote, who emigrated to
Virginia near the close of the seventeenth century, was
the son of a person of the same name who had accumulated a fortune in trade in England.   Members of this
family were owners of large estates in Cornwall, and

---

[41] Accomac County Records, Vol. 1663-66, folio, p. 82.   It is not
improbable that the Buckners of Virginia were sprung directly
from one of these London merchants.

[42] York County Records, Vol. 1657-62, p. 358, Va. St. Libr. Copy.

[43] York County Records, Vol. 1664-72, p. 189, Va. St. Libr. Copy.

[44] William and Mary College Quart., Vol. VIII., p. 256.

[45] William and Mary College Quart., Vol. IV., p. 16.

[46] British Colonial Entry Book, Vol. 1676-81, p. 182.

were entitled to bear arms; among the distinguished men
whom the family produced was Samuel Foote, who enjoyed great celebrity as an actor.[47]   John Beachamp, who
is referred to in the records as "of James River, gentleman," was a brother of William Beachamp, a member of
the guild of vintners in London; John Beachamp himself
had, at one time, perhaps, been a merchant in the same
city, for, about 1678, a person of that name was engaged
in business in St. Giles parish, Cripplegate without. The
estate which he owned in Virginia at his death was trans-
ferred by his heirs to his brother, the vintner.[48]   Samuel
Timson, a leading citizen of York county about 1683, had
formerly been a woodmonger of London.   William Fellowes, a member of the same guild, had married the
widow of Captain Philip Chesney, of the Colony.[49]
James Crews, of Henrico county, was a near kinsman of
James and Mathew Crews, who followed the calling of
haberdashers in London; their niece was the wife of
William Whittingham, of that city, whose name always
appeared in legal papers accompanied by the term "gentleman."[50]   About 1687, Otho Thorpe, a merchant of
London, bequeathed his estate in Virginia to his niece
and other relatives.[51]

A small number of prominent families in Virginia in

---

[47] Va. Maga. of Hist. and Biog., Vol. VII., p. 73.

[48] Henrico County Records, Vol. 1677-92, orig., pp. 75, 79.

[49] William and Mary College Quart., Vol. III., p. 208; York
County Records, Vol. 1675-84, orig., p. 98.

[50] Henrico County Records, Vol. 1677-92, orig., p. 306.

[51] York County Records, Vol. 1684-7, p. 270, Va. St. Libr.
Copy. This list could be greatly extended. See, for other English merchants connected by social ties with Virginia, the "Virginia Gleanings in England" in Virginia Magazine of History
and Biography.

the seventeenth century were sprung directly from sea-
captains, who, in some cases, had combined with that calling the business of active traders in the merchandize
which they imported into the Colony. As a rule, these
seamen were a superior body of men, and when they came
to settle in the community, made valuable citizens. They
had, for years, been exposed to the perils of repeated
ocean voyages at a time when these voyages were far
more adventurous than they are now; and they had thus
grown to be cool and self-reliant in the face of danger,
and to bear all hardships with firmness. As they navi-
gated their own ships, it followed that they possessed a
certain amount of general education as well as special
scientific information. Visiting the Colony year after
year, they must have grown thoroughly familiar with all
the conditions of trade and agriculture prevailing there,
and this knowledge, no doubt, stood them in good stead
when they decided to buy land and become permanent
residents. Such was conspicuously the case with Mindert
Doodes, the Dutch sea-captain who settled in Virginia
and became the ancestor of the Minor family. Thomas
Ball, the first member of the Ball family whose name
appears in the records of Lancaster county, where he was
a large landowner, was always described as "mariner"
in deeds.[52] Thomas Willoughby, of Lower Norfolk county, referred to himself in a like manner in private grants,
and William Gainge in public patents.[53] Isaac Foxcroft,
who was prominent in the affairs of Northampton about
1675, described himself in deeds as "mariner, of Kings-

[52] Lancaster County Records, Vol. 1654-1702, p. 20. Ball seems
to have been a citizen of Northampton county in 1655.

[53] Lower Norfolk County Records, Vol. 1656-1666, p. 285; Va.
Land Patents for 1624.

ton-upon-Hull."[54]   Robert Ranson and Samuel Milburn, of Elizabeth City county, were similarly designated.[55] Nicholas Jordan, a citizen of Lower Norfolk county, devised his estate, at least in part, to his brother, Robert Jordan, "mariner," of London, who probably, before his death, settled in Virginia.[56]   Land was owned in the Colony also by ship-surgeons; for instance, Dr. James Montgomery, of the man-of-war, *St. Albans,* who died at Richmond, England, about 1697, left his property in Virginia to be divided between his two brothers.[57]

The surviving county records of Virginia during the seventeenth century contain an extraordinary array of names, which have always been especially well known on account of their intimate association with English social or political history.   This is peculiarly notable in the earliest records of the Eastern Shore, where, until recent times, owing to the isolation of this fertile peninsula, the population remained perhaps more purely English in origin than in any other part of our country.   Attached to the depositions, land-grants, wills, and the like, preserved in these records, will be found such names as Whittington, Stanley, Tatham, Carew, Goring, Wraxall, Fowke, Blake, Salisbury, Walpole, Capel, Luddington,

---

[54] See Northampton County Deeds for 1675.

[55] Elizabeth City County Records, Orders June 19, 1699.

[56] Lower Norfolk County Records, Vol. 1666-75, p. 67.   Cornelius Calvert always referred to himself in deeds as "Mariner." See Records of Lower Norfolk County.   Calvert was the first of the well-known family of that name long associated with that part of Virginia.

[57] Waters's Gleanings, Will of Montgomery; see, also, York County Records, Vol. 1657-62, p. 118, Va. St. Libr.

Nottingham,[58] Empson, Ratcliffe, Cade, Pitt, Sommerville, Mortimer, Fortescue, Somerset, Bloomfield, Harrington, and Marlow. We find in the earliest Surry Records such names as Cotton, Roscoe, Osborne, Shrewsbury, Shelly; in the York, Hyde, Peverill, Cromwell, Perceval, Wentworth; in Henrico, Lisle, Napier, Milton, Bathurst; in Elizabeth City and adjacent counties, Knox, Barham,[59] and Goodrich; in Isle of Wight, Bradshaw; in Richmond, Ridley and Litton; in Rappahannock, Paget, Parr, Lowther, Gower, Swinburne, Morpeth, Burgoyne, St. John, and Blackstone; in Middlesex, Wharton and Churchill.[60] The men who bore these famous names were, in many instances, owners of large estates or held prominent offices.

Many families conspicuous in New England at this time, or at a later period, were also represented in Virginia. Among the leading ones in Accomac were the Sturgis, Smalley, Dewey, and Washburn, whilst the Ravenscroft name was as well known in Virginia as in

---

[58] After two hundred and fifty years' association with the social and political life of the Eastern Shore, the Nottingham family continues to-day to be one of the most prominent of all those seated in that part of Virginia. This is also true of many others which might be mentioned, such as the Wise, Wilkins, Kendall, Harmanson, etc. Up to a recent date, the Eastern Shore was very much cut off from the rest of the world, and in consequence of this fact, the continuity of its family history was perhaps more unbroken than was to be observed anywhere else in the United States.

[59] Anthony Barham, "gentleman," resided on Mulberry Island in James river.

[60] Many of these old English names have, in the course of time, become corrupted, such as Shrowsby for Shrewsbury and Tatum for Tatham.

the northern colonies.[61]   Colonel Isaac Allerton, of the
Northern Neck, was the son of Isaac Allerton, one of the
Pilgrims who arrived in the "Mayflower," and, through
his mother, the grandson of William Brewster, the leader
of that memorable company.   Among the planters residing in that part of the Colony were the Broughtons and
Lords, who had at first settled in New England. Several of these emigrants from the North, or their descendants of the same name, acquired some political importance; for instance, among the Burgesses elected in 1696,
were John Washburne, Michael Sherman, and Joshua
Story.[62]

It is not likely that the persons who came to Virginia
from New England exercised any Puritan influence on
the higher social life of the former Colony.   The only
trace of Puritan feeling in the more conspicuous families
is observed in an occasional given name which had really
come into common use during the period when Puritan
thought was so prevalent among the whole body of the
Church of England; it was doubtless then that Temperance became a favorite name in the Yeardley and Cocke
families, Priscilla in the Ferrer, Prudence in the Morris,
and Obedience in the Robins.

The prominent families that reached Virginia by way
of Barbadoes were as numerous as those that came in by
way of New England.   It was from this island that the
Walkes, of Lower Norfolk county, and the Perrins and
Marshalls, of Elizabeth City, emigrated to the Colony.[63]

---

[61] Samuel Ravenscroft came to Virginia from New England
about 1691-2; see Minutes of Assembly, April 25, 1692, British
Colonial Entry Book, Vol. 1682-95.

[62] Minutes of H. of Burgesses Sept. 25, 1696, B. T. Va., Vol. LII.

[63] Lower Norfolk County Records, Vol. 1686-95, p. 212². Elizabeth City County Records, Vol. 1684-99, pp. 212, 393, Va. St. Libr.

VII.

SOCIAL DISTINCTIONS.

THE quickness with which the founders of such families as the Lee, Wormeley, Jennings, Randolph, Robinson, and Beverley rose to great influence after their arrival, shows that they were in a position to acquire lands in the Colony at once, because they had brought over with them the necessary means, which they had either inherited or received from their fathers. John Page, Miles Cary, and Nicholas Spencer continued to own property in England long after they had been in possession of large estates in Virginia.[1] The earliest patents sued out by nearly all of the emigrants whose names soon became socially distinguished in the Colony, prove that they had, quite from the beginning, some fortune at their command with which to secure a share in the soil, and to establish a home; the large properties accumulated by them all were, like those of William Fitzhugh, Robert Beverley, and the elder Nathaniel Bacon, the result of extraordinary foresight and prudence, but a prudence and foresight which had something more than a mere determination to win success to start with. A marked proportion of these families, as we have seen, were sprung directly from merchants who were not likely to allow their sons to go out to Virginia in the condition of penniless adventurers.

---

[1] Bruce's Economic History of Virginia in the Seventeenth Century, Vol. II., pp. 246-247. Many other instances might be given.

Virginia was a promising community for persons without capital, who were ready to earn a subsistence by working with their bare hands, but not for persons without any capital who were seeking to make their way with their wits alone.

Apart from the few individuals engaged in the professions, there were, along economic lines, only two divisions of the population, one of which was represented by the landowner, and the other by the common laborer. The young Englishman reaching the Colony with some means of support, could at once secure an interest in the soil; if, on the other hand, he arrived without such means, he was compelled to become at once an agricultural servant. Whilst the general conditions prevailing made possible the accumulation of large estates by combining trading and planting, the chances were not so extraordinary as to allow many men of the lowest social origin to become rich by some stroke of fortune, or a succession of strokes, and thus found families in the possession of every social advantage which the Colony offered. The only prominent figure in the social life of Virginia in the seventeenth century who is known to have passed his first years there under articles of indenture, resembling those of an ordinary laborer, was Adam Thoroughgood. As his nearest relative in England, a brother, was a baronet, it is quite probable that, like a good many young Englishmen of that and a later day who established themselves in Virginia, his object in beginning in so humble a way, was to obtain a practical knowledge of planting tobacco; and that he was in the possession of pecuniary resources with which to make the most of this knowledge as soon as it was obtained.

It was a conspicuous feature of the social life of Virginia during the seventeenth century, that, like the political system, it was thoroughly organized from the beginning. There was no period in the history of that social life when it resembled the social life of a community situated on our extreme western frontier, where all social distinctions are merged in a rude social equality. From the hour when the voyagers disembarked at Jamestown in May, 1607, all those social divisions which had existed immemorially in England, took root in the soil of the new country; the line of social separation between the gentleman and the common laborer was even sharper than that between the military officer and the ordinary soldier, or between the civilian officer and the private citizen. Not even in the interval of terrible want and sickness following, during the first summer after the arrival of the earliest expedition, were these social divisions forgotten, simply because, under the influence of inherited feeling and habit, and by the force of actual law, all Englishmen recognized and acted upon differences in social rank.

When we picture to ourselves the vast wilderness which formed the background of Jamestown in 1610, a wilderness of forest tenanted only by wild beasts and painted Indians, there seems an element of ludicrous incongruity in the pomp and ceremony which De la Warr adopted on every public occasion, and in the rigid etiquette which he, as nobleman and governor, required to be observed in relation to himself. An impression is made that he was extraordinarily solemn and formal by nature, but this impression, which was undoubtedly true in a measure, did not represent all the influences directing his action. De la Warr had come out to Virginia as a great nobleman, as an almost absolute governor and captain-general, and finally as the trusted representative of that powerful company of peers, knights, and gentlemen

who had obtained the new charter of 1609. Virginia was
not a colony composed of a single village and a few small
plantations; it was a great province of England, a wilderness, as yet, it is true, but a wilderness that was certain,
in time, to become wealthy and thickly inhabited. In
exalting the authority of office so characteristic of those
times, the disposition of De la Warr was to consider
simply the dignity of his position, however nominal that
dignity really was in the light of the handful of settlers
huddled together in misery at Jamestown. And in adopt-
ing so much ceremonial in that little community, he was
only doing what any other great English noble, appointed
governor and captain-general of a part of the kingdom,
whether populous like Scotland and Ireland, or with only
a few white people like Virginia, would have done.

The spirit which governed De la Warr officially and
personally was the spirit which, in a modified way, per-
vaded the entire social life of Virginia throughout the
seventeenth century. The community, from a social
point of view, was as if some shire of England, with its
whole population, had been moved bodily over sea. In
no sense was it a community which, in its social framework, had grown along lines entirely peculiar to itself.
Every Englishman who, in those early times, went out
to the Colony, carried over the unconscious tenacity of
De la Warr in claiming every form of social consideration to which he had been entitled in England itself.
There was not the smallest desire to leave the old privileges and customs behind. Virginia was not looked upon
as a new country; it was simply an outlying possession,
like the islands of Jersey and Guernsey; and there was no
more reason why the emigrant, in going thither, should
abandon all those opinions as to the proper constitution of
society, which he had inherited, than if he were about to

make a visit to Devon or Hampshire, where marked gradations in social position had been recognized for over a thousand years. He would find no great noblemen there, it is true, but this would be the result, not of the framework of its society, but of the remoteness of the Colony from England, and its comparatively limited degree of economic development as yet.

The other proofs of social distinctions and divisions would be as conspicuous to the emigrant on his arrival in Virginia as they had been to him in England itself. For instance, one of the most ordinary social badges in use was the coat-of-arms. One distinguished student of Virginian genealogy in the seventeenth century has declared that, after a long course of investigation, he is unaware of a single person whose name in deeds is followed by the term "gentleman," who was not entitled to use a coat-of-arms. This would fulfill the definition of a "gentleman" given by Sir Edward Coke.[2] If this statement holds good for all who were so designated in public and private documents during this century, which, however, is highly questionable, then the number of persons legally entitled to coats-of-arms was as great in Virginia, in proportion to population, as it was in England. In three counties alone, namely, Essex, Lancaster, and Middlesex, the records of which for the century have been very much cut down by different vicissitudes, there were at least forty-seven families which regularly made use of coats-of-arms.[3]

There is no reason to think that armorial bearings were as freely and loosely assumed in those early times as they

[2] Lyon G. Tyler in William and Mary College Quart., Vol. I., p. 112.

[3] William and Mary College Quart., Vol. I., p. 167.

are so often now, under Republican institutions; such
bearings were then a right of property, as clearly defined
as any other, and continue to be in modern England,
what they were in colonial Virginia. In the seventeenth
century, when so large a proportion of the persons occupying the highest position in the society of the Colony
were natives of England, the unwarranted assumption of
a coat-of-arms would probably have been as soon noticed,
and perhaps as quickly resented, as in England itself. The
prominent families in Virginia were as well acquainted
with the social antecedents of each other in the Mother
Country as families of the same rank in England were
with the social antecedents of the leading families in the
surrounding shires; they were, therefore, thoroughly
competent to pass upon a claim of this nature; and the
fact that they were, must have had a distinct influence in
preventing a false claim from being put forward. In a
general way, it may be said that it was quite as natural
for Virginians of those times to be as slow and careful
as contemporary Englishmen in advancing a claim of
this kind without a legal right on which to base it, and,
therefore, when they did advance it, that it was likely to
stand the test of examination by the numerous persons in
the Colony who must have been familiar with English
coats-of-arms in general.

Before leaving England, some of the emigrants took
care to have their coats-of-arms confirmed; for instance,
in 1633, Moore Fauntleroy obtained such a confirmation
from the Office of the English Heralds, who, in their report, declared that this coat-of-arms had been enjoyed by
the Fauntleroys "time out of mind."[4]   Among the prominent families who are thought to have possessed a legal

---

[4] Va. Maga. of Hist. and Biog., Vol. I., p. 224.

right to the coats-of-arms which they habitually used, were the Bacon, Berkeley, Bland, Byrd, Bolling, Beverley, Bennett, Burwell, Claiborne, Cary, Cole, Cocke, Clayton, Digges, Farrer, Fitzhugh, Kingsmill, Lee, Ludwell, Ludlow, Milner, Page, Parke, Robinson, Randolph, Spencer, Thoroughgood, Throckmorton, Thurston, Tucker, of Lower Norfolk county, Willoughby, Woodhouse, Washington, Booth, Batte, Chichely, Colthorpe, Fleet, Jennings, Lunsford, Peyton, West, and Wyatt.[5] The English ancestry of most of the founders of these conspicuous families was as well known in the seventeenth century as the ancestry of an equal number of persons belonging to the English gentry of that day. They could follow their genealogical descent with a like precision and accuracy; in using coats-of-arms in Virginia, they were simply doing what their fathers had done before them in England, and what they themselves had done previous to their own emigration; and it appeared to them as much a matter of course to use such coats-of-arms in the Colony as it would have been had they never left their native Devon or Sussex, Staffordshire or Lincolnshire.

The possession of coats-of-arms by the leading Virginian families in the seventeenth century is disclosed in various incidental ways. Insignia of this kind are frequently included among the personal property appraised in inventories.[6] And they were also stamped on pieces of

---

[5] William and Mary College Quart., Vol. I., p. 120. The original spelling of the Farrar name was Ferrer. Not long after the family settled in Virginia "a" seems to have been substituted for "e" in the spelling of the name, probably as more in harmony with its pronunciation.

[6] For an instance see inventory of Philip Felgate, Lower Norfolk County Records, Vol. 1646-1651, p. 47.

fine silver plate. In a letter to George Mason, of Bristol, Fitzhugh requests him to invest eighty-five pounds sterling, lying in his hands to the writer's credit, in silver dishes, candlesticks, and the like, but to be careful to work no arms on them, as this could be done in Virginia by a servant under indentures to Fitzhugh, whom he declared to be "a singularly good engraver."[7] This is one of the numerous instances which shows that this prosperous planter and lawyer always maintained a thrifty and economical mind, even when there was a large sum at his command. The purchase of large quantities of silver plate, not for household display, but as a means of making a safe investment, was one of the commonest acts of wealthy Virginians in those early times, but, in the ordinary course, the engraving was done in England before the plate was shipped away to the Colony, because it was not likely that any person acquainted with so difficult an art could be found there.

The custom of carving coats-of-arms on tombs was as general in Virginia as in the Mother Country itself. If the person buried underneath was a woman who, during her life, had been married, the coat-of-arms of husband or father was used indifferently; for instance, on the tomb of Mrs. Nathaniel Bacon, the elder, who was a daughter of Richard Kingsmill, the Kingsmill's coat-of-arms is chiseled, whilst the coat-of-arms cut into the tombstone of a Miss Bassett, who inter-married with the Allans, of Claremont, is that of her husband's family.[8]

---

[7] Letters of William Fitzhugh, July 21, 1698. Richard Lee also had his coat-of-arms engraved on his silver plate.

[8] Va. Maga. of Hist. and Biog., Vol. VII., pp. 49, 211. The Allan arms were the same as those of the Allan family of Derbyshire and Staffordshire.

These elaborate grave-stones, which are the counterparts of so many belonging to the same period still found intact in the English parish church-yards, were probably, without exception, procured from England, as the coats-of-arms are, as a rule, sculptured with a skilful precision and a justness of proportion which could have been shown by trained workmen alone. It was not an uncommon provision in wills that the testator's coat-of-arms should be stamped in brass on his tombstone; for example, in 1674, Colonel Richard Cole gave directions that a slab of black marble, bearing his coat-of-arms, engraved in this metal, should, after his death, be purchased in England, brought over, and laid on the spot where he desired his body to be buried.[9]

Owing to the custom prevailing among prominent families in these early, as in later, times of burying their dead in the garden near the dwelling house, many of these costly gravestones, with their elaborate carvings of armorial bearings, have alone remained to mark the site where a colonial home once stood. The vicissitudes of time have destroyed the residence and dispersed the family, but the tombstone, as compact as ever, continues to point silently to an era when the social laws and habits of England, inherited from a remote past, but destined in Virginia to perish under new institutions, followed men in the Colony even when consigned to the dust. It is not uncommon, even at the present day, to find these ancient tombstones, with their facings blackened by storm and sunshine, but still legible, standing in an open field or meadow of Eastern Virginia.[10] Sometimes, the name

---

[9] Westmoreland County Records, Vol. 1665-77, folio, p. 186.

[10] Such is the situation of the Moseley tombs, in Princess Anne county, which, however, are still surrounded by a crumbling brick wall. The remains of the Yeardley tombs are hardy perceptible in the grounds of the Nottingham home in Northampton county.

on one of these stones has sunk into such obscurity as to have no interest even for the most learned genealogist. For instance, on what is known as the Church Pastures Farm, a part of the Brandon estate, on Lower James River, there is still to be observed the isolated grave-slab, stamped with armorial bearings, which informs us that a certain person, "gentleman," was born in London in 1649, and died in Virginia in 1700.[11] There was, perhaps, no other record in the Colony that such a man ever existed. He represented a case that, no doubt, occurred very frequently in the seventeenth century; that is to say, an Englishman of good family emigrated to Virginia, lived and died there childless, and his very name was soon lost even to tradition. If preserved at all, it was preserved, like the name of this person, on the fragment of his tombstone, tossed about a field, and trodden upon by wandering cattle.

There was the clearest recognition of class distinctions in every department of Virginian life during the seventeenth century, a fact brought out in numerous ways by the silent testimony of the different legal documents which have survived to the present day, after passing through all the vicissitudes of war and revolution. The colonial custom, following the immemorial English, was in such documents, to fix by terms, whose legal meaning was fully understood, the social position of the principal persons mentioned therein. The total omission of a term after a name was as significant in one way as the insertion of a term was in another. There were certain particular designations to show calling which were applied generally without social discrimination. In one instance alone, perhaps, did such a designation carry a distinct inference of social importance without, however, nicely

---

[11] Va. Maga. of Hist. and Biog., Vol. VII., p. 211.

defining its degree; the word "planter" probably at a late period conveyed such a meaning. Not long after the abolition of the company, we find the term "planter" applied to the lessees whose names appear in the grants of land belonging to the office of governor. The area contained in these grants was not extensive, and the lessees were men of no social consequence.[12] Not many years later, the term "planter" was applied with great freedom, whether the patentee acquired title in a large tract or in a small; whether he was a citizen of marked prominence in the Colony, or possessed no prominence at all. But, by 1675, we find, in the ordinary conveyances, recorded in the county courts, an indifferent use by the same man, as applicable to himself, of the terms "gentleman" and "planter," as if the two were practically interchangeable. At this time, the estates, in many cases, spread over many thousand acres, and whilst all who owned and cultivated land of their own, whether great or small in area, were, in a strict sense planters, the term may have come to have a subordinate social meaning as applicable to men of large estates, whose social position by force of birth, as well as of worldly possessions, was among the foremost in the community. Or it may be, which seems, on the whole, more probable, the person drawing up one of these deeds designated himself there as "gentleman" if he happened at the moment to think of his social rank, or as "planter" if he thought of his calling.[13]

---

[12] See Va. Land Patents, 1625-30.

[13] John Goode, of Henrico county, in some of the deeds in which his name appears describes himself as "gentleman"; in others, as "planter." See Henrico County Records, Vol. 1677-92, orig., pp. 189-90. The following would seem to show that the term "planter" designated simply the calling without social significance: "Know all men by these Presents that wee, Walter

Sometimes, in one deed, a grantor will designate him-self as "gentleman;" in a second, as "planter;" and in a third, as "merchant." The last two terms defined the pursuits in which he was engaged; the first, his social position. In describing himself as "merchant" or "plan-ter" in a formal conveyance, such a person may have had in mind the fact that, by the use of such terms, he made the more clear the exact identification of the grantor, and thus diminished the chance of confusion with some one else, who might bear the same name.

The calling or social rank of the grantee in a deed was stated with the same particularity as that of the grantor. One example of this fact, among many which might be brought forward, will be found in an agreement, which, about 1679, was entered into by Robert Bowman and Richard Kennon, of Henrico county; Bowman is designated as "planter" and Kennon as "merchant;" whilst in a second deed recorded in the same county, both Martin Elam and John Bowman described themselves as "planters."[14]

The men who followed a mechanical trade were as careful as the planters to apply to themselves in legal documents the terms used for their special pursuits, such as "carpenter," "cooper," "tailor," and the like, some of which callings enjoyed in the Colony the same measure of social consideration as that attached to them in England. Not infrequently a person will designate himself as "gen-tleman" in one deed, and "cooper" or "carpenter" in another. This, for instance, seems to have been the habit

---

Jones, Chirurgeon, William Wilson, gent., Richard Street, plant-er," etc.   Elizabeth City County Records, Vol. 1684-99, p. 285, Va. St. Libr.

[14] Henrico County Records, Vol. 1677-92, orig., pp. 83-84.

with George Wyatt, the son of Rev. Hawte Wyatt, and
the nephew of Governor Wyatt, a man, who, by birth and
social connections, belonged to the highest social rank in
the Colony.[15]. Major William Barber, under whose supervision the capitol at Williamsburg was built, described
himself in some deeds as "cooper;" in others as "carpenter." He was a church warden, justice of the county
court, a member of the House of Burgesses, and had
married the daughter of Henry Cary, whose name in
legal documents was always coupled with the term "gentleman," a term to which he was entitled as a member
of a family well known to be of gentle descent.[16] It was,
no doubt, equally applicable to Barber also. In those
early times, the word "carpenter" expressed more than it
does at the present day; it signified not only one who
worked in wood with his hands, but also a builder, archi-
tect, and contractor, and it was not improbable that it
was used, in this broader sense, in connection with Barber
himself. And in the same way, the word "cooper" had a
wider meaning than it now conveys.

"I was born a gentleman," exclaimed Cromwell on one
occasion in addressing Parliament, "and in the old social
arrangement of a nobleman, a gentleman and a yeoman,
I see a good interest of the nation and a great one."[17]
Nobleman, gentleman, yeoman—these were the terms
which carried a clear and precise social significance
wherever Englishmen had established a community.

---

[15] See Va. Land Patents for 1642 for patent in which Wyatt
designated himself as "cooper"; William and Mary College Quart.,
Vol. X., p. 60.

[16] William and Mary College Quart., Vol. V., p. 195.

[17] Green's Short History of the English People, chapt. viii.,
Sect. 10.

There was no order of noblemen in Virginia in the seventeenth century, but there was, to use the Protector's language, a "social arrangement" of gentlemen and yeomen.[18] The term "yeoman" appears with special frequency in the early land patents, and it was used to express exactly the same rank as the like term inserted in a contemporary legal document in the Mother Country. The fact that it was not freely used, is an evidence that, when employed at all, it was employed with discrimination. There were only about fifteen persons so designated in the early land patents; these were William Spencer, Gabriel Holland, Thomas Sully, John and Edward Johnson, John and Robert Salford, Thomas Godby, John Taylor, John Powell, Alexander Mountney, Elizabeth Dimthorne, William Lamsden, Thomas Bouldin, John Sibsey, and Adam Dixon. None of these names, with the exception of Sibsey, became prominent in the social history of the Colony. The term "yeoman" is used very often in the county records long after the names of these early settlers were entered in the land patents. In 1646, John Sawies, of Surry county, so described himself in a deed; so did James Pope, of Westmoreland county, in 1660; and Robert Beverley ,of King and Queen county, about 1694.[19] Numerous other instances of a like charac-

---

[18] Macaulay estimated that the yeoman class of England in the seventeenth century embraced one-seventh of the whole population, and that the average income of each head of a family belonging to this class ranged from sixty to seventy pounds sterling; see History, chapt. iii.

[19] Surry County Records, Vol. 1645-72, p. 37, Va. St. Libr.; Westmoreland County Records, Vol. 1653-72, p. 122; Essex County Records, Vol. 1692-95, p. 174, Va. St. Libr. The Beverleys were probably originally small land-owners in Yorkshire, and were as such perhaps designated as yeomen. It seems remarkable,

ter might be given; and they continued to occur throughout the colonial period.[20]   Originally, "yeoman" meant
simply a small landowner, and his social position in the
community lay between that of the gentleman and that of
the common laborer.   Both Pope and Beverley were in
possession of large tracts of land, and both represented
families of prominence.

In conversation, the term "mister" was, no doubt, applied to both gentlemen and yeomen, but when it appears
in legal documents as a prefix to a name, it signifies that
the person so designated was entitled to a higher degree
of social consideration than was enjoyed by a mere yeoman; the term seems, in fact, to have been reserved in
those early times in all forms of written and printed matter, such as records and books, for persons whose claim
to be gentlemen in the broad social sense, was admitted
by all.   In some cases, the term appeared to carry so
much dignity that it could only be used properly of one
who filled a high political office; for example, in the
list of gentlemen who accompanied the expedition to Virginia in 1607, the first to go over, Edward Maria Wingfield, the President of the Council, and as such the Governor of the new Colony, was the only one whose name
was preceded by the word "mister."[21]

---

however, that such a term should have been retained by the
younger Robert Beverley, one of the largest land-owners in the
colony.   Its retention was perhaps due to mere whim, "after the
order of the use," as Mr. W. G. Stanard has pointed out, "of only
wooden stools at Beverley's house, Beverley Park, in King and
Queen county; this, too, at a time when the houses of much
poorer men were full of handsome chairs."

[20] Edward Wilson James in the Lower Norfolk Antiquary (No.
I., Part 1, p. 45) gives an instance from the records of 1728:
"Thomas Lawson, gentleman, to Nat. Hutchings, yeoman," etc.

[21] Works of Capt. John Smith, Vol. I., p. 163, Richmond edition.

A similar designation accompanies the names of many
of the grantees appearing in the early land patents;
among these names were those of planters, who, like
Thomas Eaton, Adam Thoroughgood, George Menifie,
Nathaniel Hooke, and Jeremiah Clement, were men of
recognized prominence in the community. Whalley, one
of the most active lieutenants of Nathaniel Bacon, the
younger, in the Insurrection of 1676, is always honored
in the narratives of that uprising by the title of "mister,"
which was either a proof of his high social position, or a
tribute to the conspicuous part played by him in the
course of the tumult.[22]

Sometimes in the same document a man is designated
first by the term "mister," and then by the term "gentleman;" for instance, in the land patents, Adam Thoroughgood is found very often entered in grants as "Mr. Adam
Thoroughgood, gentleman." The same joint use of the
two words is observed in the county records; by a deed
preserved in Elizabeth City county, Thomas Tench, of
Maryland, conveyed property to "Mr. William Mallory,
gentleman," who was an inhabitant of Virginia;[23] and a
similar use of "mister" and "gentleman" occurs in deeds
passing between Thomas Wythe and Edmund Swaney,
who were justices of the Elizabeth City county court;
it is possible that the high position which this fact gave
them in the community, apart from birth and fortune, entitled them to the right to be so elaborately designated in
a legal document. The use of the term "mister" is observed most constantly in the lists of the county tax
levies; in these lists, the word "gentleman" does not ap-

---

[22] William and Mary College Quart., Vol. IV., p. 3.

[23] Elizabeth City County Records, Vol. 1684-99, pp. 208, 222,
246, Va. St. Libr.

pear, whilst the word "mister" is employed wherever the person whose name is mentioned could lay claim to any special social consideration. When the name entered was that of a man who belonged to a social grade below that of gentleman, it is not accompanied by a designation of any kind.[24]

Whenever the term "gentleman" appears in the records of the seventeenth century attached to a name, it was intended to convey a meaning that had been defined with legal precision. It was a term that was never used loosely, lightly, or indiscriminately in those times, even in papers without legal importance or significance; in legal documents, such as the patents and county records, it was applied as nicely and advisedly as if this had been required by a decision of the highest court in the kingdom. Indeed, its use was regulated by social customs, which, among Englishmen and the descendants of Englishmen, had all the force of a legal judgment. No one could assume the right to couple the term with his name in a legal document unless his claim was too generally recognized to be disputed. According to the great lawyer, Coke, it was an error to designate a man as a "gentleman" (when the question was one of mere social rank) unless he possessed the undeniable privilege of bearing arms. Whilst it seems improbable that the use of the term in the Colony was strictly confined to those who had the right to do this, however large the number might have been, nevertheless, it is plain that its use did not extend beyond those who, either by birth or fortune, occupied a position of influence in the social life of the com-

---

[24] A good example of a county levy from the point of view referred to in the text will be found in the levy for 1696 in the Henrico County Records for that year.

munity. In the early patents, the term "gentleman" appears as an affix only to the names of such grantees as filled the most important place in the Colony; among these names are those of Yeardley,[25] Croshaw, Sandys, Waters, Burnham, Hamor, Utie, Maurice Thompson, Spelman, Claiborne, Cheeseman, Willoughby, Felgate, Harwood, Tucker, Alington, Poole, Saunders, and Arundell. Wherever the term is observed in the county records, it is found attached to the names of persons whose social position is known to have been high. Many of the most prominent citizens never failed in ordinary conveyances to designate themselves in this manner. A father transfers an estate to a son; son and father each is referred to as "gentleman;" such was the case in a deed which, in 1637, passed between Hugh and William Bullock;[26] and other examples might be brought forward. Occasionally, there would be placed on record a deed, in which a half dozen men would be designated as "gentlemen," and one as "good-man," a term which indicated that this person alone of the entire company filled a subordinate place in the society of the community.[27]

---

[25] " Mr. Charlton told this depont., saying: ' John, I doubt you are entict away by Mr. Yeardley,' to whome this depont replied, saying: 'Mr. Charlton, you doe Mr. Yeardley much wrong, for hee is a gentleman whom I did never see in my life.' "; Northampton County Orders Jan'y 3, 1642. The Yeardley here referred to was probably Argoll Yeardley, a son of Governor Yeardley. This deposition shows the particular use of the word "gentleman" in ordinary conversation. Edward Wilson James has an interesting note on the general use of the word in England in early times; see Lower Norfolk County Antiquary, Vol. I., p. 100.

[26] Va. Maga. of Hist. and Biog., Vol. II., p. 414.

[27] See power of attorney in Northampton County Records Orders Feb'y 10, 1644-5. The "goodman" in this case may have

It was not simply in ordinary conveyances that the term "gentleman" was employed with great particularity; in such conveyances, a man, if so inclined, could press his claim to such a designation somewhat beyond what he was fully justified in doing; but in formal orders of court, no such latitude would be likely to show itself. In no legal records does the term appear more often than in orders of this kind, and nowhere is it used with greater precision. In the seventeenth century, all the work of a public character was done by the foremost men in the community; whether it was to choose the site of a new town, or to pass on a new bridge, the county court almost invariably selected the commissioners from among the wealthiest and most prominent citizens. In naming these officers in the order appointing them, the court never failed to designate them as "gentlemen," unless it happened, which was quite rare, that they were unable to claim this distinction.[28] The term "gentleman" seems to have been the only one generally used in public docu-

---

been some one from New England. It was a term which was in general use only in the Northern Colonies, having, however, been brought from England. The following is from the Elizabeth City County Records, Vol. 1684-99, p. 283, Va. St. Libr.: "Know all men by these presents yt we Pascho Curle, gent., Thomas Curle, gent., and Coleman Brough, gent., all of ye aforesaid county, gents."

[28] See Middlesex County Records, orders Jan'y 5, 1686, for an instance of the use of the term "gentleman" in a court order. " Stephen Cocke having moved this court to assigne certain gent. of this Countye to meet such as shall bee appointed by the Court of Charles Citye Countye to view and receive the bridge over Turkeye Island Creeke, it is ordered that Capt. William Randolph and Captain Fra. Eppes doe meete these gent. as shall be appointed by Charles Citye Countye." This is from the Henrico County Records Orders June 1, 1697.

ments in connection with the names of members of the House of Burgesses;[29] and this was also true of the names of the justices of the different county courts. It is only occasionally that the names of the latter public officers in the various records bear the prefix of "mister," which, as we have seen, was ordinarily the synonym of the word "gentleman."[30]   The expression "gentlemen, justices" as referring to the judges of the county courts, occurs with great frequency.[31]

A military title was considered to be so honorable that it was not thought necessary, as a rule, to follow a name, to which such a title was prefixed, with an additional term of distinction; for instance, in an order of court, bearing the date of 1697, William Randolph and Francis Eppes, of Henrico county, two of the most prominent citizens of the Colony, from a social, as well as from a political point of view, were designated simply as "captains," the military title they bore as officers in the militia;[32] but in numerous other instances of military officers, who were also conspicuous members of the society of the community, the name is as regularly followed by the term "gentleman" as it is preceded by the military title itself.   For example, Thomas Willoughby, a leading resident of Lower Norfolk county, is in the records of that county almost invariably referred to as "Lieutenant Thomas Willoughby, gentleman;" and the same use of the double designation is observed in the text of many of the early land patents; for instance, it was generally

---

[29] Hening's Statutes, Vol. I., p. 203, 1632-3.

[30] Accomac County Records for the years 1632-40.

[31] See, for an instance, Henrico County Records, orders April 10, 1696.

[32] Henrico County Records, orders, June 1, 1697.

"Captain Robert Felgate, gentleman," and "Captain Raleigh Croshaw, gentleman," instead of the one or the other designation omitted.

The term "esquire" was the most honorable and respectful in its personal application which was in use in Virginia; and from many points of view, it carried all the distinction of an English title. In England, the term was employed to designate either the son of a knight, or one who filled an office of universally recognized responsibility and prominence; in Virginia, on the other hand, its proper application seems to have been confined to the members of the Council, who, as members also of the Upper House of the General Assembly, held a position, which, in its social dignity, as well as in its relation to legislation, corresponded to that of a member of the English House of Lords. The office of Governor alone was superior to that of a member of this Upper House; and when to the importance thus derived, there was added the importance derived from being also a member of the Governor's advisory board, it can be easily seen that a Councillor was relatively as great a personage in the Colony as a leading nobleman was in England.

The Councillor was really chosen a member of the Board simply because he was a man of large estate and great personal influence in the community. Invested with this new dignity and authority, and obtaining by the office extraordinary opportunities of further enriching himself, he secured a hold upon the consideration of the Virginian population of all classes which few noblemen in England enjoyed beyond the boundaries of their own properties, and the circle of their own dependants. The name of one of these Councillors is never found entered in even the obscurest of the county records without the affix of "esquire;" this always displaces the term "gentleman;" and in some cases, seemed to cause the omission of the military titles, which are generally entered so unfailingly. The name of William Byrd, the elder, is invariably coupled with the term "esquire," whilst it is frequently recorded without the military title of "colonel," which he bore.[33] In the early land patents, however, the military title also is usually inserted; for instance, we find Roger Smith, Ralph Hamor, and Henry Browne, all members of the Council and the Upper House of Assembly, designated each as both "Captain" and "Esquire."[34] George Menifie, who, in the early patents, is described as "merchant," in the later, when he has become a member of the Council, always appears as "Mr. George Menefie, Esquire."

After 1634, when the number of patents for each year shows a remarkable increase, the designation of the patentees of the public lands as "gentlemen," "yeomen," and the like, is discontinued, but the term "esquire" is used as often as ever in these public grants. It is found in all of the county records,[35] orders of Council, and Acts of Assembly, and was invariably employed by the Councillors themselves in their private legal papers, such as ordinary conveyances and affidavits. In a document of the latter nature, which Colonel Richard Lee signed at Gravesend in 1655, he described himself as "Colonel Richard Lee, of Virginia, in the partes beyond the seas,

---

[33] "An agreement between William Byrd, Esquire, and Richard Kennon, gentleman," etc., Henrico County Records, Vol. 1677-92, orig., p. 156; see, also, orig., p. 415.

[34] Va. Land Patents for 1634.

[35] An instance: " Philip Taylor doth owe and stand indebted unto Nathaniel Littleton, Esq." See Northampton County Records, Orders, Aug. 31, 1643; May 28, 1644.

Esquire;"[36] and it was also in the same words that he referred to himself in his will.[37] By the year 1678, the term, in its unabbreviated form, had come into common use in conversation as a way of alluding to a Councillor; for instance, we find Rowland Place spoken of as "Esquire Place" in the testimony which a witness, about this date, gave in the Henrico county court.[38] Whiting, another Councillor, is designated as "Esquire Whiting" in the testimony of a second witness who appeared in the county court of Rappannock.[39] Ralph Wormeley is always so referred to.[40] The records show that the Collectors of Customs and the Naval Officers also received the title of "Esquire," but this honor was conferred the more readily because these positions were almost invariably filled by the members of the Council.[41]

The term "Honorable" seems to have been applied only to a person holding a great office, which was never filled by more than a single incumbent, such as that of Governor, Secretary, Auditor, or Treasurer. The wife of one of these officials was generally designated as "Madam;" it was by this title that the wives of Nicholas Spencer, the Secretary of the Colony, and of William Byrd, the

---

[36] British Colonial Papers, Vol. XII., 1653-6, No. 51.

[37] Lee of Virginia, p. 61. The will was drawn in England.

[38] Henrico County Minute Book 1682-1701, p. 6, Va. St. Libr.

[39] Rappahannock County Records, Vol. 1682-92, p. 73, Va. St. Libr.

[40] "To Mr. George Parks for trouble in conveying Esqr. Wormeley's negro over the river." Essex County Records, Orders, Nov. 12, 1692.

[41] Peter Heyman, who was Collector for Lower James River, was always designated as "Esquire," although he does not appear to have been a member of the Council. See Elizabeth City County Records, orders, Aug. 22, Sept. 20, 1699.

Auditor, were known; there are frequent references to "Madam Spencer" and "Madam Byrd" in the records. The wife of another Secretary of the Colony seems to have been addressed as "Madam Elizabeth Wormeley."[42] The title, however, was not restricted to the wives of such officials; for example, we find that the wife of Robert Dudley, a prominent citizen of Middlesex county, who had never filled any of these high positions, was always referred to as "Madam Dudley," a tribute very probably to her extraordinary force of character, her beauty of person, and charm of manner.[43]

---

[42] See for Madam Spencer, Westmoreland County Records, Vol. 1665-77, folio p. 79; for Madam Byrd, Henrico County Records, Vol. 1688-97, p. 148, Va. St. Libr.; and for Madam Wormeley, Middlesex County Records, orders, March 5, 1693.

[43] Middlesex County Records, Vol. 1694-1713, p. 100.

VIII.

Social Distinctions.—*Continued.*

THE English law of primogeniture does not appear to
have been in general operation in Virginia during
the seventeenth century. The reasons for this fact are ob-
vious. First, the estates of extraordinary value accumulated in Virginia in the course of the first one hundred
years were comparatively few; it followed that there
were not many heads of families, who, owing to the possession of large wealth, felt disposed to aggrandize the
family name further by concentrating in the hands of the
eldest son almost the entire family fortune. In the next
century, when sufficient time had elapsed to allow a
notable increase in the number of great estates, there was
a more marked inclination to leave the family property to
one son, though it is quite improbable that the law of
primogeniture was ever in as general acceptance in Virginia as it was in contemporary England. Secondly,
there were no mechanical trades of the higher grade in
the Colony during the seventeenth century to which
younger sons in Virginia, as in the Mother Country,
might turn when cut off in the division of their
father's estate by the law of entail; nor was there room
for many in the local professions of law, medicine, and
the church. There being no towns or cities as in England,
the transactions in mercantile life were confined to a few
general stores, and to casual dealing in tobacco and imported goods. It followed, from these different conditions, that, had a parent devised the great bulk of his
property, which consisted, for the most part, of land, to

the eldest son, it would have been impossible for him to make any special provision for the younger children by establishing them in a professional calling, or setting them up in business or in a trade, and they would have been forced, in consequence, to become common laborers. Thirdly, whilst social divisions prevailed in Virginia almost to as marked degree as in England, the absence of a recognized legal nobility very naturally tended to diminish the popularity of the law of primogeniture in the Colony by doing away with the necessity of supporting titles with ample fortune.

It very frequently happened, however, that the eldest son was allowed, by the will of his father, to have the first voice in the division of the paternal estate; an instance of this occurred under the last testament of Peter Montague, who, emigrating from England, accumulated a large property in Virginia, but was only to this extent disposed to recognize the law of primogeniture.[1] Very often, a father bequeathed to the eldest son what was known as the "manor plantation."[2] Sometimes, however, the eldest son was entirely disinherited, no doubt for the same reasons as have influenced fathers in other countries and at other periods, to take so extreme a step. An instance of this kind was, in 1678, furnished by Thomas Ball, of Northampton county, who, cutting off his eldest son, divided a large estate among his younger children.[3]

The rule that prevailed almost universally in Virginia, during the seventeenth century, in the division of property by will, was followed by William Fitzhugh in dis-

---

[1] Lancaster County Records, Vol. 1654-1702, p. 62.

[2] Will of John Williams, Isle of Wight County Records for 1691-2.

[3] Northampton County Records, Vol. 1674-79, p. 314.

tributing his estate at his death. Few men in the Colony
were in possession of a larger fortune, and few had a
greater temptation to advance the importance of their
families after their decease by leaving practically every-
thing they owned to their eldest sons. Instead of doing
this, Fitzhugh seems to have apportioned both his real
and his personal property quite equally between his five
sons. The oldest appears to have been favored only to
the extent of being made the residuary legatee of such
lands as might remain undisposed of under the will; but
that these were not expected to have much value is
proven by the equal division of the slaves among all the
sons. A specific sum of eighty pounds sterling was also
bequeathed to the eldest; and he seems to have had a
slight preference shown him in the distribution of the
family portraits, but none as between himself and the son
next in age in the division of the books contained in their
father's library.[4]

The elder William Byrd, on the other hand, disclosed
in his will a plain determination to aggrandize his oldest
child at the expense of the others, but this disposition was
quite probably due to the fact that the eldest alone was
a son, who alone could perpetuate a name only represented in the Colony by this one family.[5] In a like spirit,
carried even further, John Tiplady, of York county, in
1688, bequeathed all his lands and tenements to his eldest
son *in ventris;* his living children were daughters, for
whom it is possible he may already have made provision.[6]

---

[4] Will of William Fitzhugh, Va. Maga. of Hist. and Biog., Vol.
II., p. 276.

[5] Will of William Byrd, Byrd Deed Book, p. 114, Va. Hist. So.
MSS. Coll.

[6] York County Records, Vol. 1687-91, p. 345, Va. St. Libr.

There were a few other cases, in which the testator showed a desire to follow the principle of the law of primogeniture; for instance, in 1685, John Daniel, of York county, devised apparently all his lands and houses to his eldest son, with the direction that, should this son die without heirs, the property was to pass to the second son; and if he, too, should die without heirs, then it should pass to the third and last; and if the third should die without heirs, then the property should pass to the eldest daughter; and in case of her death, also, without heirs, to the second and youngest daughter. The whole of the personal estate seems to have been divided between the wife and children, without regard to sex.[7]

There were cases in which the testator showed a disposition to concentrate his landed property in the hands of the last survivor of his children, whether a son or daughter; in the meanwhile, all were to share in the income, but the last one to die was alone to have the right to convey or bequeath the whole property in fee simple.[8]

When an owner of land died without leaving any testament disposing of it, the whole of the real estate seems to have passed, by law, to the eldest son. Walter Bruce, of Nansemond county, drew up a will, in which he divided his plantations between his sons, but the instrument was lost, and, therefore, after his death, could not be offered for probate; and in consequence of this fact, it had no legal force whatever. The eldest son, Abraham

---

[7] Will of Daniel, York County Records for 1685.

[8] The will of Richard Patrick of Northampton county made "his children or any one of them utterly incapable of selling or disposing of any part or parcill of their lands I have now left them by this will, and I doe will and ordaine that the longest livers shall inherit." Northampton County Records, Vol. 1670-79, p. 112.

Bruce, in a deed in which he seeks to carry out his father's wishes, declares that the lands which he conveys to his brother, John, had descended to him (Abraham) as his father's heir-at-law. Had there been no such general provision in operation, the plantations of Walter Bruce, even in the absence of a will, would have been divided equally among his sons without the necessity for a deed of gift resembling the one Abraham so generously made.[9] It is quite probable that, in most cases in which lands had come to be concentrated in the hands of the eldest son, it happened, as in the instance just given, by the loss of the will distributing these lands, or by the failure of the original owner to make a will at all. Such cases must, in the long run, have been of rare occurrence, and when they did take place, many eldest sons doubtless acted upon the just impulse which guided Abraham Bruce.

If there was little disposition during the seventeenth century to enhance the social importance of a family by concentrating the bulk of its property in the hands of the eldest son, there was a very strong desire to promote the distinction of the family by concentrating among its members as many public offices as private influence could secure. All that official dignity, fees, and perquisites

---

[9] "Abraham Bruce, of Lower Norfolk County, eldest son and heir of Walter Bruce, late of Chuckatuck in the County of Nansimond, deceased, gives his brother John 600 acres of land on Boman's creek; the said 600 acres was by my father's Walter Bruce's will given to my said brother, John Bruce, but the said will, through the negligence of those that had it in keeping, is lost, and no record thereof to be found, so that the lands before recited doth honestly descend to me, the sd Abraham Bruce, as heir-at-law to my said deceased father." This deed is recorded May 16, 1689, or 1690, Lower Norfolk County Records, Vol. 1686-95, p. 123.

could confer, were seized upon during this century to increase the general consideration, which the large landowners already enjoyed in consequence of comfortable fortunes and prominent social connections. No office, provided that it carried a salary, was too insignificant to be coveted by the most conspicuous, and even by the wealthiest citizens. Coroner, appraiser of property, viewer, escheator, member of the vestry, sheriff, clerk, and justice of county court, member of the House of Burgesses, member of the Council—all could claim that, even apart from the importance of their official positions, they were the very first men in their community. Now, if a law had been adopted requiring that no person should hold more than one public office at a time, it is probable that the smaller of these offices would not have been eagerly sought after by prominent citizens, simply because the salary attached to them was insignificant, and the dignity they imparted inconsiderable; but there was no restriction, certainly not for any great length of time, upon the number of offices which one person was allowed to occupy, and it followed that every influential citizen was disposed to catch in his dragnet as many offices, great or small, as he could. One small official position by itself amounted to little, but two small official poisitions, associated with a very important one, amounted to a great deal, if not in dignity, then in point of aggregate salary.

In the interval between 1670 and 1691, every official position in Henrico county was occupied by a member of the Randolph, Cocke, or Farrer family. During the greater part of this time, the clerkship of the county court was filled by either William or Henry Randolph[10] The

[10] Henrico County Minute Book, 1682-1701, pp. 39, 49, Va. St. Libr. Henry Randolph, one of the two Randolph emigrants, was

court which came together April 1, 1698, included in its body at least three members of the Cocke family, while a fourth member served as its clerk. In 1684, Thomas Cocke filled the office of high sheriff, and a few years later, leased the public ferry, at which time, he had a seat among the county justices.[11] Such official positions as escaped the grasp of the Farrers, Cockes, and Randolphs were seized by members of the Eppes family. In 1685, the office of sheriff was filled by Francis Eppes, and that of under-sheriff by Littlebury Eppes. An Eppes is almost constantly found among the county justices. And not satisfied with the purely civil and judicial offices, ranging from the coronership and escheatorship, to the membership of the House of Burgesses, these four families were able to acquire, by force of their social influence and personal talents, the far larger proportion of the military offices of the county. A similar condition prevailed in all of the older counties of the Colony, where certain families had been seated long enough to establish a powerful social and political connection. This is another striking point of resemblance between Virginia and the Mother Country during the seventeenth century, namely, the overshadowing importance of one or two families in directing the affairs of each county, and their ability to retain this importance during a long series of years, without any general rivalry to diminish it.

The officer who was able to concentrate a larger number of official positions in his single person than any other individual whatever, was the member of the Governor's Council. Several of the positions which he combined in

---

clerk of Henrico county in 1650, and of the House of Burgesses in 1660-73; William and Mary College Quart., Vol. IV., p. 125.

[11] Henrico County Records Orders April 1, 1698.

himself were the most lucrative of all in the Colony; he was not only a Councillor, an office of great weight and dignity, but also a member of the Upper House, a justice of the General or Supreme Court, commander or lieutenant of his county, naval officer, collector of the customs, farmer of the quitrents, and escheator. It is not strange that the Council should have been described as composed of the "most noted gentlemen" of Virginia.[12] As the most prominent families grew to be more and more closely connected with each other through intermarriage, the Council came to be more and more composed of persons who were near kinsmen of each other, until, by 1703, this had reached such a point that one family, the Burwells, through themselves and their blood relations, controlled the decisions of the Board. Spotswood bitterly complained that should a cause involving a Burwell come before the General Court, a body identified in personality with the Council, seven of its members, owing to their kinship to that family, would have to retire from the deliberation of the case.[13]

In every department of life in Virginia during the seventeenth century, we discover that determined feeling that the most formal respect shall be shown to persons occupying a position of authority, which is observed in every department of English life throughout the same period. The two local bodies most powerful in enforcing

[12] Governor Andros mentions that the following "noted gentlemen of this Country" were at Jamestown Oct. 20, 1698: "William Randolph, Lewis Burwell, Philip Lightfoot, William Leigh, Gawin Corbin, Benjamin Harrison, Peter Beverley, Thomas Ballard, Miles Cary, John Taylor, William Buckner and George Marable"; most, if not all, of these prominent men, were members of the Council. See Minutes of Council, Oct. 20, 1698, B. T., Vol. LIII.

[13] Letters of Governor Spotswood, Vol. I., p. 60.

this respect were the vestries and county courts.   Vestry and county court alike were composed of the men who were, from both a social and a political point of view, the foremost in the community.   How jealous they were in protecting the dignity of leading citizens is illustrated in numerous instances preserved in the county records.   One may be given as an example.   About 1685, Humphrey Chamberlaine, of Henrico county, a man of good birth, but of a very choleric temper, was arrested because, in a fit of anger with Colonel William Byrd, he had stripped off his coat and drawn his sword with the intention, apparently, of making an attack.   The offence was committed very near the house where the court of justices was sitting, which was probably considered as greatly aggravating its heinousness, especially as Byrd had come to take part in the deliberations of that body.   Promptly clapped in jail, Chamberlaine soon broke down the bars, and but for the vigilance of the guards, would have made a clean escape.   When brought before the justices, he sought to excuse himself for his conduct towards Colonel Byrd by saying that he was "a stranger in the country and ignorant of its laws and customs."   The court, declining to accept such a palliation, declared that "no stranger, especially an English gentleman, could be insensible of ye respect and reverence due to so honorable a person" as Colonel William Byrd.   Chamberlaine was sentenced to pay a fine of five pounds sterling, and also to have repaired, at his own expense, the damage he had done to the prison.[14]

The privilege extended to persons in the enjoyment of

---

[14] Henrico County Minute Book, 1682-1701, pp. 107-8, Va. St. Libr.

the highest soical position in the community had, in many cases, been expressly established by law. For instance, at the sessions of 1623-4 the General Assembly, declaring it to be improper that persons of quality should undergo corporal punishment, enacted that, thereafter all persons of this kind should, in case of any delinquency, be merely imprisoned; if their offence was of a more serious character, they were, apparently in addition, simply to pay such a fine as the monthly court should think just to impose.[15] A regulation somewhat similar in spirit was adopted many years later on instructions from the English authorities, namely, that all male persons in the Colony, between the ages of sixteen and sixty, with the exception, it would seem, of servants and slaves only, were to be liable to be called to arms, but in doing so, scrupulous care should be taken to show the strictest respect "to ye quality of ye person" in order that officers might not be "forced to go as private soldiers, or in places inferior to their degree."[16]   Later in the century, the regard for the quality of the person in inflicting punishment for the less heinous offences was perhaps not carried so far, but it continued to be shown up to a certain point in numerous ways.

One of the few instances of a gentleman receiving corporal punishment occurred in the case of Richard Denham, of Lancaster county, who, for delivering to a member of the county court while sitting, a challenge to fight a duel, was condemned to be struck six blows on the shoulder with a whip, a punishment called for by the outrage on the dignity of the court, but which was perhaps, merely nominal as administered; and certainly in

---

[15] Hening's Statutes, Vol. I., p. 127.

[16] Colonial Entry Book, 1606-62, p. 226.

no way approached the terrible whipping which would have been inflicted had Denham belonged to a lower order in society.[17] Those persons who occupied the social position of yeomen, were not considered to be of sufficient quality to entitle them to exemption from corporal punishment; for instance, in 1647, we find a citizen of Lower Norfolk county, who is designated in the judgment of the court as "yeoman," condemned to be whipped in the presence of the justices for defamation.[18]

A large proportion of the planters were simply small landowners. Previous to the year 1650, the average size of the patent did not exceed four hundred and forty-six acres, and after that year, six hundred and seventy-four.[19] The greater number of these small estates were perhaps taken up by men of small means, who belonged to an humble walk in life, and whose names were obscure, and who personally possessed no special social influence. They were, in fact, as inferior, socially, to the gentry of Virginia in those times, as the same class in contemporary England were to the principal English landowners; but there is no reason to think that they cringed in the slightest degree to the families which wielded the greatest

---

[17] Lancaster County Records, Vol. 1652-56, p. 64. This is the only case in the seventeenth century records, of which I am aware, of a man of good position receiving corporal punishment for any offence. Denham may, however, not have been above the yeoman class, although the only fact now known about him was that he was the son-in-law of Captain Thomas Hackett, who presumably belonged to the social rank of a gentleman.

[18] Lower Norfolk County Antiquary, Vol. II., p. 13.

[19] Bruce's Economic History of Virginia in the Seventeenth Century, Vol. I., pp. 531-2.

social and political power in the community.[20]   In the
first place, it is quite probable that the bulk of the small
landowners had, in consequence of money they had
brought over from England, been able to purchase estates as soon as they arrived in the Colony, or at least to
sue out patents to public lands, by buying as many head
rights as they could afford to do.[21]   Independent pe-
cuniarily, in however small a way, in the Mother Country before they emigrated, they remained independent in
the Colony after they had established themselves there
permanently.   In the second place, the life of comparative isolation which they led nourished in them a spirit
of self-reliance, and their mastership of their own properties, though contained within narrow boundaries, fostered in them a spirit of manly pride.   Finally, they were

---

[20] William Puckett, of Henrico county, was in this respect a
fair representative of his class in the communities of that day.
When, in an altercation with him, in 1679, Major Chamberlaine
heaped on him opprobrious epithets, Puckett replied with the
utmost promptness and spirit.   See Henrico County Records, Vol.
1677-92, orig., p. 98.

[21] The following entries show the character and condition in
England, before their emigration, of many small Virginian landowners in the seventeenth century; they bear the date of 1658:
" William Webb obtains certificate from justices of Tewksbury
Borough, England, that he, his wife, and family are nowe and for
divers years last past have lived civilly and orderly within this
towne." He obtained a second certificate from the church wardens
of Bushley parish, County Worcester, that he was born in that
parish: " Besides I doe knowe that Stephen Webbe, the father,
was a freeholder of several lands within the Manour of Bushley,
and lived there for many yeares." William Webb was seeking to
prove his right to property which his brother and nephew had left
at their deaths in Virginia.   See Surry County Records, Vol.
1645-72, p. 145, Va. St. Libr.

in full possession of the suffrage, which gave them, as a body, a considerable degree of political power, a privilege, apart from all else tending in the same direction, that was certain to ensure them importance, if not individually, then as a mass.

Nor did the fact that many small landowners had at one time been agricultural hands, under articles of indenture, operate to lower the importance of this section of the community taken as a whole. Most of the indentured servants had, of their own accord, come out from England with the view of obtaining immediate employment in the Colony, and with the hope that, at a later date, they might secure a small homestead of their own there. They belonged, as a rule, to the class of English farm laborers, who were as distinguished for intelligence and industry as any laborers in that age. With the more numerous opportunities opened to them in Virginia to improve their condition, there is reason to think that a very considerable proportion of this class of emigrants, when their terms expired, became owners of small estates, which they were able to acquire by superior prudence and economy.[22]

Towards the end of the century, the estimation in which the small landowners (whether they were men who had arrived with means, or had once served as laborers in the Colony) were held was, from a social point of view, greatly raised by the steady increase in the number of African slaves introduced into Virginia. The presence of the negro bondsman had a marked tendency to promote pride of race among the members of every class of white people; to be white gave the distinction of color even to the agricultural servants, whose condition, in some

---

[22] See Bruce's Econ. Hist. of Va. in the Seventeenth Century.

respects, was not much removed from that of actual slavery; to be white and also to be free, combined the distinction of color with the distinction of liberty; and the two were all the more important if joined to the possession of considerable property.

There are numerous proofs that any suggestion as to social equality with the negro was resented even by the most indigent and illiterate section of the white population. An instance that occurred in York county in 1681, shows the feeling prevailing on this point among white working men, on whom alone a slave was likely to have intruded himself, although in this case the slave's mistress, and not the slave himself, committed the fault complained of. Mrs. Vaulx, a woman of high social position, sent her slave, Frank, to negotiate a matter of business with James Macarty and Edward Thomas, who were apparently mechanics. The latter evidently resented the selection of a black man to convey to them such an important message, for they curtly informed him that "they were not company for negroes," which seems to have ended the interview.[23]

Whilst the Indian, like the negro, could also, by law, be held in slavery, he seems, from a social point of view, to have enjoyed higher consideration with the white people; this is disclosed by the fact that there was no prohibition of the marriage of Indians with white persons, while the intermarriage of whites and blacks was strictly interdicted. There are instances in which the county courts expressly granted permission to a white man to take an Indian servant to wife; for example, in 1688, Benjamin Clamm, of Henrico county, was licensed by the justices to marry Sue, an Indian girl in the employment

---

[23] York County Records, Vol. 1675-84, orig., p. 362.

of John Cox.[24]   The marriage of John Rolfe and Pocahontas, the daughter of Powhatan, had established a romantic precedent, which, no doubt, had its influence in
diminishing popular prejudice against such unions; the
blood of the Indian princess flowed in the veins of some
of the leading men in the Colony; and this fact alone
was well calculated to remove any impression that such
alliances were dishonorable.   Moreover, the negro arrived in Virginia, not only a wretched slave, torn from
his country, but also an indescribably raw and bestial
savage, as hideous in aspect as he was brutish in instinct
and mean in intelligence. The Indian, on the other hand,
belonged to a far superior race, was brave and hardy in
spirit, and often of remarkable dignity in appearance and
stateliness of manner; and as a member of an independent nation, joined with the whites on equal terms in declaring war and making treaties of peace.   All these
facts, so promotive of his importance as a man, were not
likely to be forgotten in social intercourse.

---

[24] Henrico County Minute Book, 1682-1701, p. 206, Va. St. Libr.

IX

Social Spirit—Ties With the Mother Country.

FEW aspects of the social history of Virginia in the seventeenth century are more remarkable than the strong affection with which the people as a whole clung to all that reminded them of the Mother Country,—to the habits, the customs, the moral standards, the ideas which prevailed and governed in that beloved land beyond the sea from which nearly all the colonists were directly sprung.[1] This unswerving loyalty in all social matters was especially characteristic of the Virginians during this century because so large a proportion of the population had been born in England, and so many persons had left their native shires long after their earliest and most vivid impressions of the different communities in which they had first seen the light had been formed. It was not until the last decade of the century was reached that the native inhabitants of the Colony began to approach in number those who had emigrated from England. The sons and daughters of men and women whose first years had been passed under English skies were likely to have had almost as deep impressions of the Mother Country as their

---

[1] The Virginians, as late as 1670, seem to have spoken of themselves as Englishmen. The following is from a petition drawn up in that year: "Ye Petitioner humbly prays that since the said Biggs hath herein neglected the performance of his duty, unbecoming a good Christian, a loyall subject, and a true Englishman," etc., Va. Maga. of Hist. and Biog., Vol. X., p 376.

parents themselves, for it may be easily imagined that
these parents, especially if they had belonged to the
English gentry, omitted no opportunity of recalling
for the amusement of their children their own childhood and youth in their native land; of describing all
the varied scenes associated with those early experi-
ences; of picturing the old home; of delineating the
characters of the different members of the circle of
kindred; and relating an hundred interesting stories
drawn from the long annals of the family history. It
may be taken for granted that whatever was unhappy
or unprosperous in their condition before they went
out to Virginia faded from their memories, or became
greatly softened in the retrospect when their thoughts
flew back across the rolling waste of waters separating
them from their native shores,—that the fields, meadows, and woods of England seemed to put on a new
beauty, the ancient homes to be crowned with a new
glory, the parish church and churchyard to be clothed
in a new sacredness. Time and remoteness even created a glowing charm where none really existed and
made the charm that really did exist appear an hundred fold more attractive. Thus by the plantation fire-
sides love of all that went to compose the general social
life of England was instilled into the hearts of the
young Virginians; it was acquired at the mother's
knee; it was drawn in with the very air they breathed.

Members of all classes invariably spoke of England
as "home." There is a touch of pathos in the constant
use of this term as referring to the Mother Country.
We find it in the dryest business letters, and in the
most formal legal documents. Nor was its use confined to persons whose home England had once been;

even the natives of Virginia who had never seen England, and never expected to cross the ocean to visit the land of their ancestors, always designated it by the same loving word which, as coming from them, at least reflected the unconscious yearning inherited from parents born under English skies.   It was when he came to consider the division of his estate and to think of death that the mind of the emigrant, however long he may have resided in Virginia, appears to have dwelt with the most lingering fondness upon the scenes of his boyhood and early manhood, and upon those kinsmen who had remained behind.   It is in wills that the expression "home" as applied to England is most frequently found, and it is there that it seems to be invested with its most pathetic interest.   In some of these last testaments the writer is not content to use the word but once.   In the will of Peter Hopegood, of Rappahannock county, for instance, it appears at least six times.[2]

Had it been practicable in that century, when sailors were even more superstitious than they are now, to transport coffined bodies back to England, many wills would, no doubt, have contained a provision that the testator should be buried in the English parish church where his ancestors had long been buried; where he himself had attended services in early life, and where perhaps his nearest relatives continued to worship.   It must have been a sorrowful thought to many of these Virginians who had emigrated from England that their bones should find a last resting place so far from scenes associated for centuries with their forefathers,

[2] Rappahannock County Records, Vol. 1677-82, p. 71, Va. St. Libr.

and so far from ground that had been hallowed as the
earth to which the dust of parents and kinsmen, perhaps of their own children, had been consigned. One
of the most moving wills of the seventeenth century
was that of Robert Day, which survives among the
records of Westmoreland county. Though he followed the calling of a sea-captain, he appears to have
been a citizen of Virginia. He left directions that,
after his death, his heart should be removed from his
body, embalmed, and conveyed to England, there to
be interred beside the remains of his father, children,
and friends.[3]

It was not simply the demands of business that,
during the seventeenth century, led so many Virginians to visit England; a deep love for their old home
influenced many of those who had been born there to
return, whilst a natural curiosity to see what had been
so often described to them, and a desire to meet kinsmen whom they had never met, prompted many of the
native colonists to make the voyage. There is not a
surviving county record of the century which does not
contain numerous notices of an intention to go by the
first ship to England. As early as 1632 a special
license had to be obtained by any one wishing to depart before he could acquire a legal right to do so.[4]
This license seems to have been granted by the county

---

[3] Westmoreland County Records, Wills, 1665-77, folio p. 86.

[4] Hening's Statutes, Vol. I., p. 200. The character of the
clerk's certificate is illustrated in the following entry from Surry
County Records: "I do herebye certifye that Michael Howard
hath sett up his name and Resolution of goeing for England this
p'sent shipping according to law, at Lawne's Creek P'rish Church,
M'ch 1st, 1685-6." p' Jno Harris, Rcdr."

court; and its recordation was not infrequently accompanied by that of the last testament of the person receiving it, no doubt because the voyage was looked upon as attended with extraordinary danger. This fact must have brought a strong influence to bear to discourage many to undertake such a journey; and that the perils of an ocean-crossing were so constantly defied is only another proof of the close social bonds uniting such a large number of Virginians with the Mother Country.

There were several reasons why the law provided that all wishing to leave the colony, whether permanently or for an interval, should, before doing so, obtain a license. First, it was to prevent debtors without property in Virginia from escaping to England, whither it was possible for them to have shipped beforehand a large quantity of tobacco; and secondly, to conform to the terms of the English statutes, which required that each parish should feed and lodge its own poor, and be careful that they did not wander beyond its own boundaries to become a burden upon another parish. In spite of the necessity of securing a license to leave, there was no restriction whatever upon liberty of departure unless there was the plainest ground for refusing to grant permission; and this in reality only arose in those cases in which creditors had reason to question the good faith of a debtor with little or nothing to root him to the soil of the Colony. If that debtor left sufficient estate behind to cover his obligations, it is not probable that any obstacle was thrown in the way of his going. News of his intention was, no doubt, soon bruited abroad by persons who had been present at the session of the county court when

the license was asked for.   Such an intention must
have at once aroused the interest of the public, as a
voyage to England was an event to be discussed in
those quiet plantation communities; and if there was
any one with a right to object to that intention being
carried out, it was in his power to write at once to the
clerk of the county court asking him to refuse to deliver the license certificate until reasons for opposing
such a license could be offered.[5]

Not infrequently as many as eight persons at a
single sitting of the county court published their intention of leaving for England, and obtained the
license required.   In making such a long and tedious
voyage, it was natural that the companionship of
friends and acquaintances counted for much; and no
doubt, as far as possible, there was an effort on the
part of each person to time his departure so as to obtain on shipboard the society of others, like himself,
going out to the Mother Country.   Very often the wife
would accompany the husband to afford him the solace
of her presence.[6]   Many of those who returned to
England remained there premanently under the influence of renewed social ties with their native land, or
of an advantageous opening to follow some business

---

[5] " Mr. Francis Meriwether, Clerk of Ct., I would desire you
not to let Mr. John Waters have a certificate for goeing out of ye
Countrye untill you receive a note from me yr subscriber, for he
is my debtor a considerable sum of money in tobo, Jany 30, 1692.
Thomas Wheeler."   This is from Essex County Records, Vol.
1692-95, p. 170 Va. St. Libr.   Waters had published his intention
of going to England.

[6] A case of husband and wife going out to England together is
recorded in Rappahannock County Records, Vol. 1677-82, orig.,
p. 161.

there. Some, having probably accumulated a compe-
tence in Virginia, desired to spend their last days in
ease and quiet in the midst of the scenes which had
been familiar to them in childhood and early manhood.[7] Some, who were simply revisiting England for
a time, died there, and their wills distributing their
estates in the Colony were recorded in the general
probate office in London along with the testaments of
other English citizens.[8] Some were detained in England far beyond the period they had assigned for their
stay. There are numerous instances in which the
county courts granted a wife permission to take legal
charge of her husband's affairs owing to his unexpected detention abroad.[9] Quite frequently the trial of
a suit was deferred from sitting to sitting until one of
these visitors to the Mother Country who was a party
to the cause should reach Virginia on his anticipated
return.[10]

This constant intercourse with England must have
had a powerful influence in preserving and strengthening an affection for it, not only in the hearts of the
Virginians who revisited it, but also in the hearts of
all their kinsmen and friends, who themselves had not
enjoyed the same privilege. Doubtless, those who had

---

[7] The following is from the York County Records, Vol. 1675-84,
orig., p. 470: "Know all men by these presents that I, Anthony
Hall, late of Virginia, now of the Bogge in England, gentleman
* * * appoint Mrs. Rebecca Hethersall as my attorney."

[8] See Waters's Gleanings and also the "Virginia Gleanings in
England," which are abstracts of wills, recorded in London, con-
tributed to the Va. Maga. of History and Biography (see Vol.
X., et seq.) by Mr. Lothrop Withington.

[9] Surry County Records, Vol. 1645-72; see entries for year 1661.

[10] Elizabeth City County Records Orders, Nov. 18, 1692.

been so happy as to see the Mother Country returned with far more graphic accounts to give of its teeming cities and beautiful landscapes, its shaded streams, green meadows, and yellow cornfields, its ancient homes, hoary castles, and stately churches, than could be found in all the books in the Colony, whilst the affectionate welcome they had received from relations over sea made a deeper impression as described by word of mouth than the kindest expressions used in the letters which came from those same persons.

The little band of sea-captains, who were annually voyaging backwards and forwards, were also very active in keeping up an uninterrupted communication between English and Virginian kinsmen. These sea-captains, as we have already seen, were a body of superior men, who were freely admitted to the tables of the foremost planters. Many a verbal message and letter were carried by them from relatives in Virginia to relatives in England, or the reverse, and through them there was also a constant exchange of gifts testifying to mutual interest, affection, and esteem. William Byrd, the elder, very frequently used these agents, who were perhaps only too pleased to accommodate so considerable a man, in sending to English friends such a present as a choice assortment of hickory nuts and walnuts, or slips of sassafras and pawpaw; and through them, he was sent in return, in affectionate recognition of his good will and kindness, gooseberry and current shrubs, and the like, or the seeds and roots of such flowers as iris, crocus, tulip and anemone.[11] William Fitzhugh receives, among other presents, from English friends, a quantity of claret, and shows

---

[11] Letters of William Byrd, May 20, 21, 1684; July 29, 1690.

his appreciation of the gift by shipping in return a quantity of cider, which had been expressed from the apples of his own orchards.[12] Had all the letter books of the wealthy planters of those times been preserved, it would be seen that, with hardly an exception, they would note incidents similar to these in the lives of Byrd and Fitzhugh. Now the gift would be a cardinal red bird, the nightingale of Virginia; now the mocking bird, with its echoes of the entire choir of the colonial forests; now the flying squirrel or opossum; now the raccoon, which the first settlers took to be a species of monkey.[13] If the kindly spirit towards English kindred and friends crops out in the record of such characteristic presents as these in correspondence devoted almost exclusively to business, it can be easily imagined that the letters of a less practical and formal nature, such, for instance, as passed between the ladies of the related English and Virginia families, would have breathed a spirit of even greater kindness and affection, and in doing so gone far towards overcoming the alienating influences arising from a long separation in time and from the vast dividing reaches of the ocean.

Numerous bequests coming from both the Virginian and English branches of the same family reveal how strong the ties between English and Virginian kindred were, and how earnestly it was sought to cherish these ties to the last.[14] On the English side it is not con-

---

[12] Letters of William Fitzhugh, July 20, 1694.

[13] Some years ago, there was a Virginian raccoon caged in the courtyard of Warwick Castle, a more common sight in England in the seventeenth century than in the nineteenth, however.

[14] The gifts frequently had a sentimental as well as an intrinsic

fined to bequests from parents to their own offspring, who had settled in the Colony.[15] Such an evidence of kindness and affection as Mrs. Margaret Cheeseman, of Bermondsey, showed in her will towards the family of Lemuel Mason, of Lower Norfolk county, was far from being uncommon. She left ten pounds sterling, equal in modern values to two hundred and fifty dollars, to each one of his numerous children. In 1687 John Pargiter, of London, bequeathed an equal amount to Sarah Lovell, who also resided in Virginia; and a like amount was in 1666 left to Thomas Poulter by Hannah Wallis, of the same city. In the same year Joseph Walker, of Westminster, bequeathed property to a kinsman of his own name in Virginia, while Jane Maplesdin, also of Westminster, left a considerable legacy to John Lee, a citizen of the Colony. Among other persons in England who about the same time made bequests to friends or relatives over sea were Edward Francis and Joseph May. These are only a few typical instances among the many belonging to every decade of the century which might be mentioned.

Bequests from Virginians to their English kindred are even more frequent. For example, in 1648 Richard Simons left his whole estate situated in the Colony

---

value; for, instance, Mrs. Anne Mason left to " Mr. Gideon Mason, now living in Virginia, and to his wife, to each of them a ring of 20sh. a piece; to Gideon Mason, his son, her silver tankard; to Ann Mason, her silver porringer; to Martha, her six silver spoons." See Va. Maga. of Hist. and Biog., Vol. X., p. 412.

[15] How numerous were the bequests from English parents to their children residing in the Colony is shown by the wills which appear in the " Virginia Gleanings in England," published in the Virginia Maga. of History and Biography.

to his son, a resident of England,[16] whilst a few years later John Clarke, the owner of two valuable houses in Bocking, Essex, devised this property to his father, who was probably a citizen of that place,[17] an additional proof that many members of the highest planting class in Virginia continued to possess estates in the Mother Country long after their emigration. William Calvert, in 1665, bequeathed a large amount to his brother, whose home stood near Newark, in Nottinghamshire[18]; and about ten years later Henry Isham by will left his mother a one-third share of all the property he owned in both England and Virginia.[19] Thomas Taylor, in 1693, divided forty-two pounds sterling among his four children, a son and three daughters, who still resided in the Mother Country; and the amount due to each was, as each came of age, to be paid by the rector of the parish church of Finchley, in Middlesex.[20] George Jordan by his will directed that two thousand pounds of tobacco, which had been placed in his hands by William Jordan, should be shipped to England to be devoted to the use of the latter's children residing at Gyburne, near Skipton, in Yorkshire.[21] Such are a few characteristic

---

[16] York County Records, Vol. 1638-48, p. 431, Va. St. Libr.

[17] York County Records, Vol. 1657-62, p. 78, Va. St. Libr.

[18] York County Records, Vol. 1664-72, p. 126, Va. St. Libr.

[19] Henrico County Records, Vol. 1677-92, orig., p. 72.

[20] Elizabeth City County Records, Vol. 1684-99, p. 250, Va. St. Libr.

[21] Surry County Records, Vol. 1671-84, p. 295, Va. St. Libr. Many other instances will be found in Mr. Withington's "Virginia Gleanings in England," the first number of which was published in Virginia Maga. of Hist. and Biog., Vol. X., p. 291; see, for example, the will of Peter Ashton, Vol. X., p. 293.

instances of gifts by last testament to immediate relatives in England. The number of similar bequests and
devises to relatives more remote in blood was very
much greater.

As early as 1646, by which time considerable wealth
had been accumulated in the Colony, its citizens had
begun to leave money for the benefit of indigent persons dwelling in those English communities with
which the first part of the testators' lives had been
associated; for instance, in the course of that year,
Richard Elrington, of York county, bequeathed ten
pounds sterling to the poor of St. Martin's-in-the-
Fields, in London, subject to the provision that it
should be distributed as far as it would go, among the
oldest paupers to be found in that parish, at the rate
of two shillings and six pence a head.[22] Christopher
Robinson bequeathed five pounds sterling to the poor
of Cleasby, where he was born;[23] and in 1655 ten
pounds sterling was bequeathed by Captain John
Moon, of Isle of Wight county, for the support of the
poor living at Berry and Alverstock, in Hampshire.
As this was designed to be a permanent fund, the interest alone was to be expended in alleviating the condition of the indigent in those places.[24] Nathaniel
Knight, of Surry county, provided in his will that one-
half of his estate should be distributed among a certain
number of English persons, whom he designated in
proportion to their necessities,[25] whilst Philip Chesley

---

[22] York County Records, Vol. 1638-48, p. 135, Va. St. Libr.

[23] Va. Maga. of Hist. and Biog., Vol. VII., p. 20.

[24] Will of John Moon, Isle of Wight County Wills for 1655.

[25] Surry County Records, Vol. 1671-84, p. 260, Va. St. Libr.
Knight's father, who was to carry out this provision, resided at
Stroodwater, Gloucestershire.

left a legacy of one hogshead of tobacco to every one of his name residing in Welford, Gloucestershire.[26]

The affection and confidence in which the Virginians held their English relatives are shown in the numerous instances in which a son or daughter was, by last testament, recommended to the care of English kindred during the period the child was receiving general instruction, or preparing for some special pursuit in life. One example among many is furnished by Thomas Crosby, of Isle of Wight county, who, in 1679, bequeathed his son to Thomas Graves, of London, with the request that he should be properly educated as well as trained by an apprenticeship to earn his living in some branch of trade.[27] In many cases, to be referred to hereafter, Virginian parents during their own lives invoked the assistance of their English relatives when they sent their children to school in England. For instance, in 1684 we find the elder William Byrd seeking the kindly offices of his kinsfolk in London when his daughter was about to set sail. "She could learn nothing here in a great family of negroes," he wrote, and he was, therefore, led, in spite of her tender years, to let her go over sea to enjoy the advantage of a good English school, a step he, no doubt, would not have taken, on account of her youth, had there not been near relatives in England to show an interest in her welfare.[28]

As far as possible all the social customs and habits characteristic of England were closely followed in the

---

[26] York County Records, see Wills, for 1674.

[27] Isle of Wight County Records, Vol. 1661-1719, p. 193.

[28] Letters of William Byrd, March 31, 1684.

social life of Virginia. For example, one of the most
common provisions of wills made in the Colony during the seventeenth century was for the purchase of
mourning rings to be distributed among kinsmen and
friends; and a definite sum was generally set apart
by the testators themselves to be devoted to this purpose. The amount thus used was often very large.
Corbin Griffin, of Middlesex county, left twenty-five
pounds sterling, equal in value to six hundred dollars
in our present American currency, with which mourning rings were to be bought; and he directed that at
least fifteen of these rings, designed, no doubt, for the
persons to whom he was most attached, should cost
not less than a guinea a piece. Under the will of the
elder Nathaniel Bacon twenty pounds sterling were to
be expended in a similar way. John Page, in his last
testament, instructed his executors to buy eighteen
mourning rings; the executors of Roger Hodge were
directed to buy fourteen; and the executors of Robert
Beckingham sixteen.[29] A like provision was also often
made in wills for the purchase of gloves to be presented after the testator's death to his nearest relatives
and friends. For example, in 1676 John Emerson made
such a testamentary gift to each of thirteen persons
whom he had in life esteemed most highly; and he
went so far as to direct that each pair of gloves should
not fall below twelve pence in cost.[30]

The English custom of giving various articles the

---

[29] Bruce's Economic History of Virginia in the Seventeenth
Century, Vol. II., p. 195. When Mary, the daughter of John Evelyn, the diarist, died, sixty mourning rings were distributed among
her friends. See Diary, March 10, 1685.

[30] Surry County Records, Vol. 1671-84, p. 184, Va. St. Libr.

character of heirlooms was also very generally followed in Virginia. Even such ordinary household objects as tables and cupboards were brought into this legal category by the special provision of wills; but this was probably due to the great value in which such objects, when beautiful in design and finish, were held owing to the heavy expense incurred in their purchase and transportation across the ocean.[31] Rings, looking-glasses, Bibles—all passed very frequently subject to this same law in order that they might, like land entailed, remain in the same family for an indefinite period. The articles thus invested with the almost sacred character of heirlooms had, perhaps, in most instances, acquired an extraordinary sentimental value from their association with the homes and early lives of the testators in England, or had descended from their English ancestors. It was a frequent occurrence that a Virginian in his last will requested of the vestry of his parish church permission for his executors to inter his body in the chancel because that privilege had been enjoyed in England by his forefathers.[32]

The planter sometimes received the name of his residence as a kind of surname in accord with a custom prevailing in Scotland, and to some extent in the

---

[31] Rappahannock County Records, Vol. 1677-82, p. 53, Va. St. Libr.

[32] The will of George Watkin, of Surry county, contains the following: "My body I comit to ye earth from whence it came to be Buried in decent manner in ye Chancelle of ye Church at Lawnes Creek, as my p'r'cessors have been in ye chancell of ye P'rish Churches where they dwelt." Surry County Records, Vol. 1671-84, p. 55, Va. St. Libr. Burials in the chancel depended upon the consent of the minister. See Hening's Statutes, Vol. I., p. 243.

north of England. For example, John Parker, a prominent citizen of Accomac, is generally designated in the county's records as "John Parker of Mattapony,"[33] and other instances of the like character might be mentioned.

The names of many Virginian homes at this period bore a close resemblance to names so often used in the Mother Country. For example, the residence of Christopher Robinson, situated in Middlesex county, was known as the "Grange."[34] The name of "Exeter Lodge" was given to the residence which John Saffin had erected in Northumberland county,[35] while the residence of Thomas Bushrod, in York, bore the name of "Essex Lodge."[36] In some wills belonging to this period the home of the testator is referred to simply as the "manor house," a term in general use in England.[37] The other names which the emigrants gave their Virginian homes show a fond recollection of the English mansions in which they were born, or with which their families had been long associated. For instance, the residence of Captain Thomas Purifoy, in Elizabeth City county, had received the name of "Drayton," in honour of the ancient seat of the Purifoys in Leicestershire, the shire from which Mrs. Purifoy had come, and probably her husband also.[38] The residence of the

---

[33] Accomac County Records, Vol. 1682-97, folio p. 88.

[34] Va. Maga. of Hist. and Biog. Vol. VII., p. 20.

[35] Northumberland County Records, Vol. 1666-72, Depositions, Jan'y 20, 1666.

[36] York County Records, Vol. 1675-84, orig., p. 135.

[37] Rappahannock County Records, Wills, Vol. 1677-82, p. 75, Va. St. Libr.

[38] Va. Maga. of Hist. and Biog., Vol. VII., p. 101.

Moseleys, of Lower Norfolk county, where they had settled as early as 1649, was known as "Rolleston" in recollection of Rolleston Hall, the seat of the Moseley family, in Staffordshire.[39]   Sometimes the name of the home was suggestive of an English stateliness which was not necessarily entirely foreign to the home itself even in these early times.   For example, Richard Cole, of Westmoreland county, had given his home the name of "Salisbury Park," [40] a designation in such popular use in England, and which in this case was probably made appropriate by an extensive and magnificent growth of trees surrounding the house.   The term "Hall" as applied to a residence was also not uncommon.

---

[39] Va. Maga. of Hist. and Biog., Vol. V., p. 327.

[40] See Cole's Will in Westmoreland County Records, Vol. 1665-1677, folio p. 186.

X.

Social Spirit—Manner of Life.

FOLLOWING the shores of the lower reaches of the great rivers, the Potomac, the Rappahannock, the York and the James, we find many years before the close of the seventeenth century, a succession of large plantations, on each of which there stood a substantial mansion, occupied by a family of social and political prominence, descended from the English gentry, and using coats-of-arms, to which they were legally entitled. As early as 1675, the Colony had been established long enough for these homes, in their outer and inner physical aspect, to have acquired some of the dignity distinguishing so many of the ancient English manor-houses, and in their intimate social life, much of that charm which was thrown around the social life of England in that age by ease of fortune, refined manners, general culture, and the amenities springing from the closest bonds of kinship and friendship. In every important feature, the society of Virginia in the seventeenth century was the same as that far more celebrated society which constitutes the most romantic side of the Colony's history in the eighteenth, although, necessarily in the seventeenth century, the accumulation of wealth had not as yet gone so far, and therefore, the ability to make a display was not so great.

Before considering the most salient features of the social life of Virginia at this early period, it will be instructive to touch briefly on the material background of that life, on which I dwelt at length in a former work.[1]

---

[1] The authorities for the details that follow as relating to

First, as to the residences. The residences were, as a rule, built of wood, with the chimneys and the under-pinning of brick. Among the few constructed entirely of brick was the house of Governor Berkeley, situated at Green Spring, near Jamestown; and this was also true of the mansion in Surry county, occupied by Thomas Warren. The common use of wood in Virginia in erect-ing a residence was due to the abundance as well as to the superior quality of the timber; in England, on the other hand, owing to the smallness of the area in forest, stone, brick, and slate were generally employed for this purpose, with the result that the houses were better able to withstand the disintegrating force of time and weather, and were less open to the risk of fire. In England, as in the Colony, the floors and stairways were composed of wood, and the lower walls were lined with wainscotting. Abraham Piersey, the wealthiest merchant and planter in Virginia in the early years of the Colony, and William Fitzhugh, who possessed one of the largest fortunes of a later period, each occupied a wooden residence. The history of Fitzhugh's home resembled that of numerous others—it had gradually spread out, by the erection of wing after wing, as his family grew in size, until the whole covered a very considerable area of ground. This house contained as many as twelve or thirteen apart-ments. The residence of Mrs. Elizabeth Digges, in York county, contained, in addition to other apartments, both large and small, what were known as the "yellow" and the "red" rooms, chambers, no doubt, used only when there were guests in the house. There was also a large

---

houses and their contents, clothes, abundance of food, and the like, will be found in Bruce's Economic History of Virginia in the Seventeenth Century, Vol. II., chapts. xii., xiii.

hall-parlor, which probably served the mixed purpose of a family sitting-room and a withdrawing-room for visitors. The residence of the elder Nathaniel Bacon, a man who possessed a very large estate, and who, being very prominent in the political life of the Colony, must have entertained very constantly contained, besides a number of sleeping chambers, what were described as the "old and the new halls," which, in summer at least, were probably used at sitting-rooms. Rosegill, the home of Ralph Wormeley, who, like Bacon, enjoyed great social and political influence, contained a large withdrawing-room, in addition to numerous sleeping chambers. There was, perhaps, no other residence in Virginia more admirably appointed for the entertainment of guests. It was situated directly on the banks of the Rappahannock river, in one of its widest and noblest reaches, which thus afforded extraordinary facilities for boating and sailing. The library was, perhaps, the choicest and largest in the Colony, while the house itself was unusually spacious.

The residence of Robert Beverley, who was as commanding a figure as Bacon or Wormeley, was smaller in its dimensions than Rosegill; it contained six large chambers, one of which was, perhaps, used as a withdrawing-room. There were eight rooms in the residence of Richard Willis, one of the most prominent citizens of Middlesex county. Among the numerous rooms in the residence of William Fauntleroy was a large hall. The residence of Thomas Willoughby, of Lower Norfolk, contained, besides a hall and numerous other apartments, a parlor or withdrawing-room, and two chambers, known as "the green" and "the red," which, like the two similarly designated in the residence of Mrs. Elizabeth Digges, were, no doubt, always reserved for guests as the two handsomest rooms in the house. The residence of Southey Littleton, in Accomac county, contained, among other apartments, a hall and three sleeping chambers; the hall was probably used as a dining-room, as the expression "dining hall" appears not infrequently in the records.

These residences are fairly representative, in the point of spaciousness, of all those occupied by the class of wealthy planters, and it will be seen that they contained ample room, whether in the way of halls, dining-rooms, or chambers, for the entertainment of guests in great ease and comfort. It is doubtful whether, in this respect, the home of the average English country gentleman of that period offered a more liberal accommodation.

The inventories of the estates of the leading citizens show that these colonial residences were furnished and ornamented after the most substantial and attractive patterns which England afforded. There was every variety of bed, protected by hanging mosquito nets, and supplied with the finest linen sheets, and very often with silk counterpanes, whilst the sides were adorned with valances of gold and silver texture. There were couches, which were not infrequently covered with embroidered Russian leather, or Turkey-worked cloth; and chairs ranging in kind from those having the seat made of rushes, or rudely tanned calf skin, to those with the seat and back composed of the costliest Russian leather or cloth elaborately embroidered. In some of the residences, there were as many as twenty-four chairs, bound in the finest Russian leather; in one room alone, no doubt the parlor of Mrs. Elizabeth Digges's home, there were nine chairs covered with Turkey-worked cloth; and eleven with cloth, into which a pattern of arrows had been woven, were found in another apartment.

The large fire-places were made for the burning of

wood; in the clearing of new grounds, an annual task on each plantation, a vast quantity of fuel was accumulated, and thus furnished a supply for use in winter, which it was impossible to exhaust. Hickory was especially abundant; and cut down in the Spring, became thoroughly seasoned before Autumn had passed; the heavy logs, piled up on the great iron or brass andirons in the hall, gave out a ruddy glow, which brought the warmth back into the body of the guest who had been travelling from a remote plantation, through snow and a biting air to reach the home of his host. A fire was kept lighted in this apartment, and a little slave, hardly to be distinguished from the dogs drowsing about the hearth, was always at hand to throw on another stick as the flame began to decline. In the sleeping chambers reserved for visitors fuel was laid in each fire-place, requiring but the touch of a candle to the resinous pine knots to burst into a hot fire. The floors of the finer residences were covered with carpets, which served further to assure the comfort of the guests and inmates. Some of those used in the parlors, and, no doubt, in the handsomest sleeping rooms, also, were of the costliest material; for instance, in the home of Mrs. Digges, two of the chambers were laid with Turkey-worked carpets, while the carpets covering the floors of two other rooms were of a green color, and perhaps equally as expensive. The windows in all of the principal apartments were shaded by linen curtains, and the chimneys were hung with printed cottons. In some houses, tapestry adorned the walls of the best rooms. Pictures also looked down from many places. In the homes of such wealthy men as William Fitzhugh, Thomas Ludlow, Joseph Croshaw, and Edward Digges, there seem to have been numerous pictures, the larger proportion of which were probably copies of ancestral portraits brought over from England, as at this time there were no artists in the Colony to fix on canvas the faces of members of the leading families.

The dining-room at this period seems to have contained a great variety of tables; there was the folding, the falling, the oval, and the side-board table, some of which were so handsome that they were, as we have seen, often required by the wills of the owners to descend as heirlooms. The tablecloths were frequently of the finest stuff; for instance, Mrs. Elizabeth Digges possessed nine manufactured of damask, and the napkins, of which there was a great profusion owing to the absence of forks, were often made of the same material; thirty-six damask napkins are included in the entries of the Digges inventory. The open cupboards of the dining-room presented a very liberal display of plates and dishes. At this time, these utensils were generally made of pewter; so were the spoons, bowls, jugs, sugar pots, castors, and porringers; and so also were the cups, flagons, tankards, and beakers. In the seventeenth century, the calling of the pewterer was one of the most important of all the mechanical trades, and the art was carried to the highest state of perfection. Polished with extraordinary care, these pewter utensils shone with a brightness approaching quite near to that of silver; to the casual glance, the cupboard of the colonial dining-room of this early period seemed to be filled with utensils of the more precious metal, and, no doubt, the mistress was often gratified by compliments paid by her guests to the shining array on the shelves.

But the table service was not restricted to pewter, though that material necessarily was the one most often used. The travellers visiting the Colony in the seventeenth century comment on the quantity of silver which they saw in the residences of the different planters;

plates and dishes, cups, tumblers, mugs, tankards, flagons, beakers, porringers, bowls, sugar pots, castors, and spoons, made of this valuable material, were frequently noticed. Some of this silver had been inherited from English parents, but the greater part had been bought from English silversmiths. Planters in the possession of large fortunes were constantly purchasing silver plate through their merchants in England; and this was done not only for the more striking display which a silver table service would make, but also as a safe form of investment. On one occasion, we find William Fitzhugh giving an order to an English correspondent to purchase for him two silver dishes, to weigh about fifty ounces apiece; a set of silver castors to receive sugar, pepper, and mustard which was to weigh from twenty-four to twenty-six ounces; a silver basin, to weigh from forty to forty-five, a silver salver and pair of candlesticks, to weigh thirty ounces apiece; and a silver ladle, to weigh ten ounces. To these, there were to be added a dozen silver hafted knives and a dozen silver hafted forks. On another occasion, Fitzhugh purchased in England two silver dishes, weighing between eighty and ninety ounces apiece, twelve ordinary silver plates, and two silver bread plates, a large pair of silver candlesticks, and one paid of silver snuffers.

The elder William Byrd, like Fitzhugh, invested large sums, from time to time, in silver plate of different kinds. Mrs. Elizabeth Digges left to relatives two hundred and sixty-one ounces of such plate, and Corbin Griffin one hundred and sixty-one, whilst the silver plate belonging to Robert Beverley was valued at a figure now equal to nearly eight hundred dollars. Even the planters who had moderate estates, were in possession of a considerable quantity of silver in the shape of salt-cellars, spoons, beakers, cups, tankards, and the like. Richard Ward, of Henrico county, a planter of small fortune, bequeathed twenty-seven silver spoons; another planter of York county, of fortune equally small, divided by will twenty-four silver spoons and one silver tankard. Numerous other instances might be mentioned.

For the amusement of the guests in the house, as well as of the members of the family, musical instruments were to be found in nearly all the planters' residences; there are frequent references in the inventories to the virginal, the hand lyre, the fiddle, and violin, and also to the recorder, flute, and hautboy, as a part of personal estates. As we shall see hereafter, a small collection of carefully-selected books was one of the most ordinary contents of the Virginian home, and during those hours when the visitor was not occupied with other pastimes, an interesting volume was at hand to divert him, if his tastes were literary.

There are many evidences that, from an early date, numbers of the wealthiest class of planters possessed a large quantity of the most fasionable clothes which the English tailors could furnish. This enabled them to make an attractive appearance in entertaining in their own homes, or in visiting the homes of their friends. Among other articles of dress owned by Thomas Warnet, a merchant who died in Virginia about 1629, were a pair of silk stockings, a pair of black hose, a pair of red slippers, a sea-green scarf, edged with gold lace, a felt hat, a black beaver, a doublet of black camlet, a gold belt and sword. All this bravery must have been very imposing when seen on the streets of Jamestown, or in the houses of its citizens; but that it was not unusual, is shown by the fact that a law had to be passed before the middle of the seventeenth century, restricting the liberty of importing so much finery; it was expressly forbidden to bring in silk pieces, unless designed for hoods and scarfs, or to introduce silver, gold, and bone lace, or ribbons wrought with gold and silver texture. But this law was either repealed, or treated with contempt; silk stockings, beaver hats, green scarfs, gold lace, and red slippers were as common articles of dress in Virginia as in England itself. On gay occasions, the men strutted about in camlet coats with sleeves ending in lace ruffles; in waistcoats black, white, or blue, or adorned with patterns elaborately Turkey-worked; and in trousers made of the costliest plush or broad cloth. The whole suit was often manufactured from broad cloth or plush and dyed an olive color. About their necks they wore cloths of muslin, or the finest holland, and in their shoes, shining brass, steel, or silver buckles, whilst they carried in their hands or pockets silk or lace handkerchiefs, delicately scented.[2]

The dress of the ladies was even more remarkable for fineness of texture and beauty of aspect. There are innumerable references in the inventories of personal estates to silk and flowered gowns, bodices of blue linen or green satin; waistcoats, bonnets, and petticoats trimmed with silk or silver lace; sarsanet and calico hoods, scarfs of brilliant shades of color, mantles of crimson taffeta, laced and gallooned shoes, gilt and golden stomachers, and fans richly ornamented. The wardrobe of Mrs. Elizabeth Digges, which perhaps did not differ from that of any other woman in the Colony of equal wealth and position, contained, among its numerous pieces of finery, a

---

[2] "Brother, the five waistcoats and three felts, the 9 yards of redd kersey, the scarlett coat with silver buttons are in James's sea chest." See letter of James Clarke, 1659, York County Records, Vol. 1657-62, p. 180, Va. St. Libr.

scarlet waistcoat trimmed with silver lace, a sky-colored satin bodice, and a pair of red paragon bodies. Mrs. Frances Pritchard, of Lancaster county, possessed a printed calico gown, lined with blue silk, a white striped dimity jacket, a blue silk waistcoat, a pair of scarlet sleeves with ruffles, and a Flanders lace band. These costly articles of dress were further set off by valuable jewelry; the ladies' caskets contained numerous pearl necklaces, gold pendants, silver earrings, and gold hand rings, which were worn, if not every day, on every social occasion when the bravest ornaments seemed appropriate. Among the possessions of the Dickenson family, who resided in York county, were one gold ring, set with a single ruby, a second ring set with seven rubies, and a third, set with a white stone.[3]   Nathaniel Branker, of Lower Norfolk county, owned a sapphire set in gold, three gold rings, adorned with a blue and green and a yellow stone respectively, a diamond ring of several sparks, and a beryl set in silver. There were three other rings, and an amber necklace in addition.[4]   Among the articles owned by Denis McCarty, of Rappahannock county, was a ring bearing eight diamonds.[5]   Small gold and silver bodkins for holding together and decorating the hair, were in general use among the ladies of this period.

---

[3] York County Records, Vol. 1664-72, p. 474, Va. St. Libr.

[4] Lower Norfolk County Records, orig. Vol. I., 1686-95, folio p. 17.

[5] Rappahannock County Records, Vol. 1686-92, orig., p. 241. See, also, an account of the jewelry owned by the Moseley family given in Bruce's Economic History of Virginia in the seventeenth century. See, also, will of Mrs. Howe in Va. Maga. of Hist. and Biog. for October, 1906, under which the Hill family of Shirley, on James river, inherited valuable rings, etc. The list might be greatly extended.

Few countries of the world have possessed so abundant and varied a supply of food as Virginia during the seventeenth century. This partly explains the hospitable disposition of the people even in those early times. The herds of cattle, which ran almost wild, afforded an inexhaustible quantity of milk, butter, cheese, veal, and beef. The hams obtained from hogs that had fed on the succulent mast of the forests, was considered by travelled visitors to the Colony to be quite equal, if not superior, to the celebrated hams cured in Westphalia. Deer were shot in such extraordinary numbers, that it was said the people had grown tired of eating venison. There were few counties in which there were not many large flocks of sheep; and mutton was much relished. So abundant were chickens that they were not included in the inventories of personal estates; no planter was so badly off that he could not have a fowl on his table at dinner. The wild turkeys frequenting the woods were of remarkable weight and afforded a popular repast. The clouds of wild pigeons arriving at certain seasons in incredible numbers, were killed by the tens of thousands, and for many weeks furnished an additional dish for the planter's table. So vast were the flocks of wild ducks and geese in the rivers and bays during the greater part of the year, that they were looked on as the least expensive portion of the food which the Virginians had to procure for the support of their families. Fish of the most delicate and nourishing varieties were caught with hook, or net, or speared at the very door; among other kinds, the perch and shad, the bass, pike and sheepshead. Oysters, and shell fish, without previous planting, could be scraped up by the bushel from the bottom of the nearest inlet or tidal stream.

The numerous varieties of fruit, such as apples,

peaches, plums, and figs were more highly flavored than the same varieties grown out of doors in England, owing to the greater heat of the sun in Virginia, and a longer season in which to ripen; so extraordinary was the quantity produced that the mere droppings of the orchards formed an important part of the food used in fattening hogs. Not only were domestic grapes cultivated in profusion in the gardens, but there were also several excellent kinds, such as the sloe and scuppernong, which ran wild through the tangled brushwood springing up in every damp forest bottom. Such an abundance of wild strawberries could be gathered from the vines overspreading every abandoned field, that no attempt was made to produce the domestic berry. The cool intervals between the rows of waving Indian corn were yellow with huge pumpkins, or green with luxuriant peas; there were ten varieties of peas alone grown in Virginia, one of which, the black-eye, became, from an early date, a common article of food with persons of every class. There were two varieties of potatoes, the Irish and the sweet, both of which reached a state of perfection in a soil remarkable then, as now, for its adaptability to vegetables. The watermelon and cymblin flourished in it to an even greater degree. In hominy, the roasting ear, and the corn pone, the Virginians possessed articles of food of great excellence, which were entirely unknown to the people of the Old World. There was produced on every plantation an extraordinary quantity of walnuts and chestnuts, hazel and hickory nuts. Honey was obtainable in abundance, both from domestic hives and hollow trees in the forest. Every variety of sweetmeat, as well as oranges, lemons, prunes, and raisins were imported from England, the West Indies, or the Azores.

England itself, in proportion to its population, was not

more abundantly supplied with liquors of all kinds than
Virginia, over the sea.   A considerable share of these
liquors was brewed in the Colony, where, in one year
alone, 1644, there were six public brew-houses in operation.   By the middle of the century, home-made beer
had become the most popular draught.   Cider was consumed in almost equal quantities, and was considered by
capable judges, to be quite as good as that expressed
from the apples grown in the most famous orchards in
Herefordshire; there was hardly a residence of any pre-
tension which did not keep a supply of this liquor on
hand; and some of the planters had as much as one hundred and fifty gallons stored away in their cellars.   Perry,
which was made from the juice of pears, was also produced on every plantation, and drunk with as much lib-
erality as cider.   Among the most ordinary drinks was a
punch brewed with West Indian rum, or apple or peach
brandy; and hardly less common was mathegalin, a mix-
ture of honey and water in certain proportions.   The
wines most often found on the tables of the planters were
claret, Fayal, Madeira, and Rhenish; it was one of the
most characteristic features of those times that the rarest
French, Spanish, and Portuguese wines were drunk, not
only in private residences, owned by the wealthiest persons, but also in the taverns, which were resorted to chiefly by persons of the lower classes.

XI

SOCIAL SPIRIT—HOSPITALITY OF THE PEOPLE.

IT is evident from the brief description which has been given of their commodious residences, handsome furniture, and valuable plate, of their fine clothing and beautiful ornaments, of their abundant and varied food and wines, that the citizens of Virginia during the seventeenth century who owned large estates, were in as advantageous a position to entertain lavishly as their kinsmen among the country gentlemen of England. Servants were numerous long before African slaves began to be brought in, cargo after cargo, to take the place of the whites, whose indentures had expired. After 1675, negroes became more and more common in the household; sufficient time had now elapsed to allow a large increase in the number of slaves who had been born in Virginia, and who thus had had opportunities of receiving a careful domestic training in the planters' homes. At least one wealthy Virginian of this period, the elder William Byrd, complained of the number of negro servants who were to be found under his roof. But that they were quick in anticipating the wants of the planter's family, as well as of his guests, is shown by the many evidences which have survived of the affectionate relations existing between the master and slave. One of the most ordinary encomiums included in the mortuary eulogy inscribed on so many of the tombstones of those times is that the deceased was a "kind" master or mistress; and the wills offer an equally eloquent, and perhaps a more trustworthy, proof of the loyal and devoted spirit on the one side, and the high appreciation in which it was held on the other. The provision which Daniel Parke, in 1689, made by will for one of his slaves was far from being exceptional: "For the true and faithful service of one of my negroes, known as 'Virginia Will'," he wrote, "I leave him his freedom, and also fifteen bushels of clean shelled corn, and fifty pounds of dried beef annually as long as he lives; also one kersey coat and breeches, a hat and two pair of shoes, two pair of yarn stockings; two white and blue shirts, one pair of blue drawers, one axe and one hoe; the same to be delivered annually."[1]

The disposition to entertain and to be entertained was encouraged not only by the number of trained servants living under the wealthy planter's roof, but also by the ease with which a visitor could get from house to house; with hardly an exception, each of the principal residences was situated on a large body of water, or on a navigable creek communicating with such a body. The boat was generally the most convenient means of reaching a neighbor's home, or even a home which lay at a very considerable distance off. Born on the shores of a great stream like the York, or Rappahannock, the Lower James, or Potomac, the young Virginians of those times, as of these, acquired, at an early age, an extraordinary skill in handling a sail boat, and in making the most of every breath of wind that passed over the waters. One single sailing vessel, calling at house after house along the banks of a river, was able to carry a large party of merry pleasure-seekers to an entertainment given in some planter's home standing twenty or even forty miles away from the point where the vessel started on its voyage. If a different means of conveyance was preferred, there

---

[1] York County Records, Vol. 1687-91, p. 278, Va. St. Libr.

was the riding horse to bear both the male and the female guest to their place of destination. The rapidity and even the apparent recklessness with which the Virginians rode gave rise to an expression which became a proverb: "the planter's pace;" and in these journeys on horseback from residence to residence, the young men and women, no doubt, made the forests echo to the clatter of flying hoofs, as well as to the sound of joyous laughter.

The seclusion of the planter's life and the remoteness of his home greatly stimulated his hospitable instincts. In the instructions which were given to Governor Yeardley, in 1626, by the English authorities, he was directed to see that all newcomers were, on their arrival, comfortably lodged with those citizens who had been long established in the country;[2] but there was really little need for such a regulation, for if the newcomer was respectable, his society was considered a full return for the small cost of taking him in. Any person of distinction visiting the Colony was unable to accept all the invitations extended him. Colonel Henry Norwood, who left England after the ruin of the royal cause, relates, in his account of his stay on the Eastern Shore, that there was much rivalry among the planters there as to who should feast him first and most often.[3] Norwood himself was made doubly interesting as a guest by all the graces which he had acquired at Court, by his long experience of the great world, and by his devotion and fidelity to his King. The author of *Leah and Rachel*, writing in 1656, stated that a traveller in the Colony in proceeding on his journey, not only incurred no charge for his entertain-

---

[2] British Colonial Entry Book, 1606-62, p. 259.

[3] Norwood's Voyage to Virginia, p. 48, Force's Hist. Tracts, Vol. III.

ment, but also was received everywhere with the heartiest of welcomes. "Virginia," he declared, "wants not good victuals, wants not good dispositions, and as God has freely bestowed it, they as freely impart with it."[4] It was only in a passing moment of panic that the county courts required even of innkeepers such a report as the one provided for in 1681—no unknown guest of that time was to be allowed to remain in a tavern over a day and night without the host informing the nearest constable of the fact.[5] It was not many years since the Insurrection, led by the younger Bacon, had been suppressed, and the recollection of that terrible tumult had made the local authorities suspicious of unknown persons wandering about the country. But this was not the feeling of ordinary times; in such times, the hospitality of the colonists was carried to a point which reminds one of the Biblical age. The stranger enjoyed the right to command every comfort in the planter's residence as if he proposed to pay for it; it was as if the first homes in every county were licensed hostelries, so generous and liberal was the scale of entertainment.[6]

This spirit continued until the end of the century. Beverley declared that a traveller in Virginia needed no other recommendation to the people than that he was a "human creature;" that if he was in want of shelter and a meal, he had but to inquire of anyone he met on the road the way to the nearest gentleman's seat; and that, if on his arrival there, the master was absent, he was certain to find that the servants had received orders to

---

[4] Leah and Rachel, p. 19, Force's Hist. Tracts, Vol. III.

[5] See bond of Samuel Thompson, an innkeeper, Surry County Records, Vol. 1671-84, p. 576, Va. St. Libr.

[6] Leah and Rachel, p. 19, Force's Historical Tracts, Vol. III.

set before strangers the very best that the plantation had
to offer. And Beverley added that, if "there should be a
churl that, either out of contrariness or ill nature, would
not comply with this generous custom, he had a mark
of infamy" attached to him, and soon discovered that
he was an object of opprobrium to all.[7]

The welcome received at some of the inns must often
have been distinguished for a grace and warmth superior
to what was observed in the ordinary tavern; for in Virginia, as in England, some of the hostelries were kept
by men accustomed to the most refined society of the
communities in which they lived, but who had been
forced by ill fortune to become purveyors to the entertainment of the public. In some cases, however, we find
prominent and wealthy citizens entered in the records
as "innkeepers" because taverns were among the pieces
of property which they owned. This was probably the
case with Thomas Cocke, who, in 1685, was licensed to
keep a tavern in Henrico county; and with Thomas Jordan, who, in 1674, was licensed to keep a tavern in Surry
county.[8]

The author of "Virginia's Cure," writing about 1666,

---

[7] Beverley's Hist. of Virginia, p. 258. "Even the poor planters,"
remarked Beverley, "who have but one bed, will very often sit up
or lie upon a form or couch all night to make room for a weary
traveler to repose himself after a weary journey."

[8] Henrico County Records, Vol. 1677-92, orig., p. 330; Surry
County Records, Vol. 1684-86, p. 25, Va. St. Libr. See, also,
Lower Norfolk County Records Orders Feby, 2, 1685-6. The Jor-
dan family was one of the most prominent in Surry county, where
it had been long settled. In his will, dated 1677-8, when the
Colony was still suffering from the great upheaval of 1676, George
Jordan prayed, " God Almighty to bless this poore Colonie, and
this county especially, wherein I have lived forty-three years." See
Surry Records, Vol. 1671-84, p. 296, Va. St. Libr.

declared, as the result of his own personal observation, that the Virginians were "naturally of beautiful and comely persons, and generally of more ingenious spirits" than the people of England;[9] and the opinion formed by such an intelligent traveller as Hugh Jones, who visited the Colony many years later, was equally flattering to its inhabitants.[10] It is not strange that the spirit of manly self-reliance fostered by the independent life of the plantation, manners polished by constant intercourse with the best society furnished by the oldest colonial communities, and a natural sprightliness of mind, should have enabled some Virginians, even of this early period, to make a highly favorable impression in the most distinguished circles of London. The younger Daniel Parke and the younger William Byrd belong more distinctly to the early part of the eighteenth century than to the latter part of the seventeenth; both, however, were born in the seventeenth century, and both were the products of its highest social influences. During their stay in England, both moved in the highest society of the Kingdom, and both appear to have won its good will. As aide to Marlborough, Parke was chosen by that famous general to carry to the Queen the despatch announcing the greatest of his victories. Byrd was intimate with some of the most remarkable persons in England, and showed his versatility by securing the friendship of men belonging to such different types as Boyle, the scientist and philanthropist, and Peterborough, the fop and soldier. The history of his times, whether colonial or English, does not furnish a more charming or a more attractive figure than he. In possession of a large fortune, in the enjoyment

---

[9] Virginia's Cure, p. 6, Force's Historical Tracts, Vol. III.
[10] See Hugh Jones's " Present State of Virginia."

of all that the noblest English literary culture and the
finest school of English manners, London, could impart,
and blessed with much that Nature implants in the hearts
and minds of her children only in her most generous,
lively, and stately moods, Byrd became, at an early age,
one of the most brilliant, one of the most accomplished,
and one of the most lovable gentlemen of his time. The
very existence of such a man, who concentrated in himself such varied claims to distinction, speaks a thousand
times louder for the refinement and fertility of the social
life to which he belonged, than the most elaborate
description of its different features.

The second Robert Beverley, who, like the younger
William Byrd, was a native of Virginia, and like him,
also, born many years before the end of the seventeenth
century, was almost an equally charming product of the
social influences of his times. His "History of Virginia,"
by which he is chiefly known, throws almost as much
light on the general spirit of that day as the writings of
Byrd on the general spirit of a somewhat later period.
The fund of lurking humor which it contains, reflects the
happy temper of his Virginian contemporaries; there is
in it a freshness, a spontaneity, that is characteristic of a
youthful and growing community; a keenness and mi-
nuteness of observation possessed only by those who,
from their earliest childhood, have been close to nature
in its primeval forms; a disposition to enjoy, which,
taking all the pleasures and amusements of life as they
come, prefers to open the eyes wide to the sunshine and
to blink only at the clouds; a devoted patriotism that was
fostered by remoteness from the Old World; and a love
of freedom and a hatred of tyranny that were nourished
by the secluded and independent life of the large
plantation.

XII.

WHAT were the most popular amusements of the Virginians during the seventeenth century? All the records go to show that their diversions, whether within or out of doors, differed but little from those of their English kindred, and that these diversions were enjoyed with all that extreme heartiness which distinguished the English people in all their sports unless they had come under the gloomy influence of the austere fanaticism of the Puritans. In a former work I pointed out how far drinking in public was carried, and the extraordinary facilities for gratifying this appetite which the taverns afforded. That love of hospitality for which the planters were so remarkable gave an additional stimulus to this proclivity when indulged in in the private home. The guest was honored by placing before him at table the best liquor as well as the best food which the house could furnish; and in the fervor with which his health was drunk, glass, no doubt, followed glass with amazing rapidity. There were few residences which did not contain a great variety as well as a great quantity of wines and strong spirits. Reference has already been made to the extraordinary store of home-made liquors, like cider and perry, that were to be found in so many cellars in the Colony. The store of imported liquors was equally notable. For instance, in 1686 William Fauntleroy had in the cellar of his residence in Rappahannock county ninety gallons of rum, twenty-five gallons of lime juice, and twenty dozen bottles of wine reserved for the use of his private table;[1] and this was far from being an unusually large supply of liquors kept on hand chiefly for the gratification of the guests of the house.

One explanation of the liberal drinking both in the taverns and private residences was that a very large proportion of the population were natives of England, who had simply brought over to Virginia the habits which they had formed in the Mother Country. Perhaps the freest tipplers of that age were Englishmen, whose chill and humid climate not only encouraged an extraordinary consumption of liquors of all kinds, especially ales and beers, but also in large measure diminished the ill-consequences of excess. The great mortality which prevailed among English emigrants arriving in Virginia was to a marked degree attributable to this continued indulgence at the same rate as in England in a proclivity for which the hot climate of Virginia was far less well suited, even when the frame had become seasoned to the change.

Governor Berkeley declared that Virginia was as "sober and temperate a colony, considering their qualities as was ever sent out of the kingdom," [2] by which he meant that the Virginian planters, on the whole, drank less than the English gentlemen of the same period; and this was probably true, for we fail to find in the Virginian records for the seventeenth century any account comparable to the experience of John

---

[1] Rappahannock County Records, Vol. 1677-82, p. 80, Va. St. Libr.

[2] Letter of Berkeley to Commissioners of Foreign Plantations, July 21, 1662, British Colonial Papers, Vol. XVI., No. 78.

Evelyn, the diarist, who, on at least two occasions, notes that, at the houses he was visiting, it was the rule to ply the servants of the guests with liquor until they grew thoroughly intoxicated.[3] The indulgence in Virginia was such, however, that it became necessary at one time to pass a law that no debts made in buying wines should be allowed to be sued for in court. According to Berkeley, this law was designed to do away with the imputation so often brought against the Virginians of drinking too hard, and also to check the over-readiness with which liquors were sold on credit. As payment of all debts was made but once a year, namely, at the time when the tobacco crop was shipped away, it was the disposition of only too many persons, even before the tobacco had been planted, to enter into impossible engagements to settle at a future date simply that they might supply themselves with wines and spirits in the present. The new law forced the seller to be wary in allowing most persons a larger quantity than they had the means of paying for at once.[4] But the regulation did not touch those among the planters whose credit was not open to question. Wherever a body of gentlemen, large or small, gathered together, whether it was as appraisers to fix the value of an estate,[5] or as commissioners to accept a new bridge, or as county justices to hear causes, a goodly supply of liquor was at hand to quench their

---

[3] See entries in Evelyn's Diary.

[4] Letter of Berkeley to Commissioners of Foreign Plantations, July 21, 1662, British Colonial Papers, Vol. XVI., No. 78.

[5] Item among charges against the estate of George Proctor, 1678: "Three gallons of rum expended at the appraisement." Surry County Records, Vol. 1671-84, p. 310, Va. St. Libr.

thirst. The few letters belonging to the century, like those of William Fitzhugh and William Byrd, the elder, which have survived, show the great care with which provision was made for preventing the stock of public or private wines from running too low. Many of the leading citizens had to pay a heavy penalty for this generous style of life. Gout was as common a disease in Virginia as in England. Colonel William Randolph was a sufferer from it; so were Nicholas Spencer and John Page, as we learn from a minute of a Council held in 1687, which they were for that reason unable to attend;[6] so was Henry Hartwell, who on at least one occasion while in England was, by a violent attack, kept away from the meetings of the Commissioners of Plantations, before whom he had been summoned to testify.[7]

It was not always at their own tables, or in taverns, that the Virginians of the seventeenth century laid the ground for the inroads of gout and kindred physical ills. There is at least one recorded instance of a large banquetting hall having been built in one of the counties by a little company of wealthy gentlemen. In 1670 a formal agreement was entered into by Henry Corbin, Thomas Gerard, Isaac Allerton, and John Lee, all citizens of Westmoreland county, to erect a house in Pickatown field at their common expense. Lee was allowed ten pounds sterling, which was his share of the cost, for actually building it, under the supervision of Gerard and Allerton. Beginning May 1, 1671, each party to the contract in succession was to give a ban-

---

[6] British Colonial Entry Book, Vol. 1680-95, p. 255.

[7] Letter of Hartwell, dated Aug. 24, 1697, B. T. Va., 1697, Vol. VI., p. 133.

quet in this new hall; and he was required to invite
to it not only all of the other parties, but also their
wives, sweethearts, and friends. It was arranged that
Corbin should provide the first feast; Lee was to follow Corbin; Gerard, Lee; and Allerton, Gerard; and
then Corbin was to give his second banquet, and so on
as before indefinitely. If a party to the contract died,
his heirs were to take his place. That the hall was
erected, and the series of banquets inaugurated, we
learn from the testimony of Thomas Lee, whose father
had been present certainly at one of them. The osten-
sible object of this annual feast was to perpetuate
boundary lines, but that this method was adopted was
due, not to its superiority over the customary proces-
sioning, but to the delightful opportunity which it gave
for indulging the wealthy Virginian's love of social
entertainments.[8]

As we have seen, there were few homes of these
times in which there was not a considerable variety of
musical instruments, and in one or two instances the
number was sufficiently great to form almost a small
orchestra. At many of the entertainments some
female member of the family giving the dance, no
doubt, furnished the music by playing on one of these
instruments, but the county records show that, among
the servants and slaves, there were some who were especially valued for their skill with the fiddle, and that
this skill was called into use on many gay occasions.
Attached to the plantation of Captain Richard Bailey,
of Accomac county, was a negro slave, who, by his ac-
complishment in this respect, contributed as much to
the diversion of the neighborhood as any person in it.

---

[8] Va. Maga, of Hist. and Biog., Vol. VIII., pp. 171-2,

This fiddler is found taking a prominent part in a lively scene which occurred at the Rev. Thomas Teakle's, to the scandal of the whole countryside, though the episode seems innocent enough to modern perceptions. Elizabeth Parker, accompanied by Samuel Doe and his wife, went over to Mr. Teakle's house to visit his daughter while he was away. They carried the negro boy with them, and after their arrival it occurred to the little company that it would be pleasant in the opportune absence of the clergyman to have a dance. The fiddle which had been left behind was sent for, and the dancing began. While it was going on, one James Fairfax came for the boy, but Elizabeth Parker made him abandon his purpose by informing him with some temper that she had borrowed the fiddler of her sister, Ursula Bailey, his owner. She, however, declared that the boy should not go unrewarded for his playing, and she pulled out her purse and gave him a Spanish piece of eight. She also persuaded Fairfax to remain and take part in the dance.

Some one present seems to have reproached Margaret Teakle for "undutifulness of carriage and demeanor" towards Mr. Teakle "by making feast in his absence," but Elizabeth urged her to disregard her father, whose strict notions as to what were proper amusements she probably scorned and despised, and to take advantage of his not being in the house to enjoy herself. Mr. Teakle, who, though a clergyman, was a man of wealth, was engaged to be married to one of Elizabeth Parker's kinsfolks, "and a proud woman she was," exclaimed the fair tempter, "and wore fringes at the binding of her petticoat!" Margaret Teakle seems to have yielded only too readily to her friend's urgent appeal, and at once fetched the silk with which the fiddler might string his instrument; and as a reward for his playing gave him several yards of ribbon as well as several yards of lace, all of which, no doubt, greatly touched the negro's sense of finery. The dance started on Saturday night, and continued with spirit until nearly eleven o'clock on the next Sabbath morning. The company consisted of Elizabeth Parker, Jane Hall, Margaret Teakle, James Fairfax, and John Addison. In one interval of the dancing Margaret Teakle led her friends upstairs to show them her wedding gaiters. They seem to have overhauled the contents of her trunk, and among the articles which she presented to Elizabeth Parker were thread laces and ribbons, and also a muslin cap adorned with a yard of fine lace. When Mr. Teakle returned home a few days afterwards, and was informed of the desecration of his house by a dance on the Sabbath day, even during the hour when services at church were in progress, he was greatly scandalized, and at the next meeting of the county court formally presented Elizabeth Parker and her husband.[9]

This scene at Mr. Teakle's home throws an entertaining light on the gay spirit of the young Virginians of both sexes, who were ready to divert themselves on the most unexpected occasions, and who sometimes carried their love of amusement to a point that was well calculated to shock the piety of their elders. It was only by the indignant action of Mr. Teakle in

---

[9] Accomac County Records, Vol. 1690-97, p. 161, *et. seq*. Teakle resented especially Mrs. Parker's acceptance of the gifts of his daughter, and endeavoured to make out that the articles had been improperly taken away from his house.

having the main culprit indicted that this special incident is preserved for us, but similar instances of dances begun on the moment must have been of frequent occurrence, and have done much to brighten the social life of the Colony. Nor was dancing occurring on a Sunday a great rarity, though it never went unpunished. Among the indictments at one term of the court of Princess Anne county in 1691-'2 three were for fiddling and dancing on the Sabbath.[10] This did not show so much a disregard of the religious character of the day as a survival of the old English customs, which permitted the indulgence in a great variety of amusements after the hour of services in church had passed.[11] The authorities, however, were not as tolerant of these customs in Virginia as they would probably have been in England.

The taste for dancing did not content itself with such skill as could be acquired by the ordinary participation in this form of amusement. There is some evidence of the presence in the Colony of dancing masters who gave lessons in the art professionally. One of these was Charles Cheate, who was accompanied by his servant, Clason Wheeler, a fiddler. They

---

[10] Princess Anne County Records, Vol. 1691-1709, p. 34. In 1698, William Johnson, of Accomac, was fined for a like offence. See Accomac County Records, Vol. 1679-1705, folio p. 43. The offenders in Princess Anne county were Peter Crashley and his wife, and Thomas Dobbs.

[11] The Declaration of Sports, allowing games and the like after religious services on Sunday was reissued by Charles I. in 1633, but in 1643, when the Puritans had obtained the supremacy, the document was publicly burnt, and all sports and amusements on the Sabbath forbidden. See Traill's Social England, Vol. IV., for some account of the change.

appear to have taken an active part on the popular side in the Insurrection of 1676, and when it failed, fled to New England for safety, a harbor of refuge, however, in which their ability to teach their art was not likely to assist them in earning a livelihood.[12]   Cheate, and men following the same calling, hardly confined themselves in Virginia to instructions in dancing.   It is quite probable that they were also able to secure large fees by serving as musicians at the entertainments so frequently given in the planters' residences.   Their skill in performing on various instruments must have been superior to that of a slave fiddler like the one owned by Captain Richard Bailey, or to that of most of the planters' wives and daughters, whose opportunities of becoming proficient were necessarily rather limited.

---

[12] Boston (Mass.) Town Records, July 29, 1678.

XIII.

Popular Diversions—Acting and Games.

THROUGHOUT the seventeenth century the opinion prevailed among the great body of English-speaking people that play-acting was repugnant to good morals. In a prayer promulgated for the infant plantation in Virginia in 1612, and in that year published, actors are referred to as belonging to the "scum and dregs of the earth." [1] If there was any undertaking to have a play performed in the Colony previous to 1665, no record of the fact has survived, but in 1665, when the Stuart dynasty had been restored to the throne in England, and the theatre was fast becoming one of the most popular as well as one of the most disreputable institutions in the kingdom, a play known as "Ye Bare and ye Cubb" was acted on the Eastern Shore by three citizens of Accomac county, Cornelius Wilkinson, Philip Howard, and William Darby by name. As soon as the report of this having taken place reached the ears of the King's attorney, John Fawsett, he summoned them to court, where each was subjected to a rigid cross examination. At this session the justices contented themselves with ordering the culprits to appear at the next meeting of the court in the habiliments which they had worn in acting the alleged play, and they were also required to bring with them for inspection a copy of the "verses, speeches, and passages" which they had declaimed on that occasion.

---

[1] Neill's Virginia Carolorum, p. 315.

The justices must have found the performance to have
been of a very innocent character, for they directed
the three men to be discharged and the person who had
informed on them to pay all the expenses of the pre-
sentment.[2]

The leniency exhibited in this case shows that, if
a spirit of strong opposition to play-acting had previously prevailed in the Colony, which was not unlikely during the Puritan Supremacy, only recently
ended, that spirit had now passed away, or the justices
at least were determined not to countenance it when
the play itself contained nothing damaging to public
morality. At a time when the English theatre had not
only been revived, but also was allowed a degree of
license without precedent on account of the reaction
against Puritan strictness and austerity, it would have
been remarkable had Virginia, the Colony most in
sympathy with English feeling, condemned in a Puritan spirit all play-acting as in itself wicked and opposed to good morals, however devoid the play itself
might be of any passages to give offense even to the
most rigid censor. The large number of Cavaliers who
had settled in Virginia were, no doubt, ready at all
hours to throw their strong social influence against
so narrow and illiberal a view had it prevailed; and
led by the powerful Governor, Berkeley himself, a
playwright of no mean ability, they were certain to
create a sentiment in favor of play-acting to the extent to which alone it was possible to carry it in the
Colony, i. e., a performance on a very small scale by
amateurs in the private drawing-room of a plantation
residence. It is quite probable that this form of amuse-

---

[2] Accomac County Records, Vol. 1663-66, folio p. 102.

ment was often indulged in in this small way during the long period following the Restoration when the theatre had become the most popular resort for diversion in the Mother Country, a fact thoroughly well known to contemporary Virginians, not only by correspondence with relatives in England, but also from the accounts given by the numerous emigrants of the higher class annually arriving, as well as by the many persons returning to the Colony after a visit over sea.

Among the chief amusements of the Virginians during the seventeenth century was the game of ninepins, played either in alleys specially built for the purpose, or in large rooms in private residences. As early as 1636 William Ward, of Accomac county, is found participating in a game of this kind which took place at the house of John Dunn, and the diversion proved so absorbing that he is reported to have spent the whole day engaged in it.[3] Ten-pins was one of the diversions provided for guests at all the taverns, and it was made more exciting by betting. For instance, in 1681 Robert Sharpe and Richard Robine, of Henrico county, laid a wager of four hundred pounds of tobacco on the issue of a game of thirty-one up. Robine had been drinking quite heavily, and this probably led Thomas Cocke, Jr., who was present, to decline to serve as marksman. Three games were won by Sharpe and two by Robine, and then the playing was stopped for a time; and when resumed, two games were won by Robine, one after another. A dispute now arose as to the payment of the wager, which was afterwards submitted to a jury called together by the

---

[3] Accomac County Records, Vol. 1632-40, p. 59, Va. St. Libr.

county court. This game was played in a ten-pin alley that probably formed a part of the tavern owned by the elder Cocke[4]. A game which took place in Northampton county in 1693 was played in a private residence. Joseph Godwin, the son of the owner of the house, bet his opponent that he would tip seven pins, but only succeeded in tipping five. A quarrel arose over the payment of the wager, and a violent scuffle ensued, which seems to have brought the two parties to it into court.[5]

Betting even on the most trifling issues was one of the most popular diversions, and under certain circumstances does not appear to have been discountenanced by the county courts. The rule seems to have been for the justices, when the question of a wager was brought before them, to refer the matter in dispute to a jury. Such was the course followed in a case involving a bet of five pounds sterling which, in 1688, was made between Thomas Chamberlaine and James Brain, of Henrico county.[6] If the question to be decided was one calling for some learning, the court appears to have settled it on their own responsibility. For example, in 1687, in a suit between Captain William Stone and John Brodnax, as to whether Brodnax could be compelled to pay five hundred pounds of tobacco which he had lost in betting on the

---

[4] Henrico County Records, Vol. 1677-92, orig., p. 191.

[5] Northampton County Records, Vol. 1689-98, p. 263. Sets of ten-pins are frequently mentioned in the different inventories; for instance, among the contents of the store of William Porter, of Lower Norfolk county, in 1693, was a "sett of playing bowls." See Lower Norfolk County Records, Vol. 1686-95, p. 199[2].

[6] Henrico County Minute Book 1682-1701, p. 199, Va. St. Libr.

relative weight of gold and quicksilver, a solemn judgment was delivered by the Henrico county court on the point involved.[7]   The subject of the wager was sometimes even more abstruse.   For example, about 1690, Thomas East and Richard Ligon, of Henrico county, made a bet as to how much "one thousand foot square solid" contained.   If the two should differ as to what was the correct amount, it was agreed that the matter should be referred to Colonel William Byrd and Mr. John Pleasants, the latter the most prominent Quaker in the Colony, whose decision was to be accepted as final.[8]

Some justices appear to have taken the ground that a bet could have no standing in court because it was unlawful to indulge in gaming;[9] and in the same year in which a judgment was delivered to this effect in Richmond county we find that the bonds of tavern keepers in the neighbouring county of Essex required that no unlawful betting should be allowed to go on in their inns.[10]   Where, however, money had been staked down, or a formal contract drawn up, as the law of that day directed, and the subject of the wager was not destructive of public morality, or injurious to other people's property, the bet seems to have been, as a rule, upheld.   In a case occurring in Henrico county about 1690 the attorney for the defendant, Edward Chilton, expressly pleaded that his client was not responsible, though he had lost, simply because neither of these provisions had been followed by the

---

[7] Henrico County Minute Book, 1682-1701. p. 163, Va. St. Libr.

[8] Henrico County Records, Vol. 1688-79, p. 261, Va. St. Libr.

[9] Richmond County Records for 1694, orig., p. 30.

[10] Essex County Records, Vol. 1692-95, p. 355, Va. St. Libr.

parties; and the Court promptly sustained the contention.[11]

There are numerous references to dice playing in the county records, a game very popular with those who gamble,[12] whilst the references to card playing occur with even greater frequency. Packs of cards are among the most common forms of property included among the items in the inventories of personal estates. In 1665 Captain Jeremiah Fisher owned as many as nine packs,[13] and a few years later Jonathan Newell as many as eight.[14] Both were citizens of York county. That the cards found in the plantation residences were in constant use is shown by numerous contemporary evidences. For instance, in 1678 the grand jury of Henrico county, a county, owing to its situation on the frontier, somewhat remarkable for laxness of morals, presented Joseph Royall because, by his own confession, he had played cards on the Sabbath.[15] Three years afterwards John Hayward, of York county, acknowledged in court that, while staying at the house of James Pardoe, he and his companions fell to drinking, and after drinking all day began, when

---

[11] Henrico County Minute Book, 1682-1701, p. 279, Va. St. Libr.

[12] "Charles Stewart and Giles Webb play dice and Giles wins 500 lbs. of tobacco." This was in 1685. See Henrico County Records, Vol. 1677-92, orig., p. 313.

In 1619, the General Assembly passed an act prohibiting gambling with dice and cards. The winner was to forfeit his gains, whilst the winner and loser were each required to pay a fine of ten shillings.

[13] York County Records, Vol. 1664-72, p. 23, Va. St. Libr.

[14] York County Records, Vol. 1675-84, orig., p. 139.

[15] See Henrico County Records for 1678.

night came on, a game of cards, which ended in a violent quarrel. Pardoe and Hayward, going to bed in the room where the liquor was kept, resumed their drinking, and the game and quarrel seemed to have been forgotten.[16]

The favorite game of cards was known as put. Put was played, not only by citizens of the highest social rank in the community, but also by the domestic and agricultural servants, who belonged to the lowest. In 1686 we find John Marshall, a former servant of Mr. John Gawin, of York county, engaged in a game with Joseph Bascom, in which the latter lost a wager of five pounds sterling, a sum equal in purchasing power to one hundred and twenty-five dollars in American currency, a proof of how far the gambling went even among persons of very moderate means.[17]   In the course of the same year a game took place between Captain Soane and Richard Dearlove, of Henrico county, in which ten puts were played for a stake of fifteen hundred pounds of tobacco. Soane was successful, but as Dearlove refused to pay when called upon, a suit was entered against him in court.[18]   In 1690 Allanson Clerk, of the same county, who had won four pounds sterling of Peter Rowlett in a game of put, was thrown out of court because, when the game was played, no sum was placed in the hands of a stakeholder, or regular contract to pay such a sum was drawn up, as required by law to give the betting a legal footing.[19]   A game of cards which was played in

---

[16] York County Records, Vol. 1675-84, orig., p. 328.

[17] York County Records, Vol. 1684-7, p. 144, Va. St. Libr.

[18] Henrico County Records, Vol. 1677-92, orig., p. 300.

[19] Henrico County Minute Book, 1682-1701, p. 279, Va. St. Libr.

the house of Mrs. Judith Randolph, a lady of the highest social position, between Mr. John Piggott and Mr. Charles Featherstone, led to angry words, and finally to a suit in court for the amount of the wager involved. The stakes do not seem to have been high, as the total winnings of Featherstone, the successful party, did not exceed fifteen half crowns. In the course of the game two bottles of liquor were consumed. Piggott appears to have been especially fond of gambling. In 1682 he is found engaged in a game of cross and pile with Martin Elam and John Milner in Elam's house. The stakes were partly coin and partly tobacco; and, contrary to his experience at Mrs. Randolph's, Piggott was successful; but not quite as successful as he supposed, for, though he had won only three hundred pounds of tobacco, he claimed on the morning following the game that he had won seven hundred pounds.[20]

[20]Henrico County Records, Vol. 1677-92, orig., pp. 28, 224.

XIV.

Popular Diversions—Horse Racing.

THE most popular form of amusement in Virginia during the seventeenth century was the horse-race, and in those times, as in these, the pastime led to much betting. It was looked upon as a sport in which only gentlemen could take part, although members of every class in the community were represented among the spectators. In 1673, James Bullock, a tailor residing in York county, was fined one hundred pounds of tobacco for his almost unprecedented presumption in running his mare in a race with a horse belonging to Mr. Mathew Slader for a wager of two thousand pounds of tobacco. The county justices sitting upon the case solemnly pronounced his act to be contrary to law on the ground that racing with horses was a "sport for gentlemen alone" in which no laboring man could legally take part.[1] There are few incidents recorded in the early history of Virginia which throw a greater flood of light on the rigidity of the social divisions in the community than this incident of the unfortunate tailor, who, after winning the race, found that he had no standing in the court because the loser of the wager happened to belong to a higher social grade. It also shows the very great esteem in which horse racing was held in the Colony, and the determination to confine the sport as far as possible to the class who could give it the highest degree of distinction.

---

[1] York County Records, Vol. 1671-94, p. 34, Va. St. Libr.

Horse-races appear to have taken place in all parts of the Colony, although perhaps more frequently occurring in those parts which had been settled longest, and which, therefore, were the most thickly inhabited. The persons residing on the Eastern Shore who were fond of this pastime do not seem to have participated only in races on their own side of the bay. In 1674 Richard Awburne and Isaac Jacob, both citizens of Northampton county, undertook to run their horses in a race which was to come off on the Western Shore. The stake, formally arranged between Awburne and John Panewell, amounted to four hundred pounds of tobacco. Not satisfied with this race, Awburne and Jacob are found a few days later running their horses in another heat, but, it seems, on a track situated in their own county. This appears, however, to have been a private race; but in a third in which Jacob took part there were many other persons present as spectators, among them a number of women, whose interest in the issue was doubtless as keen as that of the men. These races in Northampton county came off on ground known as Smith's Field, where a track had been carefully laid off. Jacob, who was probably a Jew, appears so often in the records as taking part in horse-races, not restricting himself, as we have seen, to the Eastern Shore, that it is quite possible he was a professional trainer.[2]

Nowhere in the Colony did horse-races occur more often than in the lower counties of the Northern Neck.

---

[2] See Northampton County Records, Vol. 1664-1674, p. 269. There is an allusion in these records to the "fall races" (1674), as though races were held at that season regularly. See Vol. 1674-79, p. 4.

Here they seem to have taken place most frequently on Saturday, perhaps because the afternoon of that day was observed, as in England, as a half holiday. In 1696 a complaint was made to the House of Burgesses by numerous citizens of Northumberland that the celebration of the races on Saturday very often led to the profanation of the Sabbath, possibly because, in the ardor with which the sport was pursued, the racing was resumed the following morning, regardless of the sacred character of the day; or more probably what had begun on Saturday as a horse-race ended on Sunday as a drinking and fighting bout.[3]   That these races were attended by a concourse of spectators is shown by the fact that such occasions were always used by the public authorities in making announcements to the people.[4]

The principal racing track in the Northern Neck was known as the Coan Race Course, which was situated in Westmoreland county.   Persons residing in the neighboring counties seem to have often preferred this course to one much nearer to them.   For instance, in 1694 Captain Rodham Kenner, who was the high sheriff of Northumberland, left that county to try on the Coan track the running powers of a mare named Folly against those of Smoker, owned by Mr. Joseph Humphrey.   The stake agreed upon amounted to fifteen hundred pounds of tobacco.   Folly, which really belonged to Mr. Peter Contanceau, won the race, although Smoker was one of the most famous race-horses in the Colony.   Humphrey claimed that Smoker

---

[3] Minutes of House of Burgesses, Sept. 30, 1696, B. T., Va. Vol. LII.

[4] Va. Maga. of Hist. and Biog., Vol. VIII., p. 130.

had not been fairly beaten because the jockey riding
him had held his bridle tightly in order to diminish
his speed; but when this assertion was submitted to a
jury they promptly decided in favor of Kenner. Still
dissatisfied, Humphrey obtained an injunction against
further proceedings on the common law side of the
court until a point of equity involved in the case had
been passed on in chancery; and when this also went
against him, carried his cause up to the General Court
on appeal.[5] The persistency shown by Humphrey
was due not so much to a sense of the injustice which
he thought had been done him, as to his extreme jeal-
ousy in preserving the reputation of his horse, a reputation which perhaps touched him as closely as his
own. The whole case illustrates the serious spirit in
which the most ordinary horse-race at this time was
run, and how little the expense of a suit was considered if it would remove from a favorite animal the dis-
credit of defeat. At a later date we find Humphrey
and Kenner engaged in a second race.[6] In 1695
Smoker was run in a race on the same track against
Prince, a horse belonging to Mr. John Haynie, and
won. The wager in this instance was fixed at four
thousand pounds of tobacco and forty shillings.[7]

Some years previous to this race one had been run,
apparently on the Coan Race Course, between the
horse of Mr. John Stone, of Rappahannock county,
and the horse of Mr. Yewell, of Westmoreland. The
stake amounted to ten pounds sterling, or to two hundred and fifty dollars in our present currency. That
this race was not simply a private trial of speed in

---

[5] Northumberland County Records Orders, Jan'y 17, 1693-4.
[6] Northumberland County Records Orders, Jany 17, 1693-4.
[7] Northumberland County Records Orders, Aug. 22, 1695.

which only the jockeys and owners of the two horses were present is shown by the fact mentioned in the record of the event that there were many people in attendance as spectators. Mr. Stone's horse carried off the wager, but it was only after a suit that Mr. Yewell consented to make payment.[8] Yewell, who was deeply interested in this branch of sport, appeared again and again in the courts either as plaintiff or defendant in dispute as to the winning or loss of stakes. In 1688 a very important suit was tried before the justices of Westmoreland county involving a number of races in which John Hartridge and John Washington, on one side, and John Baker and Yewell, on the other, had participated. After all the various evidences for and against had been formally presented the jury left the court room and proceeded to the race track, which they examined with great care in order to obtain a more intelligent understanding of the testimony which they had just heard. But, nevertheless, they were unable to agree on a verdict. When the court was informed of that fact, the sheriff was ordered to keep them in confinement without bread, drink, candle, or fire until they should reach a decision.[9]

The race-track in Richmond county was known as Willoughby's Old Field. This designation probably shows the character of the ground on which most of the courses of that day were laid off. Land which had long been under cultivation, but had finally been abandoned to the native grasses, was not unsuited for a race-track. The plough had left the surface of the soil in a measure in a state of uniform evenness, whilst the rough, thick turf gave it both spring and compactness.

---

[8] Westmoreland County Records, Vol. 1665-77, folio p. 211.

[9] Westmoreland County Records Orders, Jan'y 11, 1687-8. The

Only the annual use of the grubbing hoe and axe, however, could prevent the course itself, as well as the rest of the field, from springing up, in a few years, in masses of tangled briars and thickets of cedar and sassafras; that this was not suffered to take place is shown by the great length of time during which races were run over the same ground. There is reason to think that the popular race tracks were kept in good condition continuously; and that as careful attention was given them as to the principal highways in the county.

Among the earliest races recorded of Willoughby's Old Field was one which took place there in the year 1693. On this occasion there seem to have been numerous horses entered for the stakes, whilst the attendance of spectators deeply interested in the upshot of the different heats was evidently extraordinary. Among those who had come to the course was Mr. John Gardiner, of Westmoreland county; and he had brought with him a horse celebrated in all that region named Young Fire, which must have been a conspicuous object even among that group of picked animals, for it was of the purest white in color. During the progress of the first races of the day, Gardiner kept Young Fire in the background, as if wishing first to observe the powers of his possible competitors; then, when several races had been run, in which all the other horses perhaps had taken part and shown what they were equal to, Gardiner suddenly led Young Fire forth and boldly challenged the owner of any horse on the track to run his steed in a race for a stake of one thousand pounds of tobacco and twenty shillings in coin. Daniel Sullivant, borrowing Mr. John Baker's

bay horse, which perhaps had exhibited its superiority
to the other horses in the races that had already taken
place, promptly accepted the guage, and it was agreed
to try the white and the bay, the one against the other,
instantly. Mr. Raleigh Travers became the security
for the payment of the wager, whilst Mr. John
Clemens and Captain William Barber were selected
to stand at the poles in order to report the name of the
winning horse. At the end of the race a dispute arose
as to whether the wager had been fairly lost and won,
and it was only finally settled by a suit in court.[10]

A third race course in the Northern Neck, hardly
less well known or less frequently used than the Coan
and the Willoughby Old Field tracks, was the one situated at Yeocomico. Here, in 1694, the race-horse
Smoker turns up again, no longer belonging to Mr.
Joseph Humphrey, but to Captain Rodham Kenner,
whose Folly had defeated Smoker, as we have seen, in
a race on the Coan Race Course a few months before.
Kenner had, perhaps, in his admiration for the speed
which the horse had displayed on that occasion, purchased him, but quite certainly only at a very high
price. In the race at Yeocomico, Smoker was run
against Campbell, a horse belonging to Captain John
Hartley. The stake agreed upon was five hundred and
seventy-seven pounds of tobacco, and the stretch was
for a quarter and a half-quarter of a mile. Campbell
soon showed himself to be so superior in speed to
Smoker that his rider was not required to ply either
whip or spur, and he was about to pass in between the

---

[10] Westmoreland County Records, Orders, April 7, 1693. The
name appearing in this entry was either Hartridge or Hartley.

poles first, when Richard Kenner, a brother of Rodham, who had been told to stand back lest his nearness should frighten the horses, rushed forward and with a loud "bellow and shout," and a violent waving of his hat, caused Campbell to shy suddenly from the track, and thus technically to lose the race. Richard Kenner was arrested for his offense, and tried by a jury, but seems to have been acquitted.[11] This incident forms an additional proof of the serious spirit in which even the most casual horse-race was run, and the popular determination that it should be conducted with perfect fairness, even if the assistance of the courts had to be invoked.

The race-course in Rappahannock was situated "at Rappahannock Church," to use the words of the records. The nearness to each other of race track and church edifice reveals how tolerant the religious authorities of these early times were towards this popular amusement; and it is not entirely a remote probability that on this Rappahannock course the young men, after the services were over on Sunday, tested the comparative speed of their horses, though unlikely that any formal racing took place. In 1676 a great race came off on this track between the horses of Robert Vaulx, Clement Trellman, and John Meader, which doubtless drew together a large number of spectators.[12] The course was still in good condition eight years later, for, in 1684, Mr. Alexander Swann and Mr. George Parkes competed on this ground for a stake of eleven pounds sterling, which had been placed

---

[11] Westmoreland County Records, Orders, Aug. 29, 1694.

[12] Westmoreland County Records, Vol. 1665-77, p. 264.

in the hands of Mr. Thomas Harwar, who was also present. A dispute arose as to whose horse had really won. One of the persons who had been chosen to act as a judge in the race declared that "Mr. Swann's horse, the black, had it of Mr. Parkes's, the gray," by at least half a head. This testimony decided the case when it first came into the county court. Parkes was ordered to pay all the costs and Harwar to deliver up to Swann the stake; but the case was brought up a second time, apparently at the instance of a second judge in the race, who was prevented from being present at the first trial. This judge testified that, instead of the black horse winning over the gray by half a head the gray had won over the black by that length. As the evidence was so directly conflicting, the court ordered the money, which was still in the hands of the stakeholder, to be returned to the persons depositing it, after a sum had been reserved sufficient to meet the expenses entailed by the first trial. These, it seemed, amounted to over two pounds sterling.[13]

The principal race-course in Surry county was known as the "Devil's Field";[14] and this, like Willoughby's Old Field, in Richmond county, was, no doubt, one of those large patches of ground formerly under cultivation, but now abandoned to a coarse turf well adapted to become the floor of a primitive race-track. In 1678 a race was run on this course between a mare and a horse, the one belonging to Mr. George Proctor, the other to John Price. Two judges, as usual, were selected to decide as to which animal won.

---

[13] Rappahannock County Records, Orders, March 5, 1684-5; Aug. 5, 1685.

[14] Surry County Records, Vol. 1671-84, p. 133, Va. St. Libr.

These were Thomas Barlowe and Thomas Adams; but instead of the goal being defined by two poles set up on opposite sides of the track it was agreed that it should be represented by a path which crossed the course at a certain point. The animal passing over this path first was to be taken as the winning one. The upshot of the race was one of those lively wrangles which were so very common in the racing at this period because the heats were so often run without the strict arrangements adopted wherever the sport was conducted with great precision and formality. One of the judges, after swearing that Price's horse "did come over the path some time before the mare," declared himself unable to say whether "the horse did carry his rider upon his back over the path, for Price did stop his horse in the path, or rather the fore parte of the horse over the path; the horse turning about, Price turned himself off from the horse's back, hanging his arms on the necke of ye horse; the first foote that came to the ground was on the path, the other beside it." The judge who uttered these words was evidently, not only a close observer, but also had a nice sense of what constituted a clean victory in a horse-race. Each of the principals seems to have acted as his own jockey.[15] Probably, most owners of race-horses during the seventeenth century, if very young men, were always ready to mount their own steeds for a heat. There are many indications that, even in these early times, the Virginians were bold and even reckless riders, and there was perhaps no form of excitement in which they indulged more ardently than in

---

[15] Surry County Records, Vol. 1671-84, p. 133, Va. St. Libr.

careering around a race-track, with a half dozen competitors careering before or behind them.

Henrico county was hardly second to Westmoreland in the lively favor in which its inhabitants held the pastime of horse racing. One of the most popular race-tracks in this county was situated at Bermuda Hundred, among the oldest settlements in the valley of the lower James River. Here in July, 1678, a race was run between horses belonging to Mr. Abram Womack and Mr. Richard Ligon. In this instance the owners did not ride their horses. One was ridden by Thomas Cocke, the other by Joseph Tanner, a servant of Mr. Thomas Chamberlaine, both of whom were still mere boys. Chamberlaine was selected to call out when the horses were ready to run, whilst Mr. Abram Childers was to act as starter. As no judges appear to have been named, it is probable that the horses were to career over a circular course with the goal situated at the point from which the race began. The persons there would thus be easily able to decide as to which horse won. The horses made a rush, but the one ridden by Cocke, after running four or five lengths, shied from the track. Cocke quickly reining him in, cried out: "This is not a fair start." Chamberlaine shouted to his servant, who was riding the other horse, to stop, but the young man, when he returned, boldly declared that the race was fairly begun, and in this contention was sustained by Mr. Childers.[16]

Both Ligon and Womack seem to have been deeply interested in horse racing. In 1683 a number of persons who had assembled at Womack's house on some

---

[16] Henrico County Minute Book, 1682-1701, p. 38, Va. St. Libr.

convivial occasion[17] got into an animated discourse on the subject, and soon there was a challenge from one of the company, Edward Hatcher, to run his horse against the horse of Edward Martin, who was also present. All exclaimed loudly: "Done, done," with the exception of Richard Ligon, who started up eagerly "Mr. Edward Hatcher," called out Ligon, "my horse shall not run any more to-day or to-night." Hatcher, uttering a great oath, shouted back that it was his horse, not Ligon's, and at once led the animal off to a pasture near by, where the races took place, followed by Andrew Martin. Ligon now came up, and seizing Hatcher as he was about to mount, said again: "Edward Hatcher, this is my horse, and he shall not run." Hatcher, seeing Ligon's determination, turned to the persons who were to act as judges, and exclaimed: "I can't help it," meaning that he was prevented from carrying out his agreement, and, therefore, should not be held as liable for the wager as if his horse had lost the race. But the judges refused to listen to him, and directed Martin to run over the track alone. When he reached the end of the course, he stopped, dismounted, and fixed his knife in the ground; then, returning to the starting point, claimed the horse which Ligon had asserted to be his own. This was probably the stake. Ligon, however, still refused to give it up, and the dispute finally found its way into the county court.[18] The account of this race which appears in the records is of interest as showing how rigid the judges in a horse race at this period were in upholding the terms of an

---

[17] The company, it would appear from Ligon's words regarding his horse, had been engaged in running races.

[18] Henrico County Records, Vol. 1677-92, orig., p. 254.

agreement even under circumstances when, it would seem, the agreement should properly have been considered no longer in force. Hatcher was held strictly to his verbal contract, though the action of Ligon had made it impossible for him to perform his part of it.

A second race-course in Henrico county was situated at Varina, and here races seem to have been run at regular intervals. Among those taking place on this course was one between the horses of the younger Thomas Batte and Richard Parker. The stake consisted of one hundred pounds of tobacco, but the fairness of the race was disputed by Batte because, as he asserted, Parker's mare had crossed in front of his horse and so thwarted his progress in the race as to prevent his coming in ahead. When the point was submitted to the county court, that body found that the only satisfactory way of settling the difficulty was to order that a new heat between the mare and horse should take place on exactly the same course. The justices, it seems, held their sessions at Varina, and it is quite probable that they attended the second race in a body. Whether they did or not, however, their decision was, no doubt, regarded with great popular favor as affording a second opportunity of enjoying the most exciting of all Virginian pastimes, a horse-race.[19]

There are numerous proofs that many other important races occurred on the course at Varina towards the close of the seventeenth century. Here, about 1687, a great race took place between the horses of Hugh Ligon and Stephen Cocke, in which Christo-

---

[19] Henrico County Minute Book, 1682-1701, p. 242, Va. St. Libr.

pher Branch was the stakeholder;[20] and in the same year a race was run in which a horse belonging to Henry Randolph participated.[21]   In 1687, also, Giles Webb won a heavy wager of John Huddlesey.[22]   In the following year William Eppes recovered in the county court twenty shillings which Stephen Cocke had refused to pay, on the ground of some irregularity in the race on which that amount had been bet.[23]   In 1690 Captain William Soane entered a suit against Mr. Robert Napier for ten pounds sterling, which he claimed to have won by default at Varina. The most important witness was the distinguished clergyman, Rev. James Blair, who requested the court to allow him to deliver his testimony simply on the word of a priest. Having acted as the endman for Captain Soane, he deposed that Napier had brought his horse to the race-track, but before the time agreed upon for the heat had led him away. The horse which had been chosen to run against Napier's, a white in color, was a sorrel owned by Mr. Littlebury Eppes. Eppes, as we have seen, had been sheriff of the county. Among the other deponents in this case were Captain William Randolph and Benjamin Harrison. Indeed, the men interested in it, whether as principals or witnesses,

---

[20] See Henrico County Minute Book, 1682-1701, pp. 170, 174, Va. St. Libr.; Vol. 1677-92, orig., p. 466. The records take notice only of the races in which there were disputes requiring settlement in court. The number of these indicates indirectly the number of races run without charge of unfairness.

[21] Henrico County Records, Vol. 1677-92, orig., p. 430.

[22] Henrico County Minute Book, 1682-1701, p. 161, Va. St. Libr. The Court allowed Webb a balance of £3 10s.

[23] Henrico County Minute Book, 1682-1701, p. 235, Va. St. Libr.

were among the first citizens of the Colony. The high repute in which the sport was held is shown by the fact that it was not considered derogatory to the dignity and usefulness of the first clergyman in Virginia at this time to take part as a judge in a horse race. The jury decided in favor of Captain Soane, and in doing so disclosed the determination so often exhibited by judges and juries alike of this period that when once two parties had agreed to run a race with their horses, both should be required to carry out the contract strictly; and that nothing short of the death of one of the horses should be accepted as a legal excuse for the withdrawal of either party from the projected heat.[24]

Among the most popular race courses in Henrico county was one which seems to have been generally known as the Ware. About 1698 there took place on this track an interesting race between a mare named Bony belonging to Thomas Jefferson, Jr., and a horse named Watt, the property of Thomas Hardiman. It was arranged that the race should cover one quarter of a mile. By the terms of the agreement the mare was to start ten yards ahead of the horse, and if she came in five lengths ahead of him, John Steward, who had borrowed the horse of Hardiman for the race, was to pay Richard Ward, who had borrowed the mare, five pounds sterling on demand. If, on the other hand, the horse came in five lengths ahead of the mare, Steward was to receive six pounds sterling from Ward. It was also agreed that the weight of each jockey should not exceed one hundred and thirty

---

[24] Henrico County Records, Vol. 1688-97, p. 147. Henrico County Minute Book, 1682-1701, p. 268, Va. St. Libr.

pounds; and that the race was to end as soon as the poles were passed. The mare, it seems, outran the horse, but a dispute arose, which brought the question of the stakes into court for settlement. Among the witnesses in this case were Thomas Chamberlaine and Stephen Cocke, whose names so often appear in the records in connection with this pastime.[25] Chamberlaine, about the same date, was a party to a race which was run on the course at Conecock. His opponent was Richard Ligon, and the wager agreed upon amounted to forty shillings. A gallon of rum was on this occasion provided for the enjoyment of the spectators.[26]

There was a fifth race track in Henrico county situated at Malvern Hill. Here, in 1699, a heat was run between the horses of William Eppes and William Sutton for a stake of half a pound sterling. It was agreed that, in the race, each horse was to be kept to his own side of the course, unless, at the very start, Stephen Cocke, who was serving as Sutton's jockey, could, by two or three leaps of his horse, get possession of that part of the track belonging to the other rider. The starter in this race was William Randolph, perhaps, after the elder William Byrd, the foremost citizen of the county. Cocke failed to leap ahead after two or three jumps, and the horses in running seem to have come violently against each other.[27]

There is nothing in the surviving records to show that the Virginians of the seventeenth century resembled their kinsfolk in England in finding pleasure

---

[25] Henrico County Records, Orders, April 1, 1698.
[26] Va. Maga. of Hist. and Biog., Vol. II., p. 297.
[27] Henrico County Records, Vol. 1688-97, pp. 74-5, Va. St. Libr.

in such rude sports as cock-fighting, and bear and bull baiting.[28] If such rough pastimes were indulged in in the Colony, no proof of the fact remains; but it is altogether probable that sports of this kind, with the possible exception of cock-fighting, found no place in the category of their amusements, if, for no other reason, because it was in the power of every man,— master, servant, and slave,—to take part in hunting some species of wild game should his inclinations lie that way. Nowhere in those times was this form of diversion followed with more ardour than in Virginia;[29] and nowhere perhaps were there more ample returns from gratifying so manly and healthy a taste. In gratifying that taste a double purpose was really served, for, as we have seen, the great variety of food which distinguished the tables of the planters in these early times was largely due to the game of different kinds obtained from the fields, forests, and streams.

---

[28] "There was now a very gallant horse to be baited to death with dogs, but he fought them all so as the fiercest of them could not fasten on him, till they ran him through with their swords. This wicked and barbarous sport deserved to have been punished. * * * I would not be persuaded to be a spectator." Evelyn's Diary, Aug. 17, 1667. Evelyn records on June 16, 1668, that he had that day witnessed cock and dog fighting, bull and bear-baiting.

[29] In some cases, the hunters never returned. See case of Geo. Watson, Lower Norfolk County Records, Orders, Nov. 15, 1641.

XV.

Popular Diversions—Hunting and Fishing.

THE landowners highly valued the game found on their estates, and in many instances carefully protected it from depredations; for example, in 1680 a guardian, in the interest of his ward, who resided in York, brought suit in the court of that county to recover damages from a citizen who had, with gun and dogs, trespassed on the ward's property, and also to prevent a recurrence of the wrong in the future.[1] Many additional cases, showing that the same position was taken by other planters, or their representatives, might be mentioned. Numerous estates, however, were so large, and such an extensive proportion of their area was in primeval forest, that it is not probable that their owners were able to keep them strictly posted even if they had wished it; and in all parts of the Colony, especially in the vicinity of the irregular line of the frontier, there were wide reaches of land, inland swamp, sea-marsh, barren upland and the like, which belonged to no man, and where everyone enjoyed the right to hunt at all seasons. It followed that it became a habit of the Virginians of every class to use the gun from the time they had strength enough to lift it to their shoulders. From the earliest date, the number of fowling pieces included among the items of inventories, was often very remarkable.[2]

---

[1] York County Records, Vol. 1675-84, orig., p. 180.

[2] See inventory of Philip Felgate, Lower Norfolk County Records, Vol. 1646-51, p. 47.

The laws of the Colony during many years required
that the head of every family should keep in his house,
ready to hand, a well-fixed gun, two pounds of powder,
and eight pounds of shot for every person under him who
was able to carry arms. The object sought in this regulation was to provide for immediate defense against sud-
den Indian attack. This was an additional reason why
the Virginians should acquire an extraordinary skill in
the use of the fire-lock; and whether directed against the
lurking Indian foe, or the different kinds of wild game,
their aim was among the surest observed in those times;
more than one writer who had had opportunities of seeing the manner in which they employed their guns, com-
ments admiringly on their "marvellous dexterity."[3]

The gun was chiefly used in the pursuit of birds, of
which there was an extraordinary abundance in the Colony, whether they belonged to those varieties frequenting
the land, or to those that haunted the waters along the
sea coast. Of the first, were the partridge, the wild
pigeon, and the wild turkey. As the area of cultivated
ground grew wider, the number of partridges steadily increased in consequence of their being able to find a larger
supply of food. On the other hand, the number of wild
turkeys perhaps as steadily diminished within the same
area, as the turkey is distinctly a forest bird, that is very
shy of human habitations. Of the two varieties of game,
it is probable that the pursuit of the wild turkey afforded
the Virginians the greater diversion, as it required much
exertion as well as wariness to come up with it and kill
it. Blinds of pine or oak boughs were erected at different
eligible spots in the woods, and here, after scattering the
flocks with trained dogs, the hunters would hide themselves, and by skilful use of the yelp, soon call up the

---

[3] British State Papers, B. T. Va., for 1692, No. 118; unassorted.

confused and unsuspecting birds within range of the guns. But this was not the only method used in taking the wild turkey; among the ingenious devices employed for its capture was the large trap built in the midst of the forest; lured by a long train of grains of corn to the hole in the ground which led into the trap, where there was piled up a quantity of the same grains, the turkey entered unhesitatingly, and once in, was too stupid to find its way out by the same hole again. Beverley informs us that sometimes as many as seventeen wild turkeys were captured at one time in this apparently simple fashion.[4]

The destruction of the turkey and partridge did not approach that of the wild pigeon, a bird which arrived in Virginia at the same season annually in the course of its migration. All contemporary observers declare that the number of these birds appearing at these times was far beyond the power of human calculation; that for hours they darkened the sky like a pall of thunder clouds; and that they broke down, by their weight, the limbs of the forest wherever an entire flock lighted in search of food. It can be well imagined that the return of this vast multitude of birds was eagerly anticipated each year by every Virginian who was fond of the sport of shooting and capturing them. So thickly did they crowd the woods in different places, and so tame had they become from fatigue and hunger, that they were struck down in great numbers with poles reaching up to their perches; nor was the work of destruction confined to the day; thousands were killed in the same manner at night, when the glare of torches served to confuse and bewilder their eyesight.[5]

---

[4] Beverley's History of Virginia, p. 258.

[5] See Bruce's Economic History of Virginia in the Seventeenth Century, Vol. I., p. 121.

The pursuit of the great flocks of wild geese and ducks along the sea coast, and by the shores of the inlets and creeks, afforded the Virginians of these early times as much diversion as the pursuit of the game birds frequenting the upland fields and forests. The gun had not yet been able to decimate the myriads of aquatic fowl which had been feeding in these waters from the earliest ages; practically throughout the seventeenth century their number remained undiminished; steal upon the flocks as often as they might, the sportsmen of that day could not make even a perceptible impression in reducing the incalculable multitudes, that often, in one string, spread over several miles of the surface of the Bay. In hunting the duck and goose, the device of the blind used in pursuing the wild turkey was employed, and in this way, the greatest success in killing them was obtained.

The game hunted with dogs alone was as abundant as the game hunted with guns. There appear to have been in Virginia, in the seventeenth century, a great number of dogs of a mongrel breed, whose chief use was in destroying the smaller kinds of animals running wild in the woods and fields. How valuable they were considered to be by their owners is shown in a case which occurred in Northampton county about 1691; a complaint was, in the course of that year, lodged in the county court against Mike Dixon, on the ground that he permitted his dogs to rush out and bark at the heels of persons passing along the highway, which was situated immediately in front of his door. Instead of proposing to kill or restrain them, Dixon simply petitioned the court to have the public road removed some distance back from his dwelling house, "because it was necessary," he declared, "to keep dogs for the preservation of creatures from vermin."[6] The crea-

---

[6] Northampton County Records, Vol. 1689-98, p. 86.

tures he referred to were poultry and young pigs, and the vermin were wolves, foxes, minks, polecats, and the like.

Though foxes were hunted, there is no record of wealthy planters breeding packs of hounds for the enjoyment of this sport. Hares were caught in large numbers by pursuing them with dogs, or by smoking them out of the hollow trees, or the holes in the earth, in which they hid themselves during the day. Raccoons and opossums were tracked at night with ease. According to Beverley, the plan followed by the hunters of these animals was to go with three or four dogs to the parts of the woods where they were always to be found, owing to the abundance there of the wild grape, or whatever other food they were most fond of; as soon as an opossum or raccoon had been driven up a tree, the nimblest climber among the hunters was sent up to shake the animal from the limb on which it had taken refuge; but, generally, it was only after a scuffle that the game could be made to loosen the grip of its claws and to tumble into the midst of the yelping hounds below. A moonlight night was usually selected for this special sport, or if the night was dark, the hunters carried pine-knot torches to light them on their way. The dogs were kept in easy reach by calls on a cowhorn, the mellow note of which at that silent hour in the forest could be heard at a great distance. Several large dogs were always taken along, as wolves, bears, and panthers were now abroad.[7]

Bears and panthers were found as late as 1683, even in those parts of the Colony which had been longest settled. In that year, rewards were offered in Accomac county for the destruction of these beasts, which must have

[7] Beverley's History of Virginia, p. 258.

greatly encouraged the pursuit of them, already very exciting from the very unusual danger attending it.[8] Bears were especially numerous in Lower Norfolk county, where they were able to obtain a secure refuge in the fastnesses of the Dismal Swamp. What was known as "wolf-driving" was, in many counties where this kind of animal still prowled about freely, one of the most popular forms of sport; it was the annual custom in Northumberland, for instance, as late as 1691, for the county court to make public arrangements within regularly appointed limits for the thorough scouring of the forests for these hated vermin.[9] They seem to have been hunted on horseback with dogs, as if they were so many foxes. Beverley states that he had often, while going at full speed, run down wolves in the recesses of the woods. Beaver, otter, and deer hunting was also among the most popular diversions of Virginian sportsmen at this period.

But the amusement of this general character which they are said to have most delighted in, was the pursuit of the horses that ran wild in the forests. So many foals were annually dropped there, that a large proportion of each herd was as shy of man as so many deer browsing within the same area of country. Under the custom then prevailing, these wild animals belonged to whoever could seize and brand them; thus, in addition to the excitement of the sport, the young Virginian had as an inducement to pursue them, the prospect of getting possession of a very spirited steed. It was, however, such a difficult task to overtake them, that Beverley, after his own ardour perhaps had been cooled by advancing years, remarked that the chief result of trying to capture one

---

[8] Accomac County Records, Vol. 1682-97, p. 35.

[9] Northumberland County Records, Orders, Sept 16, 1691.

of these unbroken horses was to ruin one already broken.[10]   Almost equal sport was afforded by hunting the numerous wild cattle roaming in the woods.

Another popular diversion consisted in taking fish in various ways.   This was done chiefly with hook and line, but seines, cast and stationary nets, as well as gill lines, were also in general use.   The most exciting branch of this sport was known as "striking," a method that had been adopted from the Indians.   A blazing light was obtained by burning pine knots in a brazier raised above the bow of a boat, and as the boat glided along over the surface of the stream in the darkness, this bright light attracted the fish, and also made them clearly visible in the water below. A person skilful in handling the weapon employed in this sport, was able to secure a great number of very fine fish in a single night.[11]

---

[10] Beverley's History of Virginia, p. 258.

[11] Beverley's History of Virginia, p. 258.

XVI.

THE most important occasions of a partly or wholly public character in Virginia during the seventeenth century were the horse-race, the funeral, the wedding, the meeting at church on Sunday, the general muster, and county-court day. I have already referred to the popular gatherings at the principal horse-races. From an early date, the funeral had some of the aspects of a festive event, however decorously conducted. In the remote rural neighborhoods, especially where the extraordinary seclusion and monotony of the life in narrow clearings in the primeval forests seemed to emphasize the sombre side of human destiny, it would have been supposed that a funeral would have reached the very height of solemnity, not only in the actual ceremony itself, but also in all that immediately followed. Moreover, it was in such a community as this that the deceased was most likely to have been known to every individual in the assemblage of people, a fact that, by imparting to all a sense of personal loss, would have made a mournful feeling universal, and for that reason, if for no other, left the gloom of the funeral unrelieved by even a suggestion of cheerfulness in any form. But it was in these very neighborhoods that the people in attendance at a burial were most certain to find, as soon as the ceremony was finished, a means of consoling themselves in the liveliest fashion, at least temporarily, for the bereavement which had befallen their community. Having in such a neighborhood to travel the furthest in order to be present at the funeral, they stood in the greater need of refreshment when the ceremony was over. This fact was clearly recognized by the surviving members of the deceased person's family. It would have been looked upon as most inhospitable to have permitted those who had come such a distance to show their respect for the dead, to go away thirsty and hungry, to arrive more thirsty and more hungry still at their homes, at perhaps a late hour at night. Under the influence of this feeling, the persons attending a funeral were regarded as possessing an even more sacred character than ordinary guests, and the amplest provision that the house could afford was made for their entertainment.

The eating and drinking was often preceded by a furious fusillade. About 1650, Thomas Wall, of Surry county, instructed his executors to fire over his grave "three volleys of shot for the entertainment of those who came to bury him."[1] At this time, the firing off of guns at funerals was permitted by law;[2] but this was not always allowed, as there were years when powder and lead had to be carefully husbanded, owing to fears of Indian invasion. So many accidents occurred at funerals by the wild firing indulged in by persons present who had been drinking too freely that, in 1668, the county court of Lower Norfolk entered an order that no such firing should be suffered on a like occasion thereafter, unless an officer was on the ground to regulate it.[3] At the funeral of Major Philip Stevens, in York county, as much as ten pounds of powder were used up in doing honor to his memory.[4]

The expenditure of powder, however, was insignificant

---

[1] Surry County Records, Vol. 1645-72, p. 246, Va. St. Libr.

[2] Acts of Assembly, 1655-6, Randolph MS., Vol. III., p. 265.

[3] Lower Norfolk County Records, Vol. 1656-66, p. 143.

[4] York County Records, Vol. 1657-62, p. 86, Va. St. Libr.

in comparison with the consumption of liquor of all kinds. The quantity seems extravagant, even in those cases in which the deceased left a large estate; in the cases in which the estate was small, the quantity often provided appears incredibly disproportionate to the estate's value; for instance, at the burial in Surry county, in 1673, of John Grove, a planter of very moderate means, the cost of the liquors amounted to as much as one thousand pounds of tobacco.[5] The personal property of Walter Barton, of Lower Norfolk county, was valued at fifty-four pounds sterling and fifteen shillings only, and yet his funeral expenses were estimated at eight pounds sterling. The burial of William Vincent, who was also a man of small means, led to an outlay of fifteen hogsheads of tobacco.[6] At the funeral of Mrs. Elizabeth Eppes, of Henrico county, five gallons of wine and two gallons of brandy were drunk by the persons in attendance; and, in addition, a steer and three sheep were consumed. At one funeral occurring in York county, in 1667, it required, for the assuagement of the mourners' thirst, twenty-two gallons of cider, twenty-four of beer, and five of brandy; and to sweeten the drinks, twelve pounds of sugar had to be provided.[7] At another funeral, which took place in Lower Norfolk county, in 1691, the consumption of liquor amounted to sixty gallons of cider and four gallons of rum; and of sugar, to thirty pounds.[8] The expenses incurred in burying John Griggs, of York

---

[5] Surry County Records, Vol. 1671-84, p. 33, Va. St. Libr.

[6] Lower Norfolk County Records, Vol. 1664-72, p. 549; Vol. 1686-95, folio p. 171.

[7] Henrico County Records, Vol. 1677-92, orig., p. 258; York County Records, Vol. 1664-72, p. 221, Va. St. Libr.

[8] Lower Norfolk County Records, Vol. 1686-95, f. p. 171.

XVII.

PUBLIC AND PRIVATE OCCASIONS.—THE WEDDING.

ONE of the most curious features of the social life of Virginia during the seventeenth century, was the number of marriages often made by the same individual, and as a corollary, the quickness with which the loss of a partner was repaired by remarriage. Instances of the same person having married at least three times were far from unusual; and there were even instances in which a person had been married six times, without having, like Bluebeard or Henry VIII., shortened the length of a single one of the six unions by murder or divorce.[1] The frequency with which remarriage on the part of a woman took place was due, in some measure, to the fact that she was always married off at a very early age. When a father made an important gift to a daughter, it was customary for him to insert in the deed conveying it, a clause providing as to what should be done with the gift in case she should become a wife before she had reached her sixteenth year.[2] Ursula, a daughter of the elder William Byrd, who died when seventeen years old, had been married to Robert Beverley long enough to give birth to a son.[3] There is an instance of a clandestine marriage re-

---

[1] The mother of Mrs. Elizabeth Carter, of Lancaster county, married six times. See Va. Maga. of Hist. and Biog., Vol. II., p. 237.

[2] Surry County Records, Vol. 1645-72, p. 408, Va. St. Libr.

[3] Writings of the second William Byrd, Bassett's edit., p. xxxiii. See an entry in Evelyn's Diary, May 16, 1681, in which he states as his opinion that a young lady was not "capable of disposing of herself judiciously till she was sixteen or seventeen years of age."

corded in Northampton county, in which the wife had not yet passed her twelfth year.[4]

Many of these women, who assumed all the cares of family life at such an immature age, became, in time, broken in health, and after bearing from ten to twelve children, died, leaving their husbands to marry again and to surround themselves with second broods, perhaps equally as numerous. But very often the young wife was left a widow in a few years, and if endowed with beauty, charm, or a fine plantation, she soon consoled herself by marrying a second or a third time, as the case might be. So great was the haste in some instances that the second husband was granted the probate of the will of the first.[5] In 1696, Rev. James Boulware obtained, in the Essex county court, a judgment against Edward Danneline for fees which were due to him, not only for having performed the marriage service of Mr. and Mrs. Danneline, but also for having preached the funeral sermon of John Smith, the first husband of Mrs. Danneline, for whose estate the second husband had been appointed administrator.[6] In this case, the funeral baked meats had furnished forth the marriage tables. There is one instance recorded in this century in which the husband took such a cheerful and philosophical view of his widow's remarriage that he left his whole estate to her children by a second husband, should she remarry again and have offspring —an example of serene generosity probably then without precedent, and probably never since imitated.

But perhaps the most remarkable case of quickness

---

[4] Northampton County Records, Vol. 1657-64, p. 154.

[5] Case of Alexander Shipworth, York County Records, Vol. 1664-72, p. 70, Va. St. Libr.

[6] Essex County Records, Orders, June 11, 1696, Va. St. Libr.

with which a widow's hand was sought in marriage after the death of the first husband, occurred as early as 1623. Rev. Greville Pooley was the hero of this episode, which was characterized by all the romance that ardour at least could give. The husband of Mrs. Jordan had been dead only three or four days, when Mr. Pooley, fearful lest a rival should start up, earnestly requested Captain Isaac Madison to broach for him, to the widow, a proposal of marriage. Madison, no doubt, struck with the unseemly haste of such conduct, at first declined to act as intermediary; naturally enough, he said that he did not wish to "meddle in any such business;" but finally, being a warm friend of the clergyman, and feeling sure that Mrs. Jordan would soon marry some other man, if she did not marry Pooley, he yielded. When Madison told her of his mission, the lady declared that she had as soon marry Mr. Pooley as anyone she knew, but she did not think it quite decent to do so so quickly. Having received this answer, Pooley plucked up courage to visit Mrs. Jordan himself. During the course of the interview, he desired a dram of her, and on her bidding one of the servants go and fetch it, he declared very gallantly that he would have it of her fetching, or not at all. She then went into the next room for it. A verbal contract was now entered into with all the formality of a marriage ceremony, and the couple drank to each other's health. He kissed her and exclaimed: "I am thine, and you are mine until death do part us." A few minutes afterwards, Mrs. Jordan began to fear lest she should be criticised should she be too precipitate in remarrying. Pooley, however, protested "before God that he would not reveal" the engagement until she thought "the time fitting." But being very full of the secret, and perhaps thinking to bind the lady more firmly, he soon told it. Mrs. Jordan was so angered that she declined to carry out the contract, and in so doing increased the clergyman's chagrin by saying that "if he had not revealed it, he might have fared ye better."[7]

The quickness with which so many women of this period remarried was not due to a lack of tender feeling for the memories of their deceased husbands; it very frequently had its origin in reasons of practical necessity that could not be carelessly put aside. On a large and secluded plantation, where numerous unbroken negroes, recently brought in from Africa were at work, or white agricultural servants, who, in some cases, were transported criminals, the position of a widowed mistress, however firm in character, or however accustomed to command, was environed with dangers as well as exposed to serious inconveniences. The reasons for apprehension were more urgent when she had been left with very young children. The men seemed to recognize at once that widows were made, by these peculiar conditions, which, as a rule, surrounded them, the more easy of conquest, and they pressed their suits with a proportionate degree of confidence and ardour.

The frequency of remarriage on the part of the women of this period was also due, in some measure, to the fact that the number of persons of the male sex exceeded the number of persons of the female in the different communities of the Colony. Among the native inhabitants, there was, no doubt, a numerical equality between the two sexes, but the disproportion in favor of the male sex in Virginia throughout the seventeenth century was annually maintained by the very much larger number of men than of women among the new settlers, whether they came over with independent means, or with no other re-

[7] British Colonial Papers, Vol. 1622-3, No. 30.

source but the labor of their hands; whether, in short, they were planters on their own account, or merely agricultural servants.   There were, naturally, more persons of the male than of the female sex among the English emigrants; and it followed that the supply of possible husbands was greater than the supply of possible wives, and that, if a woman remained single, whether from birth, or after the death of her husband, it was for no want of suitors for her hand.   One means adopted by brothers who had prospered in the Colony, of aiding their families left behind in England, was to invite their sisters to visit them in Virginia, where, as in the case of William Fitzhugh's sister, they would soon be able to make eligible matches.   Bullock informs us that no maid whom he had brought over failed to find a husband in the course of the first three months after she had entered his service.

At the time when Rev. Greville Pooley made such haste to distance all possible rivals in the graces of Mrs. Jordan, the numerical superiority of the men was perhaps the most extraordinary in the history of the Colony. It was only a few years before that the London Company had found it necessary to import wives for the different tenants engaged in working the public lands; in one year alone, there appear to have been settled on these lands one hundred and ten tenants,[8] none of whom seem to have been married until the company provided wives for them.   The social rank of these tenants was the same as that of the large body of men renting farms from the great English proprietors, from among whom they had perhaps been taken, owing to their experience in culti-

---

[8] Works of Captain John Smith, Vol. II., p. 40, Richmond edition.

vating the soil. They certainly did not occupy a higher social level than English yeomen.

The young women who went over to become the wives of the tenants, though belonging to the lower orders in England, were chosen especially for their previous good character. No indiscriminate or irregular method of selecting them was countenanced in the slightest degree by the company. Owen Evans, pretending to have received the royal commission to impress maids for shipment to Virginia and the Bermudas, visited Somersetshire, and there caused such consternation among the young unmarried women, that forty are said to have fled from one parish alone, and so successfully concealed themselves that their nearest friends did not know what had become of them. Evans was soon arrested.[9] It is probable that the whole number of maids imported did not exceed one hundred and fifty. The largest band arrived in 1620, when ninety landed.[10] In a letter from the company to the Governor and Council in Virginia, dated August, 1621, it was stated that one widow and eleven maids had been dispatched, and that fifty more maids would soon follow.[11] In September of the same year, the company again wrote that thirty-eight maids had been sent out; and it is probable that this number was additional to the fifty previously referred to.[12] Each one was acquired at the rate of about one hundred and fifty pounds of tobacco, or twelve pounds sterling, which went to reimburse

---

[9] Dom. Cor. Jas. I., Vol. CIII., No. 42.

[10] Abstracts of Proceedings Va. Co. of London, Vol. I., p. 67, Va. Hist. Soc. Pub.

[11] Randolph MS., Vol. III., p. 165.

[12] Randolph MS., Vol. III., p. 166.

those members of the company who had borne the expense of transporting the maids to the Colony.[13]

That these young women did not become the wives of the tenants within a few days after they reached Virginia is shown by several facts. First, the company gave orders that they should be well cared for until married, and the Assembly requested of the company that they should always bring victuals with them for their support in this interval.[14] Secondly, in choosing a husband among the large body of men who occupied the public lands, each maid was to have as much freedom of selection as she would have enjoyed had she been marrying in England. There was probably a proportion of three single tenants to each maid, and her choice, therefore, instead of being confined to one man, practically lay between three men, any one of whom she could accept or reject as under normal circumstances in her native country. If no one of the three touched her fancy, it was in her power to abandon the thought of marriage altogether; by disposing of herself as a domestic servant or agricultural laborer, in response to the extraordinary demand for her in either character that existed, she could easily have secured the amount required to cover all the charges entailed by her transportation to the Colony; and this was perhaps the course pursued by some among this memorable company of women, who have so often furnished a theme to romantic writers.[15]

An impression prevailed in England in these early

---

[13] Randoph MS., Vol. III., p. 166.

[14] Randolph MS., Vol. III., pp. 165, 166.

[15] No writer has used this celebrated episode more effectively than Miss Mary Johnston in her popular novel, " To Have and to Hold."

times that the Virginian residing alone on his plantation on the other side of the world, was willing to marry any woman rather than not marry at all; for instance, in 1612, the Spanish Ambassador in London, Don Pedro de Cunega, reported to the King of Spain that at least forty or fifty of the settlers in the Colony on James river had found wives among the Indians, and that a clergyman who had opposed their doing so, had been strongly reprehended.[16] In reality, the only marriage between an Indian woman and an English settler occurring in Virginia during the existence of the company's rule, was the celebrated union of Pocahontas and John Rolfe, which was made possible by the fact that Pocahontas was the daughter of a king, however barbarous in spirit and aspect. The earliest English marriage to take place in the Colony was that of Anne Burras and John Laydon. Laydon himself followed the pursuit of a carpenter, while Anne Burras was the serving woman of Mrs. Forrest, the wife of a prominent settler.[17]

The marriage contract was quite as common in Virginia during the seventeenth century as it was in England. The terms of some of these ante-nuptial agreements secured to the woman the right to retain the whole of her property,[18] a right that was, perhaps, always reserved in those cases in which the future wife was a widow with children, whose first husband had left her his entire estate in fee simple. In a marriage contract between John Hurst and Elizabeth Alford, of Lower Norfolk county, dated 1675, it was carefully stipulated

---

[16] Calendar of British State Papers, Colonial 1574-1660, p. 13.

[17] Works of Captain John Smith, Vol. I., p. 203, Richmond edition.

[18] Surry County Records, Vol. 1671-84, p. 265, Va. St. Libr.

that Hurst should not "meddle" with his wife's property, and that she should be fully authorized, not only to manage, but also to sell it, should she so desire, as if she were still unmarried.   In addition, she kept in her own hands the power to convert to her own use the bills of exchange, tobacco, and other merchandize, which she should at any time send out of the Colony; above all, she reserved to herself the right to distribute her estate by will in such manner as she chose.[19]   It is evident that this lady was shrewd enough to make the most of the eagerness of her lover by preserving her complete independence in all matters relating to her own business.

There is recorded of this period at least one instance in which a woman bound herself by a formal contract not to marry any one but the other party to the agreement, but apparently not binding herself absolutely to marry this person.   Such was the case of Sarah Harrison, daughter of Benjamin Harrison, who after "cordially promising" never to become the wife of anyone but William Roscoe, boldly repudiated her written obligation by becoming the wife of Rev. James Blair.   Her conduct at her wedding gave additional proof of her eccentric character; when called upon by the clergyman who performed the ceremony to say "obey," she replied: "no obey;" and when the clergyman read that part of the service again, she again replied "no obey;" and gave the same answer when he read it a third time.   The clergyman now ignored her words and proceeded with the ceremony to its conclusion, probably in his heart wishing Mr. Blair well of a very capricious partner.[20]

There were great strictness and exactness in the Colony

---

[19] Lower Norfolk County Records, Vol. 1666-75, p. 185.

[20] Va. Maga. of Hist. and Biog., Vol. VII., p. 278.

in throwing around marriage all the safeguards which the law could create and enforce. Under a proclamation issued in 1672 it was declared that the ceremony should not be valid unless a license bearing the Governor's signature had been first obtained, or unless the banns had been published at least three times in the church of the parish in which the parties resided.[21] When one of the latter was under age, the consent of the parents or guardians was required before the license would be granted;[22] and the license itself had to be returned to Jamestown for final recordation.[23] About 1683, the presiding justice of each county court was impowered to issue a marriage license after receiving a certificate from the clerk of the same court that the marriage bond called for by Act of Parliament had been given.[24] The penalty named in this bond was twenty thousand pounds of tobacco. The bond itself seems to have been generally signed by the bridegroom and a friend, who had come forward as his security, but in many cases it appears to have been signed by his friends alone.[25] The publication of the banns in the parish church shows how closely English customs were followed in the Colony; this method of legalizing an intended marriage was probably, in most cases, preferred to the license, if for no other reason, because it entailed smaller expense, since a fee of one hundred pounds of tobacco had to be paid for the license, but of only forty

---

[21] Robinson's Transcripts, p. 73.

[22] Acts of Assembly, Randolph MS., Vol. III., p. 216. See, also, Hening's Statutes, Vol. I., p. 157.

[23] Henrico County Records, Vol. 1677-92, orig., p. 225.

[24] York County Records, Vol. 1675-84, orig., p. 517.

[25] Three marriage bonds will be found among the records of Essex county for the year 1693. See Vol. 1692-5, pp. 290-1, Va. St. Libr.

pounds for the banns.[26] It seems to have been usual at times for the prospective bridegroom to set up at the court-house door, a written notice of his intention to marry; this was done, in 1657, by Richard Markham, who was engaged to Frances Yeates, and, in 1659, by John Manning, who was engaged to Lydia Richardson. Both were citizens of Lower Norfolk county.[27]

Runaway matches occurred very frequently throughout this period. To such an extent had Maryland, by 1673, become the Gretna Green of Virginian lovers, whose marriages for one reason or another were obstructed in their own Colony, that the Virginian Assembly, in the course of that year, requested the Governor to appoint a committee with the power to negotiate with the Governor of the neighboring Province for the adoption of regulations that would make it illegal for Catholic priests or Protestant clergymen there to marry the couples who had by stealth left Virginia and crossed the Potomac for that purpose.[28] But it was not always necessary to pass that river in order to make a clandestine marriage; in 1662, a prominent citizen of Northampton county ran off with Elizabeth Charlton, a girl only twelve years of age, an heiress and a member of one of the most conspicuous families on the Eastern Shore. At the time, she was staying at the home of Captain Jones, where she was receiving her education. The marriage in this case occurred on the other side of the Bay, whither the couple had fled in a sail-boat. The license was probably obtained there, as there the two were unknown.[29]

---

[26] Hening's Statutes, Vol. I., p. 243.

[27] Lower Norfolk County Records, 1656-66, pp. 90, 253.

[28] Orders of Assembly, Oct. 20, 1673, Colonial Entry Book, Vol. LXXXVI.

[29] Northampton County Records, Vol. 1657-64, p. 158.

As early as 1632, it was provided by law that, except in a case of necessity, the marriage ceremony should be performed in a church;[30] and that it should take place between the hours of eight in the morning and twelve midday.[31] The close of the ceremony at this period seems to have been followed by a lively fusillade; but this, finally, led to such an alarming expenditure of powder that it was restricted, if not forbidden altogether, in those years when there was fear of trouble with the Indians.[32] It is not probable that the legal requirement that the marriage ceremony should be celebrated only in a church edifice remained in force down to 1700; in some of the parishes, the church was situated so remotely from many of the inhabitants that this would have made a journey of perhaps two days necessary to reach it. For several years previous to the middle of the century the local magistrates were impowered to perform the ceremony, but this resulted in so much confusion that a law was passed confining the right to clergymen;[33] this change very probably did not alter the rule, which must have prevailed during the time the magistrates could marry couples, namely, that the ceremony could take place in a private house. As soon as the settlements began to spread out, convenience required that this should be allowed; and no doubt also the social spirit of the people, which sought to make the most in their secluded life of every enlivening event, caused it to be greatly preferred. When the wedding came off at the bride's home, the feasting and dancing, usually so freely indulged in, could be started as

---

[30] Hening's Statutes, Vol. I., p. 158.

[31] Randolph MS., Vol. III., p. 216.

[32] Randolph MS., Vol. III., p. 210.

[33] Westmoreland County Records, Vol. 1653-64, p. 80.

soon as the ceremony ended. Very often this could not be done for hours when the ceremony took place in the parish church.

There is no surviving record of the festivities accompanying a Virginian wedding in the seventeenth century; but little reason exists to doubt that an occasion of this kind closely resembled a like occasion occurring in England in those times. Quite probably it was attended by even greater and more prolonged gaiety, owing to the desire of the people, whose lives were, as a rule, secluded and uneventful on their remote plantations, to make the most of every opportunity that arose to brighten their existence. We have already seen that even the funerals were not devoid of their bright and cheerful side; if there was a disposition to extract even from a funeral all the social enlivenment which it could possibly afford, whether springing from the reunion of friends and acquaintances, or from the enjoyment of whatever was good to eat and drink, it can be easily perceived that the spirit with which the guests would enter into such a joyful occasion as a wedding, would be almost unrestrained. The county neighborhoods were not, as a rule, so thickly settled that an occasion of this kind re-occurred with extraordinary frequency, thus to dull by rapid repetition the edge of the pleasure derived from attending it. When a wedding did occur, it was an event all the more important because it did not happen so often as at this time it did in the more crowded parishes of England. Moreover, the majority of the guests, in order to reach the home of the bride, were compelled to travel a considerable distance either by boat or horse; it was not a matter of a few hours for both going and returning, but sometimes of a whole day; indeed, it was not uncommon for twenty-four hours to be consumed in the journey

to or fro alone, and knowing this, the guests were in no
mood to shorten the festivities when they had once arrived at the residence where the wedding was to take
place.   The parents of the bride required no other influence but the knowledge of the many miles their guests
had come to lengthen these festivities to the last moment
to which they could be drawn out.

When a wedding came off, it seems to have been made
an excuse for general relaxation among people of all
classes, and sometimes for the most open disregard of
duty.   A witness in a case that was tried in the court of
York county in 1656, testified that, on his arrival at Mr.
Thomas Bushrod's residence, he was surprised to find
his tobacco crop in a neglected condition.   "Mr. Bushrod," said he, "what do you mean by suffering your tobacco to run up so high; and why do you not topp itt?"
Mr. Bushrod replied that "his overseer, Richard Barkshyre, had gone to a weddinge att Pyanketank without
his consent, and he knew not how to helpe it."[34]   When
the Dutch men-of-war entered James River in 1666, and
carried such havoc among the merchant-men lying there
under the supposed protection of the guard-ship, the
latter vessel was rendered practically useless at the critical moment by the absence of the captain, on shore in attendance at a wedding.

It does not seem to have been always customary at this
period for the bridegroom to procure the wedding ring.
In 1655, Henry Westgate directed in his will that a hogshead of tobacco belonging to his estate should be used
for the purchase of two wedding rings, one of which
was to be given to his daughter, Elizabeth, the other to

---

[34] York County Records, Vol. 1657-62, p. 125, Va. St. Libr.

his daughter, Anne. These rings were to be bought in England.[35]

The marriages which took place in Virginia in the seventeenth century, whether the ceremony occurred in church or in a private residence, were rarely followed by divorce. Writing in 1681, William Fitzhugh, a lawyer of distinction, who was thoroughly familiar with the Colony, declared that he had never known but one couple residing there to obtain from court even an order of separation. This couple was Giles Brent and his wife.[36] Other cases, however, had occurred, but at very long intervals. In 1655, Alice Clawson, of Northampton county, secured a divorce from her husband on the ground that he had, for many years, lived among the Nanticoke Indians in the character of their principal chief, and had refused to give up his Indian concubine.[37] In this case, the heathen associations of Clawson, even more than his prolonged desertion of his wife were probably the main reason why the justices granted the divorce so readily. It was rare that a decree of separation was prayed for, and still rarer that it was allowed. In 1699, Mrs. Mary Taylor, of Elizabeth City county, complained to the county court that her husband was "so cross and cruel" that she could not live with him. She begged that he should be required to provide her with a maintenance, but in a home of her own, where she would be "secure from danger." The court promptly ordered him, not only to deliver up to her her furniture and wearing apparel, but

---

[35] Lower Norfolk County Records, Vol. 1651-56, p. 182.

[36] Letters of William Fitzhugh, June 8, 1681.

[37] Northampton County Records, Vol. 1654-5, p. 135. There is a petition for divorce entered in Lower Norfolk County Records, Vol. 1656-66, p. 354².

also to contribute twelve hundred pounds of tobacco, or six pounds sterling, annually to her support.[38]

---

[38] Elizabeth City County Records, Orders, Jan'y 18, 1699. The following item relates to a midwife's fees: "Agnes Williams, aged 24 years, sayeth that Maudlin (Magdalen), wife of John Major, did bargain with Susan Helline, widdowe, for to keep her while she lay in childbed, and did promise to give her 12 hens." This was in 1682. See Accomac County Records, Vol. 1632-40, p. 16, Va. St. Libr.

XVIII.

Public and Private Occasions.—Church, Court-Day and Muster.

FUNERALS and weddings partook in some measure of a private nature, although, in these early times, the line between them and occasions strictly public in every sense was perhaps not always strictly drawn. The three most important public occasions in the social life of the people at this period were the meeting of the congregation in the parish church, the general muster and the gathering on the monthly county court day at the county court-house.

In Virginia, throughout the seventeenth century, the holding of services in the parish church on Sunday gave rise to an occasion which was as remarkable for its social as for its religious aspects. In this edifice all the people of the entire parish were supposed to assemble every Sabbath morning, and as there was a considerable penalty for remaining away, it is probable that few who were without a good reason to be absent failed to attend. Apart from any desire to join in public worship, the prospect of meeting friends and acquaintances must have had a strong influence in bringing a large number of persons together under the church roof. Both before and after the hour of service they had a full opportunity to mingle in the closest social intercourse. It was at this time that friendships were formed or cemented, courtships begun or advanced, and the latest news and gossip of the neighborhood banded about. Advantage must have been taken of this occasion also to wear some of that costly finery which, as we have seen, members of either sex very often possessed in a great quantity. The women were not so conscious of the sacred character of the hour as to be indifferent to arousing the envy of their acquaintances by the display of a beautiful dress, while among the younger men at least there must have been many who sunned their foppish instincts in the eyes of the congregation by the exhibition of their bravest waistcoats or most brilliant shoe-buckles.

The old church which still stands near Smithfield, in Isle of Wight county, one of the noblest monuments of the colonial era in existence,[1] must have beheld in these early times as notable a gathering of planters and their families in the shadow of its embowering trees as has ever taken place on the soil of Virginia. Here, and at other churches like it, a spirit of social kindness as well as of religious devotion, was nourished from Sunday to Sunday, the bonds of mutual sympathy and helpfulness were made closer and more intimate, the more innocent vanities were aired, the manners of the young improved by inter-

---

[1] A very interesting account of the Smithfield church, its historical and personal associations, will be found in a sympathetic, learned and thoughtful paper read by Major R. S. Thomas before the Virginia Historical Society, Dec. 22, 1892, and published in its collections. Major Thomas possesses a fund of information about the history of this part of Virginia; and it is due to his extraordinary zeal and industry as an antiquarian that many facts of importance in illustration of that history have been preserved.

course with their elders, and the minds of the old refreshed by renewed association with their neighbors. For a few hours the parish church was a centre of overflowing life. If the services were in progress, there was the large congregation listening to the words falling from the lips of the clergyman, or joining in the singing of one of those immemorial psalms which required no instrumental music to increase their impressiveness; and if the services had ended, there were the groups of persons within the edifice and the groups without under the trees laughing and conversing, while in the surrounding thickets horses, impatient to carry their masters and mistresses home, were neighing and stamping the ground.[2] An hour later the character of the whole scene had changed; the church building was closed in door and window; not a man or horse was to be observed; and the silence was only broken by the occasional cry of a wandering bird, or the bark of a squirrel. And so it continued until, on the following Sunday, the church doors were thrown open again.

A general muster, while sharing in some of the

[2] The peacefulness of the occasion was sometimes, in the frontier counties disturbed by rude interruptions, as the following entry in the Henrico County Records for 1687 shows: " Upon ye p'sentment of one of ye grand jury on his own knowledge that Henry Ayscough did on a Sunday (ye tenth of July last) come drunk to ye Church, and there unbutton his coat and offer to fight with two persons then there; likewise he swore that he would ride into ye church and did attempt it; It is ordered that ye said Henry Ayscough, for his said drunkenness, swearing, and other misdemeanors, be fined, and doe pay according to ye lawes in such cases made" * * * Henrico County Minute Book, 1682-1701, p. 185, Va. St. Libr.

social features of the assemblage at church, was naturally distinguished for much more stirring and exciting incidents. As a meeting of this kind was held for an entire county, it drew together persons from a far wider area of country than the area contained in a single parish; from the remotest points within these extensive limits the people came, some trudging on foot, some perhaps travelling in carts and rude carriages, but the greater number riding on horseback. Women perched up behind on pillions accompanied their fathers, brothers, or husbands. The military spectacle afforded by a general muster, the finest which the Colony had to offer, no doubt had the same burning interest for all classes of persons at that day which it would now have. These musters must frequently have lasted longer than a few hours, but even when confined to a single day, the occasion for all who had to come from a distance really spread over two days, as they were unable to return home before the following morning.[3] There was thus an opportunity after the close of the exercises for a general commingling of the people. As every freeman was subject to military duty, the muster brought together numerous representatives of every class in the community above the grades of servant and slave, and even servants and slaves were there in attendance on their masters. All who were most prominent and influential among the gentlemen residing in the county must have

---

[3] In 1696, as already stated, a petition was offered in the House of Burgesses by citizens of Northumberland county praying that no musters should be allowed to take place on Saturday, as it led to the profanation of Sunday. See Minutes of House of Burgesses, Sept. 30, 1696, B. T. Va., Vol. LII.

been present, and this fact alone, no doubt, served to impart a special social distinction to the occasion in the eyes of the opposite sex, and had its effect in increasing the number of ladies present. The muster itself, by varying the character of the day by a military display, gave a fillip to the social pleasure of the reunion such as it would not have possessed had the people come together without a special object. The event very probably also had its darker side in the presence of many who were disposed to take advantage of it to indulge too freely in liquor, but the presence of so many soldiers fully armed was always a guarantee that no serious disorder would occur.

The diversions of the monthly court day were entirely confined to men. This occasion was far from being purely social in its character. It had also its political and business aspects, all of which were removed from the sphere of feminine participation. The absence of women, in a measure, accounts for the lack of restraint which so often distinguished the day in these early times. There are numerous proofs that the meeting of the monthly court created an opportunity, not only for the general discussion of the merits of candidates for the House of Burgesses, for making bargains for the sale of tobacco and live stock, and for an exchange of county news, but also for a free enjoyment of rough horse-play. Above all, it was enlivened by a great deal of drunken revelry, which was not entirely confined to members of the lowest class. A minute of Northampton county court, dated 1678, records the fact that it had become the practice of several persons to attend on the occasion of the court's meeting in order to get intoxicated, quarrel, and fight;

and that they had had the "impudence" to enter the court-room whilst the judges were sitting, and be abusive to their face. A strict measure for repressing these roughs was adopted, and the keeper of the ordinary near the court-house was warned that, unless he preserved perfect order in his tavern, his license would be withdrawn.[4] When George Mayplis petitioned the county court of Lancaster for the right to sell cider at the court-house on court day, it was granted on condition that its exercise should be "in no ways injurious or prejudicial in ye disturbing of ye court in ye time of its sitting."[5] In spite of all these precautions on the part of the justices, much drunkenness seems to have prevailed by the time night arrived. This fact was so well known that the indentured servants very often took advantage of the relaxed vigilance of that hour to make their preparations for flight. About 1680 a servant confessed in Northampton county court that he had been waiting for a court day in order to steal a bridle and saddle. This he said he could do as soon as night came on when he knew the people would be too much in drink to observe his action. The bridle and saddle he intended to hide in the woods until he could run off with one of his master's horses and thus make good his escape to Maryland.[6] Nicholson, during the course of his adminstration offered prizes to all who should excel in riding, running, shooting, wrestling, and cudgeling.[7] These contests probably took place on court days.

---

[4] Northampton County Records, Vol. 1674-78, p. 374.

[5] Lancaster County Records, Orders, July 12, 1682.

[6] Northampton County Records, Vol. 1679-83, pp. 52, 53.

[7] Beverley's History of Virginia, p. 79.

XIX.

DUELLING.

IN a life so frequently marked by controversies and brawls on the occasions when the people came together, it was to be expected that every now and then a duel would occur, which would end in a tragedy. As early as 1619 Captain William Eppes killed Captain Stallinge in a private quarrel. At a later period, owing to heated words that had passed between them while together making a journey to Jamestown, a duel took place between Richard Stephens and George Harrison, in which Stephens received a cut in the knee from his opponent's sword. At the end of two weeks he was dead, but the autopsy showed that he could not have lived long even if he had come off uninjured in the duel with Harrison.[1] Actual or threatened duels must not have been uncommon about 1643, as in the course of that year an order was adopted that, should a justice of the peace send a challenge to a member of the Council, he should be disabled from holding office.[2] This special order was, no doubt, called forth by a particuular instance in which such an offence had been committed by a judge of one of the county courts.

A decade had hardly passed when we find a justice in the position of the councillor in this case. About 1653 Richard Denham, acting for his father-in-law,

---

[1] Letter of George Menifie to John Harrison in England, April 27, 1624, British Colonial Papers, Vol. III., 1624-5, No. 15.

[2] Robinson Transcripts, p. 238.

Captain Thomas Hackett, delivered a challenge to Mr.
Daniel Fox at the very moment he was sitting with his
fellow justices on the bench of Lancaster county court.
Denham admitted, when sternly questioned by the
court, that he was aware he bore a challenge, and he
boldly demanded of Fox what answer he proposed to
return to Captain Hackett. One of the justices here
spoke up in sharp reproof: "An action of that nature,"
he exclaimed, "I would not be ye owner of for ye
world." To which Denham replied in a slighting manner. The court then very emphatically declared that
Denham was a "party in ye crime" of Captain Hackett,
and that for bringing the challenge, whose character
he well knew, and for delivering it while the justices
were sitting, as well as for his contemptuous manner
and peremptory words, he should receive on his bare
shoulder six strokes of a whip at the hands of the
sheriff. The latter officer was also instructed to arrest
Captain Hackett and hold him without privilege of
bail until he should "answer for his crimes" at the
next session of the General Court at Jamestown. The
cause of the challenge seems to have been a reflection
cast upon Hackett by Fox during a session of the
county court, which Hackett asserted had its origin in
"malice and an evil disposition." He invited Fox to
meet him at eight o'clock in the morning at a point
situated on the line bounding their two estates, where,
as it lay in a valley, the combatants would be removed
from observation or interruption. Hackett selected
the rapier as his weapon, and the only particular in
which he failed to follow the regulations was in not
leaving the choice to his opponent; but he was scrupulous to inform Fox of the length of the special rapier

he proposed using in the duel. He requested Fox to bring his second with him. "If you please," he adds with great courtesy.[3]

Some of the servants appear to have been as fiery in nature as their masters, and as quick to resent an affront, real or imaginary. In 1661 a servant belonging to Christopher Calvert, who resided on the Eastern Shore, sent a peremptory challenge to Goslin Van Netsen, a citizen of Dutch origin. The challenge was accepted, a duel fought, and the servant badly wounded. Calvert was ordered by the county court to pay for the present all the fees which Dr. George Nicholas Hacke should charge for medical attendance on the injured man, but they were ultimately to be shared equally with Van Netsen, who had inflicted the wound. Calvert was to be finally compensated by an extension of the servant's term.[4] It is probable that, in this case, the servant sending the challenge really belonged to a higher social grade than would appear from the entry in the records. Many of those bound

---

[3] Lancaster County Records, Vol. 1652-56, p. 64. "The challenge ran as follows: ' Mr. ffox, I wonder ye should so much degenerate from a gentleman as to cast such an aspersion on me in open Court, making nothinge appe-ar but I knowe it to be out of malice and an evil disposition which remains in your hearte, therefore, I disyre ye if ye have anything of a gentleman or of manhood in ye to meet me on Tuesday morninge at ye marked tree in ye valey which partes yr lande and mine, about eight of ye clocke, where I shall expect yr comeinge to give me satisfaction. My weapon is rapier, ye length I send ye by bearer; not yours at present, but yours at ye time appointed. THOMAS HACKETT. Ye seconde bringe along with ye if ye please * * * I shall finde me of ye like."

[4] Northampton County Records, Vol. 1657-64, orig., p. 132.

by articles of indenture were young men of gentle connections, whose social antecedents were inconsistent with the position in which they placed themselves; or it may be they had signed the articles in order to learn some special pursuit, like tobacco planting, before embarking in it on their own independent account. It is not likely that Van Netsen would have accepted a challenge from an ordinary domestic or agricultural servant, as that would have signified a confession on his part that he did not hold himself higher than the lowest social class in the community.

A curious instance is recorded in the history of the Insurrection of 1676 of a wish on the part of one of its leaders to have recourse to the old custom of single combat in order to find out with which side lay the true equity of the quarrel between the two parties. On one occasion, when the opposing soldiers were facing each other, Major Bristow, a supporter of Governor Berkeley, offered to fight any follower of Bacon who had a right to be considered a gentlemen. Ingram, one of the most conspicuous officers in the popular army, promptly accepted the challenge, but when he made a motion to advance, with sword and pistol in hand, his own man caught hold of him and forced him back, because, as the chronicler of the event slyly observes, they were doubtful of the justice of their side, but more probably because they saw that Ingram was no match in physical strength for his proposed antagonist.[5]

Giles Bland, who was destined to end his life on the gallows for the part he took in the Rebellion of 1676, had on one occasion a heated altercation with one of

---

[5] Ingram's Proceedings, p. 40, Force's Historical Tracts, Vol. 1.

the Ludwells, which ended in an exchange of gloves, and an appointment to fight a duel on the following morning. Bland appeared punctually at the hour agreed upon, but Ludwell failed to come. In his resentment Bland nailed the glove to the door of the State-House.

Neither the transplanted Englishman nor the native Virginians were, when angry, scrupulous respecters of persons or places, however distinguished or sacred. In 1684 a quarrel arising in the court-house of Lower Norfolk county during a session of the justices, two brothers, John and Henry Gills, drew their swords on their opponents, and but for the prompt interference of the by-standers a bloody combat would have been fought on the floor of the room. Both brothers were at once committed to prison.[6]

---

[6] Lower Norfolk County Records, Vol. 1675-86, Orders, May 15, 1684. "So many horried murders and duels were committed about this time as were never before heard of in England, which gave much cause of complaint and murmurings." See Evelyn's Diary, Dec. 18, 1684. Again he writes: "Many bloody and notorious duels were fought about this time."—Diary, Feb'ry 18, 1686.

XX.

Conclusion.

NOW that the varied aspects of the purely social life of Virginia in the seventeenth century have passed under review, it is seen that the most remarkable general feature of that life was its close resemblance to the social life of England in the same age, in spite of the modifying influences of a new and developing country remotely situated from the Old World. There were several reasons why this close resemblance should have been maintained long after the community had had time to acquire a distinct character of its own. These reasons, which have been incidentally touched upon in the preceding pages in other connections, may now be grouped together in conclusion.

First, the great bulk of the population was of unmixed English blood. At no period during the century did the alien element, whether Dutch, French, or Celtic, become important from the point of view of number, although individuals of foreign origin, from time to time, exercised great influence.[1] In nearly every instance the person of foreign birth intermarried with a Virginian, or English man or woman. Not only was his alien temper and sympathies thus moderated unconsciously to himself, but the chance of his transmitting his own national traits to his offspring was thus lessened, if not destroyed. His descendants in the third generation, if not in the second, gave no indications whatever of foreign descent. The original

---

[1] For a detailed account of the foreign elements, see Appendix.

foreign strain had in them at least been practically ob-
literated. They were as thoroughly English in instinct, feeling, aspiration, moral standards, and general
attitude of mind, as if no alien blood whatever coursed
in their veins.

In the second place, the population was not only of
pure English blood as a whole, but also distinctively
representative of the mass of persons residing in the
Mother Country. Virginia was not, like New England, settled by people out of sympathy in their religious observances, social customs, and general views
of life with the majority of Englishmen. The emigrants were drawn almost entirely from that majority,
and as they shared all the social, religious, and political
leanings that characterized it as a body, they, from
the very beginning, planted in Virginia all the immemorial habits, customs, and traditions of their native
land. Wave following wave simply confirmed these
habits, customs, and traditions, because forming a part
of their own lives before finding a home in the West.

The English spirit prevalent in that age is reflected
in a more or less vivid degree in all the peculiarities of
Virginian social life, from the sharp division into
classes down to the indoor and outdoor diversions of
the people. The gentleman was as distinctly differ-
entiated from the yeoman, and the yeoman from the
agricultural servant or mechanic, as in England itself.
Such men as William Byrd, Richard Lee, Adam
Thoroughgood, and the elder Nathaniel Bacon, men who
owned many slaves and thousands of acres of land,
besides filling the principal political offices, occupied in
their respective parts of Virginia the same position of
influence as that occupied by the largest landowners

in the English shires. The social barriers which separated these men, and men of the same class, from persons belonging to a lower rank, were as clearly recognized in Virginia as in the Mother Country. From the beginning there was never there any of that rude social equality which characterizes all pioneer communities in our own times. All the ceremonial terms indicating social superiority, all the badges and signs long adopted as marks of gentle descent, were in constant use in the Colony from its foundation. It is true that an unrestricted suffrage prevailed for many decades, but as soon as the artistocratic influence became completely predominant the right to cast a vote was made dependent upon the conditions which had long been enforced in England.

The English spirit was reflected not simply in the strict preservation of social differences. It was equally conspicuous in all the social habits and customs of the Virginians,—in the manner in which they celebrated their funerals and weddings; in the general character of all their public gatherings; in the nature of their indoor diversions, such as card-playing, betting, dancing and the like; in their love of horse-racing; in their taste for hunting and fishing, and in their cheerful recognition of all the claims of hospitality.

The third influence promoting a close social resemblance to England was a corollary of the first and second, namely, with few exceptions, the most conspicuous citizens of Virginia in the seventeenth century had been born, reared, and educated in the Mother Country. By the time they emigrated to the Colony their characters had been formed and their opinions fixed in the English mould, to which they had been subjected during their childhood, youth, and early manhood. They were Englishmen, not simply by descent and nativity, but also by consent and intimate personal associations during the most susceptible and receptive period of their lives. Under English skies they had obtained, unconsciously to themselves, a thorough knowledge of all the social laws of their nation; had become familiar with all that nation's forms of social diversion; had acquired all the culture which the English schools could impart, and had become versed in all that the Anglican Church could teach of religious dogma and religious ceremony. In short, all their preferences in the matter of ecclesiastical, political, and social government had all been finally shaped before they saw the shores of Virginia. Their readiness to leave their old home in order to try their fortunes in the remote West was a proof that they were possessed of an unusual degree of self-reliance, energy, and enterprise; and men of that character were the very ones who were least likely to be disloyal to the impressions of their formative years. It was these men who were most instrumental in giving direction to the history of the Colony in the seventeenth century, whether religious, social, or political, and not unnaturally their influence, after their emigration, was cast on the side of all those ideals which had prevailed in the Mother Country for immemorial generations.

A fourth influence promoting the Colony's social resemblance to England was the existence within its settled area of a system of extensive landed estates. This system had its principal origin in the needs of the tobacco plant. A virgin soil was required for the production of that plant in its highest perfection, and to secure this the landowner was constantly compelled to increase his holdings. But the tendency towards the engrossment of the soil did not spring entirely from economic influences; it sprang in part from a feeling which the landed proprietor had either brought over from England, or inherited from an English father, namely, that the possession of a large landed estate was the firmest basis on which the social distinction of his family could rest. Moreover, it would enable him to gratify one of the strongest of his inherited social instincts; that is to say, his desire to maintain a strict privacy in the surroundings of his home. Love of isolation in the situation of his dwelling house has always been a characteristic of the Englishman. If his estate is small, he plants a hedge, or erects a wall to shut out the public gaze; if large, he builds his house behind groups of trees. There was no need to grow hedges or to build walls in Virginia to conceal the mansion from public view. A site could always be found where the most complete privacy was assured by the natural screen of hill or grove. This secluded life confirmed in the emigrant all those moral and intellectual tendencies which he had inherited or imbibed in his native land. Indeed, those tendencies really expanded and flourished more freely in the atmosphere of Virginia than they could have done had he remained in England, because the atmosphere of the Colony was less conventional and less artificial in its pressure than the atmosphere of the Mother Country. The life of the plantation simply accentuated all his native traits. He became only more jealous of his personal and political freedom; only more intense in his love of home and family; only more scrupulous in his recognition of the claims of hospitality, and if religiously disposed, only more obedient to the authority of the church, and more submissive to the dictates of his early religious training.

A fifth influence promoting the Colony's social resemblance to the Mother Country sprang from the presence of the slave and indentured servant. The system of indentured service in its social effects differed but little, if at all, from the system of slavery. It really accentuated the social divisions among the whites more distinctly than the presence of the institution of slavery itself did. The indentured servants were as much a legalized lowest class in Virginia as the noblemen were a legalized highest class in England. It gave purely class distinctions a recognized standing in the Colonial Courts of Law. It was not until the end of the century that negro bondsmen became numerous on the plantations, and yet in social spirit the seventeenth century in Virginia did not differ from the eighteenth. The ever-increasing multitude of African slaves after 1700 simply confirmed the social tendencies which had previously been fostered by the presence of the indentured whites. The black slave took the place of the white servant, with the result of strengthening and extending, and not of modifying and narrowing, the prevailing social conditions.

Finally, the Colony's social resemblance to the Mother Country was promoted by the fact that its whole system of government, whether as relating to its religious and legal affairs, or to its military and political, was modelled on the system prevailing in England. Virginia, like England, was divided into parishes under the control of vestries composed of the foremost citizens of their respective communities; and, like England, it supported an Established Church subject to all the Anglican canons and regulations. Like England, it had placed the administration of the law in the hands, first, of a County Court, and, finally, of a Supreme Court; only in Virginia there was but one Supreme Court, which enjoyed all the powers of the English co-ordinate highest courts combined. Like England also, Virginia relied chiefly upon a militia for defence; and like England too, her political affairs were directed by a single Executive and an Upper and Lower Legislative Assembly. The emigrant saw around him all the institutions which he had been accustomed to over-seas, only modified slightly in their application to a less populous and less wealthy community. It was in agriculture alone that he observed an important departure, but the social influence of this divergence was diminished by the presence of the indentured servant and slave, which, as we have seen, had such an important effect in maintaining the class differences inherited from England.

To the cursory glance the social life of Virginia in the seventeenth century seems doubly narrow and provincial; first, because it was a community occupying a site only comparatively recently stolen from the primeval forest; and, secondly, because it was a Colony lying several thousand miles away from the Old World, and all the controlling currents of those times. But that life at once assumes its true character of universal interest and importance when it is recalled that this was the beginning of a social system which was to make a lasting impression upon the history of the Western Hemisphere, and which was to produce

that memorable body of men,—Washington, Henry,
Jefferson, Madison, Monroe, and Marshall,—the transmitted influence of whose political careers has, with
the growth of the United States in power, steadily
broadened until it has now come to touch the affairs
of the entire globe.

APPENDIX.

As early as 1658, a very liberal naturalization law was passed by the Virginia Assembly in order to encourage foreign immigration. This law was renewed in 1671, and again in 1680. But at no time during the seventeenth century was the number of citizens of alien birth residing in the Colony so great as to exercise a marked influence on its general history. Long before the persecution of the Huguenots in France became systematic and pitiless, a considerable number of persons of French origin had settled in Virginia. It is most probable that, in nearly all these cases, the French immigrant had either himself lived for some time in England, or was sprung from parents who had done so. If the former, he had stopped there long enough to become largely anglicized in spirit; if the latter, he was certain to have been to all intents an Englishman, as he had been born under English skies, brought up in an English community, and educated in an English school. His name alone in this last case betrayed the original seat of his family.

Among the few Frenchmen arriving at an early date in Virginia from their native country, were the Vigna-roons, whom the London Company were, by the luxuriant growth of the indigenous grape, encouraged in 1619 to bring over in order to test the capacity of the soil for the production of the finest varieties of wines. Others emi-grating to the Colony about this time, by way of London, were John and Peter Arundell. Peter Arundell was a native of Normandy, and this was probably the case also with John. Martin Slatier emigrated by way of Canada previous to 1624. At a later period (about 1652), we find in Northumberland county a family of Roziers; in York, families bearing the names of Sebrell and De Long respectively. In 1656, there resided in Lower Norfolk county Hugh Wood, originally Dubois, and John Forbesson; in York county, in 1666, John Pettit, Peter Godson, and Francois a Pluvier; in Surrey, during the same year, John la Grand; in Lower Norfolk, Roger Fonteine; in Northumberland, in 1669 (about which time there was a close trade connection between the Northern Neck and the Channel islands, so largely inhabited by people of French origin and names), John Montone, a prominent physician, Andrew de la Briere, John Contanceau, son of a Frenchman naturalized in England, Michael de Contee, Andrew Pettigru, John Crallé, and Clement Lemprière.

One of the most conspicuous and useful citizens of Lower Norfolk county about 1680 was James Thelaball, a native of France. Dr. John Fontaine, residing in Virginia in 1686, was a native of Rochelle. About the same date, a band of Frenchmen, driven from their country by religious persecution, settled at Brenton, but the greater number in a short time removed to Maryland. Among the clergy of Virginia at this time were Revs. Stephen Fouace, James Boisseau, and Lewis Latane. In 1688, John Foissin, who was born in Paris, owned a store in Henrico county, which contained a varied assortment of rare French goods, such as muslin neck-cloths, silk-fringed gloves, embroidered waistcoats, lace and velvet caps, lace shirts and ruffles, and the like. During the same year, Bertram Servant, a wealthy planter of French origin, resided in Elizabeth City county; among other citizens of the same county, in 1692, were David Du Puy, Gyles Du Berges, and James Lascelles. Philip Pardoe and Richard de Barry owned plantations in Isle of Wight county.

The largest number of Frenchmen who ever emigrated to Virginia in a single body, came out in 1700, and settled at Monacan above the Falls of the James River, but they arrived too late to exercise any social or political influence on the history of the Colony during the seventeenth century.

Although there was a continuous commercial intercourse between Virginia and Holland down to the passage of the Second Navigation Act, neither the Dutch nor the German emigration to the Colony in the seventeenth century attained the proportion even of the French. In the first place, Holland was a Protestant country, and religious persecution played no part in prompting many of its people to remove to alien colonies over sea; in the second place, New Amsterdam naturally attracted to itself nearly all those Dutchmen who sought fortune in the West. Nevertheless, a considerable number of both Dutch and Germans settled in Virginia from time to time, drawn thither, no doubt, in the course of the tobacco trade. In 1653, there were so many natives of the low countries residing on the Eastern Shore that Deputy-Governor Claiborne found it necessary to protect their lives and property from the hostility aroused against them among the people at large by the war which had just broken out between England and Holland. In 1657, the most highly educated citizen of Northampton county was, perhaps, Dr. George Nicholas Hacke, a native of Cologne. John Sigismond Cluverius, probably also of German birth, was at this time the owner of a considerable estate in York county. Among the residents of the Eastern Shore in 1660 were Hugh Cornelius Corneliuson, Hendrick Wageman, Daniel Derrickson, Peter Jacobson, Abram

Van Slot and Abram Jansen. Five years later, a large
addition was made to the laboring population by the arrival of the Dutch soldiers, who were captured when New
Amsterdam fell into English hands. These were distributed among the planters. In 1666, Henrick Van Doveracke resided in York county. Among those obtaining
naturalization at this time were Andrew Herbert or Hobart, John Young, William Martin, Bartholomew Engel
bockson, Lawrence Van Slott, Henry Wagemaan, Nicholas Koch, Thomas Harmanson, Mindert Doodes, Hendrick Fayson, Herman Kelderman, John Peterson, and
Michael Vallandigham. Thomas Harmanson, a native of
Brandenburg, became a citizen about 1622. A considerable number of the Dutch immigrants had been citizens.
of England before they settled in Holland, or were
sprung from Englishmen who had become Dutch citizens.
This was the case, apparently, with John and William
Custis, of Accomac, and William Moseley, of Lower Norfolk county.

Traces of the presence among the English population
of the Colony of other Continental peoples beside the
Dutch and German are hardly observable. One of the
persons arriving with the first supply was Edward Gargana, probably of either Italian or Portuguese descent.
Of undoubted Italian origin were Bernardo and Vincen-
zo, the two Venetians imported by the London Company
in order to manufacture glass. Albino Lupo, whose
brother was a merchant of London, was perhaps of Portuguese blood. Amaso de Tores was probably a Spanish
Jew. Among the persons residing in Lancaster county
in 1652, were John Pedro, and Silvedo and Manuel Rodreguez; in Rappahannock county, Giacimo Debello,
Edward Mazingo, and Richard Iago.

In 1690, many Irishmen captured at the Battle of the Boyne were imported into Virginia as agricultural servants. A like addition to the population had been made during the supremacy of Cromwell at an earlier date. But the most important emigrants from Ireland settling in the Colony in the seventeenth century were men of English blood, whose fathers had received grants of confiscated lands in that unfortunate country, or who had removed thither in the course of business. Such was Daniel Gookin, who, in 1622, patented lands at Newport News, and such, no doubt, were Anthony Lawson, of Lower Norfolk, and others whose names might be mentioned.

INDEX.

Abbot, 41.
Adams, 203.
Addison, 183.
Alford, 230.
Alington, 50, 118.
Allan, 108.
Allerton, 89, 100, 180.
Andros, 20, 132.
Archer, 40.
Armorial Bearings, 105.
Arundell, 118, 258.
Ashton, 73, 90.
Aston, 51.
Awburne, 195.
Ayscough, 241.

Bacon, 53, 59, 60, 95, 101, 107, 108, 153, 159, 251.
Bailey, 41, 95, 181.
Baker, 199.
Ball, 97.
Ballard, 132.
Barber, 113, 200.
Bargrave, 75.
Barham, 99.
Barkshyre, 236.
Barlowe, 203.
Barnard, 55.
Barry, 260.
Barton, 220.
Bascom, 192.
Bassett, 59, 108.
Bathurst, 66.
Batte, 75, 91, 107, 206.
Beachamp, 96.
Beadle, 42.
Beckingham, 153.
Bennett, 55, 91, 107.
Bentley, 41.

Berkeley, 60, 81, 107, 158, 178, 187.
Bernard, 55.
Beverley, 53, 72, 101, 107, 114, 132, 159, 163, 176, 215, 225.
Biggs, 140.
Bishop, 77.
Blair, 207, 231.
Blanchard, 44.
Bland, 63, 91, 107, 248.
Boisseau, 259.
Bolling, 93, 107.
Bolton, 75.
Booth, 51, 95, 117.
Bouchler, 48.
Boulware, 224.
Bowman, 112.
Bradlock, 85.
Brain, 189.
Branch, 207.
Branker, 166.
Brent, 63, 237.
Brenton, 259.
Brett, 63.
Brewer, 85, 89.
Brewster, 40.
Briere, 259.
Bridger, 76.
Bristow, 248.
Broadhurst, 70.
Brodnax, 76, 77, 189.
Brooke, 88.
Brough, 119.
Broughton, 100.
Brown, 6.
Browne, 40, 122.
Bruce, 128, 129.
Buckner, 94, 132.
Bullock, 34, 118, 194.
Burnham, 118.

Burrus, 230.
Burwell, 107, 132.
Bushrod, 155, 236.
Byrd, 5, 79, 91, 107, 122, 124, 127, 133, 147, 152, 163, 170, 175, 180, 190, 209, 223, 251.
Calthorpe, 54, 107.
Calvert, 98, 150, 247.
Carter, 73, 223.
Cary, 64, 93, 101, 107, 113, 132.
Cavaliers, 31, 61, 76, 79.
Chamberlaine, 133, 189, 209, 204.
Charlton, 118, 233.
Cheate, 184.
Cheeseman, 118, 149.
Chesley, 151; see Chesney.
Chesney, 96.
Chew, 86.
Chicheley, 61, 107.
Childers, 204.
Chilton, 190.
Claiborne, 51, 88, 107, 118.
Clamm, 138.
Clarke, 63, 150.
Clawson, 237.
Clayton, 5, 107.
Clemens, 200.
Clement, 116.
Cluverius, 260.
Coats of Arms, 105, et seq.
Cocke, 100, 107, 130, 174, 188, 204, 206, 207, 209.
Codd, 63.
Codrington, 42.
Cole, 107, 109, 222.
Collin, 95.
Contanceau, 196, 259.
Contee, 259.
Corbin, 71, 90, 132, 180.
Corneliuson, 260.
Cox, 74, 139.
Cralle, 259.
Crews, 96.
Crosby, 152.
Croshaw, 49, 118, 121, 161.
Culpeper, 65, 77.
Curle, 119.
Custis, 24, 261.

Dale, 58.
Daniel, 128.
Danneline, 224.
Darby, 186.
Davison, 48.
Day, 143.
Dearlove, 192.
Death, 89.
Debello, 261.
Denham, 134, 245.
De La Warr, 42, 103, et seq.
De Long, 259.
Derrickson, 260.
Dewey, 99.
Dickenson, 166.
Digges, 58, 107, 158, 160, 162, 163-5.
Dimthorne, 114.
Dixon, 114, 214.
Doodes, 97, 261.
Douthat, 74.
Du Barges, 259.
Dudley, 124.
Dunn, 188.
Du Puy, 259.
Dutch, 260.

East, 190.
Eaton, 116.
Edwards, 74.
Elam, 112, 193.
Elrington, 151.
Emerson, 153.
Engelbockson, 261.
Eppes, 119, 120, 131, 207, 209, 220, 245.
Evelyn, 70, 153.

Fairfax, 182.
Farrer, 107, 130; see Ferrer.
Fauntleroy, 106, 159, 177.
Fawsett, 186.
Fayson, 261.
Featherstone, 41, 193.
Felgate, 44, 89, 118, 121, 211.
Fellowes, 96.
Ferrer, 87, 100; see Farrer.
Finch, 52.
Fisher, 191.

Fitzhugh, 5, 34, 65, 74, 91, 101, 107, 108, 127, 147, 158, 161, 163, 180, 237.
Fleet, 48, 107.
Fontaine, 259.
Foote, 95.
Forbesson, 259.
Forrest, 230.
Fouace, 259.
Fowke, 79.
Fox, 76, 246.
Foxcroft, 97.
Francis, 149.
Freeman, 94.

Gainge, 97.
Gardiner, 199.
Gargana, 261.
Gastwick, 65.
Gawin, 192.
Gerard, 180.
Gibbes, 47.
Gills, 249.
Godby, 114.
Godson, 259.
Godwin, 189.
Goode, 111.
Gookin, 262.
Gower, 40.
Grand, 259.
Graves, 152.
Green, 69.
Greenspring, 158.
Griffin, 153, 163.
Griffith, 92.
Griggs, 220.
Grove, 220.

Hacke, 247, 260.
Hackett, 135, 246.
Hall, 146, 183.
Hammond, 76.
Hamor, 87, 118, 122.
Hardiman, 268.
Harmanson, 99, 261.
Harmar, 74.
Harper, 41.
Harrison, 42, 72, 77, 132, 207, 231, 245.

Hartley, 200.
Hartridge, 198.
Hartwell, 180.
Harvey, 45, 52.
Harwar, 94, 202.
Harwood, 118.
Hatcher, 205.
Hayden, 6.
Haynie, 197.
Haywood, 90, 191.
Hethersall, 146.
Heyman, 66, 123.
Higginson, 89.
Hill, 166.
Hinton, 52.
Hobart, 261.
Hodge, 153.
Holland, 114.
Holt, 42.
Honeywood, 76.
Honeyman, 59.
Hooke, 116.
Howard, 143, 186.
Huddlesey, 207.
Humphrey, 196, 200.
Hurst, 230.
Hutchings, 115.

Isham, 62, 150.

Jackson, 47.
Jacob, 195.
Jacobson, 260.
James, 6, 115, 118.
Jansen, 261.
Jefferson, 208.
Jennings, 64, 107.
Johnson, 114, 184.
Johnston, 229.
Jones, 76, 90, 112, 175, 233.
Jordan, 98, 150, 174, 221, 225.
Juxon, 75.

Keith, 6.
Kelderman, 261.
Kemp, 55.
Kendall, 99.
Kenner, 196, 200.
Kennon, 112, 122.

Killingbeck, 41.
Kingsmill, 107, 108.
Knight, 151.
Koch, 261.

Lamsden, 114.
Landon, 79.
Langley, 221.
Langston, 77.
Lascelles, 259.
Latane, 259.
Lawson, 115, 262.
Laydon, 230.
Lear, 70.
Lee, 56, 90, 93, 107, 122, 149,
    180, 251.
Leigh, 42, 132.
Lempriere, 259.
Lightfoot, 74, 132.
Ligon, 190, 204, 205-6.
Littleton, 55, 122, 160.
Lloyd, 86.
Lockey, 92.
Lord, 100.
Lovell, 149.
Ludlow, 62, 107, 161.
Ludwell, 20, 63, 91, 107, 249.
Luke, 65.
Lunsford, 61, 65, 77, 107.
Lupo, 261.
Lyddall, 60.
Lytcott, 55.

McCarty, 166.
Macarty, 138.
Madison, 225.
Major, 238.
Mallory, 116.
Manning, 233.
Maplesdin, 149.
Marable, 132.
Markham, 233.
Marshall, 46, 100, 192, 205.
Martin, 261.
Mason, 48, 79, 108, 149.
Mathews, 52.
May, 149.
Mayplis, 244.
Mazingo, 261.

Meader, 201.
Menifie, 86, 116, 122, 245.
Merchants, 36, 83, et seq.
Meriwether, 145.
Michael, 221.
Milburn, 98.
Milner, 107, 193.
Minor, 97.
Molesworth, 76.
Montague, 75.
Montgomery, 98.
Montone, 259.
Morris, 100.
Morryson, 20, 53.
Moon, 66, 151.
Moseley, 109, 166, 261.
Mountney, 114.
Munford, 92.

Napier, 207.
Newell, 191.
Newman, 75.
Nicholson, 244.
Norton, 42.
Norwood, 5, 36, 58, 76, 172.
Nottingham, 99.

Page, 71, 101, 107, 153, 180.
Pardoe, 191, 259.
Parke, 70, 107, 171.
Parker, 155, 182, 206.
Parkes, 46, 123, 201.
Pargiter, 149.
Patrick, 128.
Pawlett, 46.
Peachey, 70.
Peake, 60.
Pedro, 261.
Pennington, 40.
Perkins, 41.
Perrin, 100.
Perry, 93.
Peterson, 261.
Pettigrew, 259.
Pettit, 259.
Peyton, 63, 67, 94, 107.
Phelps, 42.
Philpot, 42.
Piersey, 86, 158.

Pinder, 75.
Place, 66, 123.
Pleasants, 190.
Pluvier, 259.
Pocahontas, 49, 139, 230.
Poole, 118.
Pooley, 225.
Pope, 114.
Porter, 189.
Pory, 46.
Poulter, 149.
Powell, 114.
Prat, 42.
Price, 202.
Pritchard, 166.
Proctor, 179, 202.
Pryor, 74.
Puckett, 136.
Purifoy, 155.

Quiney, 87.

Reade, 54.
Randolph, 78, 107, 119, 120, 130, 180, 193, 207.
Ranson, 98.
Ravenscroft, 99.
Richardson, 233.
Robine, 188.
Robinson, 75, 107, 151, 155.
Rodreguez, 261.
Rolfe, 48, 139, 230.
Roscoe, 231.
Rosegill, 58, 159.
Rossingham, 46.
Rowlett, 192.
Royall, 191.
Rozier, 259.
Russell, 41-2.
Rydeing, 69.

Salford, 114.
Sandford, 95.
Sandys, 40, 118.
Saunders, 118.
Saweis, 114.
Scarborough, 64.
Sebrell, 259.
Servant, 259.

Sharpe, 188.
Shelley, 47.
Sherman, 100.
Sibsey, 114.
Singleton, 75.
Skipwith, 61.
Slader, 194.
Slaughter, 6.
Smalley, 99.
Smith, 20, 25, 41-2, 59, 73, 95, 122, 224.
Smithfield Church, 240.
Soane, 192, 207.
Spelman, 47, 118.
Spencer, 65, 101, 107, 114, 124, 180.
Stallinge, 245.
Stanard, 6, 50, 56, 115.
Stanford, 92.
Stephens, 65, 245.
Stevens, 76, 219.
Stewart, 191, 208.
Stone, 189, 197.
Story, 100.
Strachey, 48.
Street, 112.
Sturgis, 99.
Sullivant, 199.
Sully, 114.
Sutton, 209.
Swaney, 116.
Swann, 201.

Tanner, 204.
Tatum, 99.
Taylor, 114, 122, 132, 150, 237.
Teakle, 182.
Tench, 116.
Thelaball, 259.
Thomas, 138, 240.
Thompson, 50, 86, 118.
Thoroughgood, 52, 102, 107, 116, 251.
Thorpe, 48, 96.
Throckmorton, 40, 48, 58, 107.
Thurston, 107.
Timson, 96.
Tiplady, 127.
Tores, 261.

Travers, 200.
Trellman, 201.
Tucker, 47, 86, 107, 118.
Tyler, 6, 77, 105.

Utie, 118.

Vallandigham, 261.
Van Doveracke, 261.
Van Netson, 247.
Van Slot, 261.
Vaulx, 92, 138, 201.
Vincent, 220.

Wageman, 260.
Walke, 100.
Walker, 149.
Wall, 219.
Waller, 40.
Wallis, 149.
Walthrop, 40.
Ward, 164, 188, 208.
Wardley, 95.
Warnet, 164.
Warren, 158, 221.
Washburn, 99, 100.
Washington, 61, 92, 107, 198.
Waters, 118, 145.
Watkin, 154.
Webb, 136, 191, 207.
Welsford, 61.
West, 41, 46, 52, 107.
Westgate, 236.
Westover, 46.
Wheeler, 145.
Whitaker, 48.

Whiting, 123.
Wilkins, 99.
Wilkinson, 186.
Williams, 238.
Williamsburg, 113.
Willis, 159.
Willoughby, 48, 97, 107, 118,
    120, 159.
Wilson, 112.
Windebanke, 54.
Wingfield, 40, 115.
Withington, 146.
Wise, 99.
Womack, 204.
Wood, 259.
Woodhouse, 52, 107.
Woodward, 59.
Woorey, 65.
Worley, 41.
Wormeley, 57, 123-4, 159.
Worsley, 49.
Wotton, 40.
Wraxall, 85.
Wyatt, 61, 107, 113.
Wythe, 116.

Yarington, 42.
Yate, 44.
Yeamans, 66.
Yeardley, 45-6, 100, 118, 172.
Yeates, 233.
Yeo, 70.
Yewell, 197.
Young, 261.

Zouch, 51.

DATE DUE
